SCIENCE, SCRIPTURE,
—— *and* ——
SAME-SEX LOVE

John & Susan
So glad you
are back in SoCal!

[signature]

"I am deeply grateful for Mike Regele's book. Mike writes with a deep compassion to all sides of this contemporary issue but never compromises on spiritual integrity or solid research. He helps all of us, especially us in the mainline church, sort through the complexity of issues and come to a balanced examination of our feelings and attitudes."

—Grant Hagiya, Resident Bishop, Greater Northwest Area, The United Methodist Church

"Mike Regele writes about human sexuality humbly, graciously, simply, and wisely as husband, father, Presbyterian pastor, social commentator, and friend. His book is stimulating not only for an academic but also for pastors and persons in the pew. He helps us to listen, think, and speak about deeply held convictions in the spirit of a civility that builds others, affirms differences of opinions, and leads to reconciliation between conservatives and progressives within the church. Through serious Bible study, theological/scientific reflection, personal experience with others, and church debate, he has come to strong convictions about Christian sexual ethics and the power of God's love to heal the brokenness of our lives. His is a voice that we need at the table of our continuing dialogue as we seek to 'promote the peace, unity, and purity' of the church."

—Jerry Tankersley, Senior Pastor, Laguna Presbyterian Church, Laguna Beach, California

"While our world debates the holiness or sinfulness of homosexuality, Mike Regele offers a perspective everyone should read: the reflections of a father with a gay child. Human sexuality is a complicated and sensitive subject. In this book, Mike offers the genuine, thoughtful, heartfelt story of how he learned to take the Bible so seriously that he couldn't take it literally. He holds his values of faith, family, and friends together with thoughtful integrity. If you are struggling with your own understanding of human sexuality or need tools to talk to others, this book is for you."

—Cameron Trimble, United Church of Christ pastor,
executive director for the Center for Progressive Renewal

"With the tender heart of a father and the sharp intellect of a theologian, Mike Regele writes about his own journey in understanding the issues of gay and lesbian love in a Christian context. This poignant and savvy work belongs on the shelf of any pastor, parent, or layperson who is ready to struggle with science, experience, and faith. I found this book to be so rich in research and personal insight that my copy appeared yellow and green from the highlighter I used! It is a profound challenge to the church to look seriously at God's inclusive creation, the covenant available to all of us, and the reminder of our promises in baptism."

—Jill M. Hudson, author of *Congregational Trauma* and *When Better Isn't Enough*,
retired Associate Stated Clerk of the Presbyterian Church (U.S.A.)

"This is a book for those willing to take the next step beyond mere repeating of the texts and arguments that are all too familiar. Mike Regele trusts an authoritative scripture. He also is willing to look at evidence from all fields of inquiry. All data are examined with great care as befits someone who manages a company doing demographic research. His very readable style is enhanced by lists of most-asked questions and answers that are supported by the evidence given. Graphs and other models help make the conclusions clear. This book begins with the question that should have been the starting point for all discussions of homosexuality. Is it chosen or innate? For Regele science is a 'game changer.' It affirms what all of us know—we are born with our sexual orientation. He then helps us work through the consequences of that reality."

—Jack Rogers, Professor Emeritus of Theology, San Francisco Theological Seminary,
Moderator of the 213th General Assembly of the Presbyterian Church (U.S.A.)

MICHAEL B. REGELE

FOREWORD BY BRIAN D. McLAREN

SCIENCE, SCRIPTURE,

and

SAME-SEX LOVE

 Abingdon Press™

Nashville

SCIENCE, SCRIPTURE, AND SAME-SEX LOVE
Copyright © 2014 by Abingdon Press

Library of Congress Cataloging-in-Publication Data

Regele, Mike.
  Science, scripture, and same-sex love / Michael B. Regele.
    pages cm.
  Includes bibliographical references.
  ISBN 978-1-4267-9829-0 (binding: soft back, trade pbk. : alk. paper)   1. Homosexuality—Biblical teaching.
2. Homosexuality.   I. Title.
  BS680.H67R44 2014
  241'.664—dc23

                                                                    2014034762

14 15 16 17 18 19 20 21 22 23—10 9 8 7 6 5 4 3 2 1
MANUFACTURED IN THE UNITED STATES OF AMERICA

For my daughter

A Prayer

O God, you made us in your own image and redeemed us through Jesus your Son:
Look with compassion on the whole human family;
take away the arrogance and hatred which infect our hearts;
break down the walls that separate us;
unite us in bonds of love;
and work through our struggle and confusion to accomplish your purposes on earth;
that, in your good time, all nations and races may serve you in harmony around
your heavenly throne;
through Jesus Christ our Lord. Amen.

The Book of Common Prayer
The Episcopal Church

Contents

Foreword

Mike Regele begins his new book with an Episcopal prayer that includes these words: "take away the arrogance and hatred which infect our hearts; break down the walls that separate us; unite us in the bonds of love."

It is hard to think of a more important venue for that prayer to be answered than in regard to the issues of human sexuality that affect all our churches.

Many who address this issue do so with a concern for gay, bisexual, and transgendered people, but they have little understanding of the church.

Others have a great concern for their churches, but little experience and understanding of LGBT people.

Of the few who have deep understanding and love both for our churches and for LGBT people, some focus primarily on theology and others focus primarily on science, statistics, and evidence.

To find someone like Mike who holds all of these concerns and perspectives together is rare indeed. So rare, I think, that it's safe to say the book you're holding is truly one of a kind.

If you're after serious theological reflection on the biblical passages that play a key role in debates over homosexuality, you'll find that reflection here.

If you're after an intelligent engagement with current medical, psychological, neurobiological, and sociological data on sexual orientation and identity, you'll find that engagement here.

If you're after pastoral insight that takes seriously the challenges of organizational change in both local congregations and larger denominational bodies, you'll find it here.

And if you're after something more personal and even confessional, you'll find in this book not just theology, science, and pastoral insight; you'll also find the warm heart of a father who writes every page with his own daughter in mind.

On top of that, Mike is an eminently clear writer. He is thorough but not wordy. He is logical but not mechanical. He loves to ask an important question and then set about to answer it. He never wanders from his central pursuit of making sense of scripture, science, and homosexuality.

Mike and I have a lot in common. We're both from evangelical backgrounds where homosexuality was condemned with terms that ranged from "abomination" to "less than God's best." We are both parents of gay children whom we love and respect. And we both have devoted much of our lives to the well-being of the Christian church and the vitality of its mission.

And perhaps most important, we both pray that God will "work through our struggle and confusion" to accomplish God's purposes on earth. If you share that prayer, you will be as grateful as I am for the gift of this book.

Brian D. McLaren (brianmclaren.net)

Preface

When I began my Christian pilgrimage over forty years ago, I would never have imagined writing a book on homosexuality and certainly not about homosexuality and the church. I avoided the issue for most of my life, sitting somewhere in that space just outside the formal institution but deeply involved through the consulting firms I led. I watched many denominations struggle with the issue, with one side constantly trying to politically or theologically outmaneuver the other. The constant conflict made me sad and at times very frustrated. Why? Because it is hard to promote and support healthy and vigorous churches when they use their time, money, and energy fighting over homosexuality. I have close friends on both sides of the issue, and I know they see this consequence as well.

Until recently I would say, "This is not my fight." But the revelation that my daughter is gay changed all of that for me. Suddenly it is *my* issue. At first it is private, something within our own family. Then my denomination (PCUSA) took an action that allowed each presbytery to decide whether to ordain gay and lesbian persons who are in intimate partner-relationships. After years of wrangling, a group of tall-steeple pastors decided they had had enough, and they began a process that resulted in the formation of A Covenant Order of Evangelical Presbyterians (ECO) shaped initially by The Fellowship of Presbyterians (FOP).

My family was a part of a local Presbyterian church for nearly thirty years. The issue of gay marriage and ordination was never a significant problem within our church. I am sure some people felt strongly one way or the other, but it was not a topic of conversation. In 2011, this changed. Some within our church decided to start attending the FOP events, and a groundswell of enthusiasm for involvement began. In a public meeting an alternative denominational option was presented as a direction for our church, and I realized I could no longer remain quiet. *Science, Scripture, and Same-Sex Love* comes out of that moment.

But, of course, Presbyterian churches are not alone in disagreement over homosexuality. In The United Methodist Church, congregations align with similar polarities. On one hand, some United Methodist churches are known as Reconciling congregations, and on the other hand, some lean toward conservative affiliations. Likewise, in the Episcopal Church of America, congregations and dioceses have forged new alignments and affiliations. Similar discussions are found in the Evangelical Lutheran Church of America, the Southern Baptist Church, and others. Our Roman Catholic friends are also engaged in their own form of this conversation.

I believe there are many thoughtful Christian people in churches from many traditions who are struggling or who have simply never really explored this issue from an alternative viewpoint, one that is based upon substantial biblical, theological, and scientific reflection. I devote this book to them.

Respectfully,
Rev. Michael B. Regele
May 2014

Visit http://www.cokesbury.com/forms/digitalstore.aspx?lvl=free+downloads to download a free corresponding **study guide** PDF for use in small group discussions. **Password: 8s97rpWzRn**

Acknowledgments

Many people have made important contributions to my journey writing this book. Some I do not even know. I "met" them when I came across their stories. Reading real stories of real individuals and their families is a necessary ingredient in the formation of one's views on same-sex attraction and love. If more people in churches, especially leaders, would allow themselves to hear these stories, I believe a different ethos would emerge within many churches. That is not to say they would agree with those of us supporting same-sex relationships. But humanizing people is always a good thing.

Two of the people who made an important contribution to this book's journey are Linda and Rob Robertson, whose story, "Just Because He Breathes: Learning to Love our Gay Son," I came across in *The Huffington Post* one day. I am grateful for Linda and her husband Rob's efforts to help other LGBT young people and their families, especially those from within the faith community. To those like Linda and Rob and others who have shared their story in some way, I say thank you.

There are of course many people I do know, and I want to acknowledge and thank them, though given the topic, perhaps somewhat indirectly. In 2012 my wife and I started meeting with a small group from our Presbyterian church. Most of the couples were parents of an LBGTQ child (*child* may not be quite right, for some of them were in their fifties). One couple does not have a LGBT child, but they are our dear friends and felt a deep desire to show solidarity with us. And our group has grown over the years as others have found their way to us. We have laughed and we have cried together. We have studied and we have prayed together. We have counseled one another. We have created a safe space together. And we have eaten many fine meals. It is rare in life to have such a strong supportive group of friends.

The two-year period in which this book was written became a tumultuous time for my wife and me. We found ourselves outside our church of nearly thirty years. But two colleagues in ministry came alongside me (us), providing encouragement, wisdom, and a listening ear. Jerry Tankersley, pastor of Laguna Presbyterian Church, was someone I had known for thirty years but only at a distance. We don't even agree on everything I have written. But when I reached out to him, he opened his schedule and let me bare my heart in total safety. He has become a dear friend. Similarly, Kirk Winslow, pastor of the new worshipping community called Canvas OC, also became a source of great encouragement. We have been friends for many years but the recent years have become the most precious. My wife and I are also thankful for the communities of Laguna Presbyterian Church and Canvas OC. Both have become a welcoming home for us.

Many friends read the manuscript and gave me feedback. Some agreed with me, some did not, but together they helped me shape my argument. They also allowed me to discern if the spirit in which I was trying to write was coming through as I hoped. You know who you are and I am grateful to you.

I especially want to express my gratitude to those who have read, commented on, and endorsed the book and its message. Some are old friends, some new. They include Rev. Jill Hudson; Rev. Brian D. McLaren; my old seminary professor, Dr. Jack Rogers; and United Methodist Bishop Grant Hagiya.

It will become very apparent as one reads the book that I am heavily indebted to N. T. Wright for my historical and theological frameworks and exegesis. Wright has reopened my Bible for me over the past ten years and made the text more accessible. The Jesus I find in the text is more real and the context in which Paul wrote is better grounded by providing insights into his worldview. This influence is so great that I must acknowledge with gratitutde the contributions to this book that Wright has made.

Writing a book takes time, and I do have a day job. The initial manuscript was written with no timeline and in my spare time—early mornings and late evenings. But once there was a publisher, timelines were fixed. Morning and evenings would no longer be enough time to complete additional research and make manuscript edits. Consequently I began working on it during the day. The impact upon my business partners and staff became real. Thankfully they all believed in the project and granted me the space to close my door day after day to complete my editorial tasks. Thank you all.

A special note of appreciation must be extended to my new friends at Abingdon Press. Paul Franklyn was willing to fulfill my request that he read the entire manuscript, not just a couple of chapters, before deciding if they would consider publishing it. Additionally his scholarship pressed me to make sure I was as current as possible on biblical and theological research. I learned many new things after the initial manuscript because of Paul's input and direction. Kathryn Armistead (Kathy) was my primary editor. A more gentle and kind person I have not met. She could press me here and redirect me there and sometimes provide additional research to explore in the psychology domain.

Finally and most importantly, I want to thank my family. This was a family project. It was a nonstarter if any of them would have said no. All five of my children, my one daughter-in-law, and my wife were given the early manuscript. In many ways this book is part of our family story. Therefore they each were given the freedom to give me a "thumbs up" or "thumbs down." All said go for it! And so to my wife, Debbie, my children Jonathan and Laura (his wife), Justin, Jordan, Kiersten, and Elissa: I love you all and thank God every day for each one of you.

Chapter 1

A Father's Quest for Answers

Why Am I Writing about This?

"Faith, Family, Friends"

Robin Roberts[1] of *Good Morning America*, the network TV show, displayed these words on a sign one morning to represent the three most important things in her life. I share these same values. My faith has shaped every part of my life since that late January evening when I was seventeen years old. My family is second only to my faith. Every day I think about my children and wish they were closer. I want them to chase their dreams and follow the road that is laid out for them, but those roads led many of them extremely far from our home in Irvine, California. Then there are friends. We have had many for many years. Some have gone through painfully difficult times with us. We have gone through difficult times with them. We have agreed and disagreed on many things and sometimes not elegantly.

I now find myself in a position in which all three of these values are in conflict with one another. One of our daughters informed us a few years ago that she is a lesbian. For most in our faith community, homosexuality and homosexual practices are sin. If that is true, then the reality of my daughter's confession on first glance pits us against our faith. We find it likewise pits us against some friends. What I know for certain is that regardless of the other two, I must stand with my daughter. She is my daughter. She is a wonderful gift from God, and I love her with my whole heart. This means I have some work to do between God and me. It means I have some work to do with some friends as well.

Over the course of several years, my wife and I worked through some of the difficult questions raised by the confluence of our faith, family, and friends on the issue of homosexuality. We had many long discussions. We

1

have read and explored some of the varied resources that are available. I did research on topics from theology to psychology to biology. This book has come out of these discussions and the research. Although it will present findings, it is still a work in progress—as am I.

The Questions

One will not be able to read far before numerous questions emerge, for which one would like answers, if possible. I list them here so the reader knows the terrain we will travel. At the end of the book, I will return to each of these and provide summary responses.

- Is one born a homosexual or transsexual person, or is homosexuality something someone chooses? In other words, is sexual orientation a choice an individual makes?

- Is same-sex attraction sinful?

- Within the scope of the healing and restoration of creation, is homosexuality a disease to be corrected?

- Is it true that Lesbian, Gay, Bisexual, and Transgender (LGBT) people are more promiscuous than heterosexual people?

- Is it true that same-sex relationships do not last as long as hetero-sex relationships?

- Is abstinence for life the only choice for a Christian LGBT person? Or can they enter into intimate and sexual relationships and still be active participants in a Christian community?

- Is same-sex marriage acceptable from a Christian standpoint?

- Should LGBT persons be allowed to become ordained leaders in the church if they are in committed same-sex relationships or marriages?

- Does support of same-sex marriage disqualify one from leadership and teaching ministries in the church?

My Personal Story

Discussions about homosexuality can become incredibly abstract quickly, and we can easily forget that we are talking about real people. So I begin with my story, which I believe sets this quest in a real-life context.

Not Raised in the Church

I was not raised in the church. For a short period in the fourth grade I think I went to Sunday school and sang in the youth choir at the First United Methodist Church in Corvallis, Oregon. But that all faded away for reasons I do not recall. Life was not easy for our family. My dad owned an ARCO gas station, which included an auto repair shop. I worked there from junior high through high school. I was a bit wild, loving fast cars more than English, history, math, or science; so unfortunately I spent a little too much time in the parking lot and not enough in class. It was the late 1960s, so there was a fair amount of "experimentation" going on, and I was all for experimentation! One January evening of my senior year in high school, I stopped by an old friend's house. We had been fellow experimenters in the past, and I wanted to see how the experimenting was going for her. I found that my friend and another young man had become Christians and were part of the Jesus movement. That night changed my life. I learned just a little bit of the story of how God loved me just as I am. Despite all the ways I had been a moral failure, still Jesus forgave me. I didn't know Genesis from Revelation, but I did know that I was a sinner, and forgiveness with the offer of a fresh start sounded pretty good.

I moved to Seattle and graduated from Seattle Pacific College. I worked for a brief time in a coffeehouse where I met a seventeen-year-old high school student named Debbie, whom four years later I would finally marry. We have been happily married now since 1976 and together have produced five great kids, all *very* different. Early in my Christian journey, my interest in the Bible and theology seemed insatiable. We moved to the Bay Area in northern California to study at Peninsula Bible Church (PBC) and intern under the singles pastor. I learned to love my Bible through that church, and I learned that we are supposed to love people, all kinds of people. I also learned that many churches spent more time determining who was in and who was out than they did acting like God's people with wide-open doors. PBC however, was different. All kinds of people were welcome there, which was demonstrated through its radical and innovative (for the late 1960s and '70s) Body Life service.[2]

Singles Class in San Francisco in 1979

I served as an intern in the singles ministry at PBC. The main group was in Palo Alto, but there were satellite groups throughout the Bay Area. These were usually started by a single person who had been part of the ministry in Palo Alto but whose work had taken them to more distance places around the San Francisco Bay.

One such group was founded in San Francisco. A modest number of singles found themselves employed in the city, and so they lived there. As part of my internship, I was invited to teach in some of these satellite groups, and so I found myself scheduled to teach a few weeks in the San Francisco class in the late 1970s.

This period was the high point in the Gay Pride movement. By the late 1970s, the sexual revolution of the 1960s had evolved into a sexual revolution for same-sex persons. The center of all of this was Castro Street in San Francisco where a large number of gay bars were located. On a particular Sunday the leadership of the singles class decided that my wife and I needed an "immersion experience," so they took us to a gay bar/restaurant. For us, it was a scary proposition. But the reality was far from scary. It was a restaurant filled with people—a little unusual looking to us but not scary. Sadly the sexual revolution of the 1970s turned into the devastating HIV/AIDS era of the 1980s, which ravaged the gay community.

Singles Pastor at Mariners Church

Following the two years in the Bay Area at PBC, I was called to be the singles pastor at Mariners Church in Newport Beach, California. The group was called the Salt Company, named after the ministry of the same name in the 1960s at Hollywood Presbyterian Church. Several young single folks—many graduates of either UCLA or USC—had formed a singles group as part of Mariners Church, and it was flourishing. They wanted a pastor, so my exceedingly pregnant wife, our young son Jonathan, and I packed up and moved to Southern California—where we have been ever since. Several experiences during my tenure as the Mariners singles pastor would further shape what I thought about homosexuality.

My primary responsibility was to teach Sunday mornings in a restaurant where between two hundred and three hundred single people would gather. I decided to teach a series on sexual ethics and indicated that I would be addressing topics such as premarital sex, abortion, homosexuality, marriage, and some other related matters. Singles groups love teaching about sex, so it was the most well-attended series we ever had—on some Sundays more than four hundred attended! Once the topics of the series were made known, several men in the group approached me privately and revealed that they were gay. Some were handling it OK. Some were not. One young man asked me to meet with him and his parents when he came out of the closet. Another worked closely with me, hoping that I would conclude that committed same-sex partnerships were morally acceptable for a Christian. The core of his argument was (a) that he was born the way he was and (b) that the practices that Paul the Apostle observed were not the same as the committed relationship he was describing. He based much of his argument on the newly released (at that time) book by John Boswell, *Christianity, Social Tolerance, and Homosexuality* (1980).

I had two objectives when I taught on the subject of homosexuality. First, I wanted to express to this group of single Christians that many of their assumptions about homosexuality were wrong. At that time, the prevailing belief was that homosexuals "chose" to be gay and that the choice was a choice against God and what was right. I taught that the research (which was not extensive at that time) would demonstrate that same-sex attraction is an innate trait—how a person is born—and not a choice. This was a little radical in 1982, especially in a conservative Bible church, but for the most part, the group accepted what I was teaching.

My second objective was to emphasize the point I had been making throughout the series: the central moral imperative of Christian faith is not finding the rules and living within them. It is to promote life in all of our human interactions by trying to love as Jesus loved. Unfortunately for the young man who had been so committed to helping me understand things from a gay man's perspective, at that time, I felt I could not support homosexual expression as promoting life. I am grateful to this man for his patience with me. I came closer to him than anyone else in that conservative community, but I did not come close enough.

I don't know how many gay men there were in our singles group, but I estimated between 5 and 10 percent based upon the number that I personally knew. I did not know any lesbians because none confided in me. One young single, from a conservative Christian home and also a Christian college, confessed to being bisexual. He had several gay encounters while at college but was conflicted when he met with me some years later. The unsettling part of his story was how depressed he was. I feared for him.

During those years as singles pastor, a man I knew from San Francisco (we shall call him Bill), came to Southern California to visit me. He confided that he was gay. He had been raised in a conservative Christian home and had attended a well-respected Christian college. He said that he had tried really hard not to be gay, but after years of struggle, he had finally come to understand that he was gay. That was not going to change. But he was also deeply committed to Jesus and his Christian faith. Though he knew the two were not easy to pair, he was going to try. Both were part of his identity, part of who he was. At the time I remember feeling sad and confused. Here was this young man who was so committed to his faith, and he was gay. I knew God loved him. I did too! He was a good friend. I didn't know what to say, but what I knew I could not say was anything that condemned him.

Another young man, again from a conservative Christian home, struggled terribly to come to grips with his same-sex attraction. We spent many hours in pastoral counseling together. More important, he was also being treated by a psychiatrist and was on antidepressants. Unfortunately he could not resolve the inner conflict and one day jumped off a building, committing suicide. I have presided over two memorial services in my life. His was the first. I will never forget looking into his coffin and wondering how to put all of this together—faith and his reality.

A clear pattern ties all of these stories together. They were people raised as Christians who took their faith very seriously, but in their young adult years the reality that they were also gay pressed down heavily upon them. In the 1980s there was not much reconciliation happening within the church between a homosexual/bisexual orientation and Christian faith. I often wonder what happened to these men.

Daughters' Gay High School Friends

When I was in junior high and high school, any boy who showed effeminate behavior was made fun of and called a "fag" or other demeaning epithet. Few if any would admit to being gay or lesbian. Much had changed by the time our daughters were this age. They were both involved in theatre and brought home friends who were openly gay. It was no big deal to them. It just "was." We found that their nonchalance about this made it a nonissue for us as well. These were just kids who came to our house and interacted with us, and we found them totally delightful. Sexuality was a nonissue. We were horrified when one young man's family put his belongings out on the street. If he was going to be gay, he was not going to be in their family. Again and sadly, they were a conservative Christian family, and when confronted with the choice between their beliefs and their son, they chose, at least for a moment, their beliefs.

Our Own Daughter's Coming Out

As I indicated earlier, we have five children, and our entire lives are wound around them even now that they are adults and most live—sadly—far from us. Our first three were boys, and the last two, twin girls. Twins, especially same-sex twins, are a force to be reckoned with. There is a bond there that we singletons do not understand. As I learned early on, one steps between them at one's peril. A fight between them becomes a dual assault on anyone who tries to intervene between them.

Both daughters went away for college to different places. That was a hard transition for them but good as well, for they learned that they could live separate lives. But we found that one of them was getting more and more distant from us during her first two years of college. Whereas one would come home for visits or would call, the other would not. Prior to this, we had all four been close, so this shift became increasingly disconcerting. One daughter, after two years at University of Arizona, decided that New York was where she wanted to be, so she transferred to a college in Manhattan. The other, who had become distant, after a couple of starts and stops, ended up in New York for a year as well to live with her sister. We had started to wonder, based upon some conversations about ballot issues in California, whether the one who had started and stopped was a lesbian. It was not until later in that year that we were to have that confirmed.

I suspect most parents when first informed that their child is gay go through something similar to the stages of grief—from denial, to anger (at yourself?), to hopefully acceptance. Regardless of what you believe about homosexuality, it hits you hard. You realize that many of the unspoken expectations you hold will not happen as you had imagined. There is a grieving; there is a loss. What will their future be? How will the world receive them? What about the church? What about our friends? How will the family receive them? Will it even make any difference? What do *you* think about it? How will *you* view your child? Dozens of questions in rapid succession are repeated over and over and over in your head.

In that same moment my wife and I each had to make a decision. Would we abandon our daughter over her sexual orientation, or would we stand with her? There really was never any question, but until one faces the actual decision, it is extremely abstract. We had had gay church members and friends, but for us, it had become, in a moment, extraordinarily real. In the midst of a great deal of confusion and uncertainty, we would side with our daughter.

But it was not as simple as that, because, like that of many Christians of all denominations, our faith is an essential part of our identity. The gospel

7

story for me was and continues to be the greatest story there is. It is the one story that makes sense of life and gives me hope. I had to wrestle these two pieces of my life to the ground. Curiously, the foundations of that process were laid back in my singles ministry years when I taught on sexual ethics. Promote life in all you do by loving to the extent you can as God loves us.

The rest of this book is my journey, if possible, to bring these two together. But it is not just my journey. It is a journey that many mothers and fathers must make when sons or daughters reveal they are gay. It is a journey for those who are friends who want to understand and support a mother, father, or gay friend. It is a rocky journey that I hope many Christian leaders have taken or will take. It is not an easy journey. One will find oneself confronting all kinds of fears, loss, confusion, and uncertainty—especially where one might have thought there was certainty.

My Approach

The homosexuality issue can be a case study in how various fields of inquiry should come together to provide greater understanding. I believe that when we allow them to do so, we obtain a richer appreciation for a complex phenomenon. In the simplest terms, heterosexual expression alone (at least historically) assures the continuation of the human species—or any other species that persists through sexual reproduction. And yet the phenomenon of same-sex attraction and behavior can be observed in multiple species, including humans, over time. Why is this?

This is actually a fairly complex question to answer. To do so, we must consult fields of inquiry beyond our biblical traditions. Reality is multifaceted, so we must consult many different fields or domains of study to understand it. Our biblical traditions are one domain, but there are others. Each has a contribution to make. Each sheds its light, and the result is a better understanding of the whole, if we allow them to. So in my study, I shall attempt to consider an integrated approach to my questions, looking to multiple relevant fields of inquiry for explanations.

My approach to this range of homosexuality questions is this: we must allow each domain of inquiry to speak and from that conversation draw an integrated multidimensional understanding of the lesbian, gay, bisexual, and transgender (shorthand—LGBT) phenomenon and the moral implications that attend this. In the case of this topic, the domains to consider are theology, science (biology and psychology), and history.

I begin with creation theology. The focus is not on specific persons and their behavior but upon God's creation and God's intended role for humans. Following this, I turn to what modern science (physics and cosmology) tells us about the way the universe works, beginning with the factors that drive the large-scale evolution of the universe. I then zoom in on what biology and psychology reveal. The question we want to understand from these different but complementary fields of inquiry is this: What kind of universe has God created? More specifically, I want to ask: How does the kind of universe we live in relate to the phenomenon of LGBT people? I will not presume to provide exhaustive expositions, especially of the science. I would most certainly misrepresent it because I am not a scientist. I was trained to interpret scripture. So while I will attempt to capture the "topline" view, for more detail, I must direct the reader to other papers and books, many of which will be found in the "Works Cited."

In the following chapters, we look at scriptures referencing same-sex sexual expression. There are not many, and in most cases they are a relatively small part of a larger narrative. I will attempt to present each text with interpretations that are supported by solid scholarship. My goal, as always in all of my biblical interpretation and teaching, is to understand a text within its context. This will require looking to the field of historical inquiry as well. If this entire discussion is about LGBT sexual expression, how is it similar to and different from the past, especially within the Greek and Roman worlds of, at least, the New Testament? These can be "muddy waters" to pass through, and there is always the possibility that my conclusions are inaccurate in some respect and wrong in others. But it is also possible that those who oppose same-sex marriage and LGBT persons in ordained leadership are incorrect in many ways as well. We each simply must give it our best, follow the strands of inquiry, and see where they lead and what kind of "fabric" they weave when all are allowed to speak from their domain.

Throughout this study, regardless of the specific domain of inquiry in which one happens to be working at a particular moment, there are always moral questions standing in the background. People draw all kinds of moral conclusions from the various data and domains of inquiry. I will lift up possible conclusions at various moments along the way. Ultimately I will speak directly to them. I do believe, regardless of where the issues take us, there are moral issues to consider.

As you read this book, it will become clear early on that I am compelled to support same-sex marriage and gay ordained leadership in the church because it is the right thing to do. But please journey with me and hear me out because I believe that you might see things differently if you "walk in my shoes." In writing on such a topic, the issue of a proper objectivity is often—rightfully—raised. It would be easy to dismiss my conclusions by simply saying that it is just personal for me (which has in fact already happened). Well, yes, it is. I admit that from the beginning. But there are many things that are personal to each one of us that still require us to work hard to obtain real data and follow the results wherever they lead, even if the data lead to conclusions we don't initially like. I approach the topic with this clearly in mind and so have strived to remain as objective as possible. Hopefully, my conclusions reflect this.

With all of this in front of us, my final concern will be how one who supports LGBT marriage and ordained leadership in the church can continue to serve in churches that actively reject such views. This question is important because it was this question that launched me on this journey.

Where to Begin

It is fairly typical to begin such a study with one's assumptions. It is only fair that these be placed on the table before I begin to dive into the content. These assumptions (which we all have, even if we are unaware of them) will determine avenues of inquiry one might take and the conclusions one might draw. In a simple example, if one assumes that Genesis 1 describes a literal seven-day creation, then certain research choices will be closed off, except perhaps to deny them. It is to be expected that certain conclusions about how the universe came into being will be shaped by the choices of what fields of inquiry we explore and allow to speak to us.

My Assumptions about Domains of Inquiry

I hold the scriptures in the highest regard as true testimonies of the story of God's redemption of creation and, as such, a faithful expression of the faith we are called to and the life we are to live. Consequently, when some scientists say, "There is no God; there is only the universe," my faith in the story of the scriptures trumps such a statement. This reflects my basic assumptions about scripture and other fields of inquiry. I believe (as do many respected theologians and scientists) that biblical study and theology, science and historiography are each their own domains of study. Each has its own assumptions, rules, and methods that guide its explorations. In other words, each is its own domain of inquiry. I believe we make a grave error when we try to employ the assumptions, rules, or methods of inquiry for one domain in another domain. When a scientist, having drawn certain conclusions within her domain of inquiry, then uses those tools and jumps over into the theological domain and makes theological statements, she makes an error, a category mistake. I call it domain jumping. Carl Sagan did just that in a famous quote at the beginning of his fascinating series, *Cosmos*. He begins with full cinematic drama saying, "The Cosmos is all that is or ever was or ever will be" (Kennard, Haines-Stiles, and Malone 1980). This is a theological statement or at least a metaphysical one. It is not a cosmological statement from within the physical sciences, which is his domain of expertise. He is domain jumping here. But because he is speaking so forthrightly as a distinguished scientist, his audience believes he is making a scientific statement. As a physical sciences specialist who explores "how" the cosmos works, he makes a statement beyond his domain. He cannot demonstrate any evidence for his assertion. His field of inquiry begins and ends with the physical universe. From his stance as a scientist, he does not and cannot know if there is anything, any reality beyond the physical universe.

The same is true when those within the domains of theology and scriptural study use their methods and conclusions and then jump over into the domain of science and make scientific statements like, for example, "The universe came into existence by the spoken word of God." What is wrong with this statement? Nothing if I as a theologian speaking as a theologian were to say it. But when I, as a theologian, make such a statement as a scientific fact, I have jumped domains, and the statement is not legitimate to the field of inquiry, because I cannot produce physical evidence of it as would be expected from within the physical sciences. Furthermore, attempts to prove this assertion by quoting the Bible not only do not add anything, they actually hurt the cause of the gospel. Just because the assertion cannot be proved using the rules and methods of the physical sciences does not mean it is not true; just that it cannot be demonstrated in accordance with the canons of the physical sciences.

Here is one last example to try to make this clear. Science tells us *how* the universe works. It cannot tell us *why* there is a universe. That question is a question for the domain of theology or perhaps philosophy. Science can help us understand the mechanisms at work in nature that result in LGBT persons. As a result, we must let them teach us. But how LGBT persons are to live a moral life is within the domain of theology and ethics.

So, this book rests on three assumptions.

1. I believe that we must study the findings of modern science vis-à-vis homosexuality and allow this domain to add to our overall understanding of this phenomenon in nature—just as we must

11

do relative to heterosexuality—and restrain the urge to insert theological statements into our inquiries into how natural process works.

2. I believe we must do our historical homework—to make sure we really understand how sexuality was expressed in the ancient world and how same-sex sexual expression fit into that. We must also make sure we understand the current expressions vis-à-vis the ancient and not assume they are the same.

3. I believe we must let the scriptures clarify for us how God views the gay person and how God would have gay persons live as part of God's dearly loved creation. In addition, we must let the scriptures clarify for nongay persons how we are to live in community with LGBT persons. This point is proper to the field of theology.

In line with these assumptions, I am a theistic evolutionist. I believe the findings of modern science provide great insight into how the universe came into being and how it continues to unfold according to a wonderful interplay of natural causes within an open system. There is necessity determined by the laws of physics and chemistry, and yet there is contingency that creates surprises, contributing to fruitfulness of the universe and its diversity. These are statements from within the scientific domain.

I also believe that there is a God behind all there is, and it is God's love and desire to share Godself that, for reasons beyond our comprehension, resulted in God's Word of creation. Finally, I believe creation is not yet complete (see discussion on Romans 8 below, p. 28), but the promise is that one day it will be. Until then, it struggles and groans. We humans were created to fellowship with God and participate with God in the creative process as stewards of God's creation. All of these are statements from within the theological domain.

My Assumptions about Biblical Authority

It is often said that much of the debate about same-sex expression, same-sex marriage, and ordained leadership of active LGBT persons is about biblical authority. In other words, what role does the Bible have in giving direction on this issue? Those on the progressive[3] side accuse the conservatives of demanding of the biblical text what it cannot bear, when it is set against our modern world. And so when the progressives speak, they are likely to present a more nuanced direction on the issue. But those on the conservative side maintain that those on the more progressive side walk loose with the text, not granting it the authority over faith and practice that the conservative side believes it should have. Conservatives will quote specific verses that presumably speak of homosexuality as being evil. However, if the person receiving the comments questions whether or not the texts actually reflect modern same-sex relationships, they are told that they have compromised the Bible's authority.

So let me begin with making a strong statement about my belief in biblical authority. The Bible is one of the main ways Jesus is mediated to us. I have spent most of my adult life studying it and teaching it in one venue or another. I love the scriptures. They tell the story of God's great love and commitment to creation and to me. The biblical text must be respected as it is, and it must be studied appropriately so that it can tell its story to every people in every place and every time. This is part of the teaching role of the church. So for me, as a Christian, it is my rule of faith and practice, and I believe it speaks truthfully about both. As an ordained Presbyterian pastor and teacher, I join other clergy, but also laity across many church traditions, who want to look more deeply into how the Bible can speak to us today. And as a father, I take seriously my responsibility to pass the good fruit of my faith to my children.

It is also true that people with a strong commitment to biblical authority differ on the interpretation of the scriptures from time to time. From my perspective, that is the case on this issue. Good people can and will draw different conclusions. But I do not mean by this that there is no truth or that truth is relativized. I am a critical realist[4] (Wright 1992). I believe truth exists and that it can be known, though always partially. I believe a true reading of a text is possible. I also believe we all are wrong on some interpretation of the text all the time. Nonetheless our task is to faithfully study the text to the best of our ability and the resources available to us; because truth matters! We will never get it perfectly right, but as a faith community together, we must pursue that end nonetheless.

My Assumptions about Biblical Interpretation

While I am laying out my assumptions, I think it is important to reveal something about my approach to biblical interpretation. The interpretation of texts will be governed by the assumptions one employs, consciously or not, about how to approach a text and what we think it says. Each of us reads a text through our twenty-first-century eyes. We cannot help it. We live in the twenty-first century. But because of this, we may read an ancient text's words and fill them with twenty-first-century cultural meaning. When we do this, we most likely not only miss the author's meaning but also draw conclusions that are contrary to what the author meant.

We must allow the Bible to be what it is and not insist that it be something it is not. I believe that to insist that it be something it is not is to dishonor the text and diminish the authority of the story it tells. It is ironic that many of the views I hold would be considered liberal by a fundamentalist. Yet in reality, we both try to conserve the original ideas of the author or editor and the message he or she was trying to deliver to a particular people at a particular moment in time. Jesus started with the particular, laying the groundwork there for his message to become universal, embracing all people from all cultures. We will see that when we look at his message and how that message was extended by the Apostle Paul.

Although I believe the Bible is a divinely inspired compendium of writings that reveal deep and wonderful things about God and what God is up to in creation, it is not written according to the standards of modern historiography or science; these are different domains. Does this mean that the Bible offers no history at all? No! But to insist that any statement the Bible makes must be scientifically accurate is to cause the text to bear a weight beyond what it is intended and certainly beyond what those who wrote and compiled it could have thought and known. So I ask:

- Is it really fair to expect the text written by someone in the sixth century BCE to provide modern scientific descriptions along with whatever theological point one was trying to make?

- Is it reasonable to assume that though the writers could not have understood what they wrote, they wrote true twenty-first-century scientific descriptions anyway?

I do not believe it is either fair or reasonable, and too often such expectations and assumptions obscure the real story that it is trying to tell—and that our world needs to be told!

In Summary
What do I believe the Bible is? It is a book of religious writings compiled over a couple thousand years that tells of a particular people's religious and cultural pilgrimage. It is that, plus, it is a book that represents (reveals) the purposes of God in history to redeem creation from decay and destruc-

tion and ultimately death. In the language of N. T. Wright, it tells the story of how God intends to set the world right. It is infallible in this regard, in matters of religious belief (i.e., faith and practice). It provides a true witness to the redemptive purposes of God and is a reliable testimony to those purposes and how we ought to respond.

How do I approach the Bible? I attempt to read it within its historical, literary, and cultural context. I use all of the tools of literary interpretation and exegesis available to me. I attempt to follow biblical scholarship. My goal is to understand what the author or authors/editors were trying to say in their time and place to the people of Israel in their time and place for both the Old and New Testaments. It is only after having some grasp of its original context that I believe we can begin the process of asking ourselves, "What is the more universal message, and how does it apply to us in our context?" This is of course an ongoing process, for none of us ever gets it just right.

One of the major dangers to readers of the Bible, who hold it in great honor, is to take some of its words out of the context in which they have a particular meaning and use those words to support a particular point of view. The danger here is that the words being used from the Bible may not support the view they have been quoted to support. When this is done, harm is done to people and to the text itself. I do believe this method is used by some on both sides of the LGBT debate. More than one example will be exposed when I get to the exegesis of some of the common texts used against homosexuality.

Finally, my roots are in the Reformed tradition. We subscribe to the hermeneutical principle that the central and universal message of the scriptures must help us understand the particular (Rogers 2010). (This does not mean other traditions do not subscribe to this principle of interpretation, just that this is my personal background.) For me, this means that all of scripture must be interpreted in the light of the death and resurrection of Jesus the Christ. In my reading of the entirety of the biblical witness and specifically within the life, death, and resurrection of Jesus, the central message is one of God's love for all of God's creation, and that is expressed through God's promise to heal, restore, and finish creation. I believe our reading of all texts should be governed by this fundamental principle. The application of this principle will be clear in the subsequent discussions; and like our historic compatriot, John Wesley, we understand that "our reading should likewise be closed with prayer, that what we read may be written on our hearts" (1835, 546).

Summary

To summarize my approach, the following statements reflect my perspectives, which shape how I will proceed to answer the basic questions stated earlier.

I am convinced:

- Theology and biblical studies provide us with authoritative direction about why there is a creation and how we are called to live within it. They address the moral domain of life and specifically God's redemptive purpose for humanity and the completion of creation.

- Science (psychology, biology, and so on) and history are domains of inquiry that provide us with descriptions of how the physical universe works and how humans have acted within it as it has unfolded over time.

- These domains are not in conflict. They are different descriptions that together provide us with a fuller understanding of the whole of reality.

- The Bible is a religious book speaking to a specific people at a specific time to address specific issues. The task of biblical study is to understand that to the best of our ability.

- The task of teachers of the church (theologians, pastors, and other professional teachers trained in theological inquiry) is to express their understandings in ways that clarify for the church its understanding of the faith and how it ought to be practiced.[5]

- We must study the findings of modern science vis-à-vis the phenomenon called homosexuality and allow this domain to add to our overall understanding of this phenomenon in nature and restrain the urge to insert theological statements into the inquiry of natural processes.

- We must let the scriptures clarify for us how God views the gay person and how God would have gay persons live as part of God's beloved creation.

- We must let the scriptures clarify for nongay persons how we are to live in community with LGBT persons.

This is where I begin. Not everyone will agree with me, but I have laid my cards on the table.

Notes

1. When I originally wrote this introduction, Robin Roberts, though long rumored to be gay, had not made a statement one way or the other. What she has made clear for years is her deep faith. But at the end of 2013 she acknowledged her longtime relationship with her girlfriend, Amber. She posted this on her Facebook page: "I am grateful for my entire family, my longtime girlfriend, Amber, and friends as we prepare to celebrate a glorious new year together."

2. I would refer the reader to the book by Ray C. Stedman, founding pastor of Peninsula Bible Church, titled Body Life (1995). It is an old work now, but it was a radical concept in the 1970s. The church, located near the Stanford University campus, opened its doors widely to all of the "hippie" boomers who made their residence somewhere along the Bay Area Peninsula.

3. I really don't like the label of "progressive," but it provides a shorthand label for nonconservative. It is often also referred to as "liberal" or "liberal/progressive." Additionally, in recent years within the evangelical community, some have begun to distance themselves from traditionally evangelical positions such that now there are some who consider themselves "post-evangelical" or "emergent."

4. In the field of theological studies, critical realism is a way of talking about how we know something. N. T. Wright, in his book *The New Testament and the People of God*, writes, "I propose a form of critical realism. This is a way of describing the process of 'knowing' that acknowledges the reality of the thing known, as something other than the knower (hence 'realism'), while fully acknowledging that the only access we have to this reality lies along the spiraling path of appropriate dialogue or conversation between the knower and the thing known (hence 'critical')" (Wright 1992, 35).

5. Although there is great consistency across the millennia, there have also been moments when the church concluded it did not have it quite right. The Protestant Reformation is of course the "gold standard" on this point even though some of the basic theological innovations of the Reformation are today being challenged by biblical theologians. See N. T. Wright on the meaning of justification by faith as an example (Wright 2009).

Chapter 2

Creation Theology: The Place to Begin

The Jewish and Christian faiths are rooted in creation theology. By that I mean that God is the source of all that is and that from the word of God came all of creation. In modern terms, we would say that the entire physical universe came into being by an act of the divine being. To subscribe to this is an affirmation of faith. Although science seeks to tell us about the mechanics of the physical universe, it is bounded by a line before and after the "big bang," if we follow the standard model. Any conversation on the other side of the big bang is a conversation that enters the domain of faith, even if one has no religious faith.

What are the alternatives if one does not subscribe to divine creation? There are basically two. The first is that the universe just is. Such a view does not try to ask the "why the universe?" question. It simply accepts the universe as a "brute fact." The second alternative, popular among some cosmologists, is the "multiple worlds theory," which explains this universe as just one of many popping in and out of existence. Neither of these alternatives can be proved, and so they are taken as an explanation on the basis of some belief. I choose the third option: divine action created the universe.

All three require faith!

Having said this, there are significant ideas about life and its purpose, humans and their role in creation that are addressed when one starts from a creation perspective.[1] A certain framework for the moral dimension of life finds its source in creation theology because it is the root of human dignity and respect for our environment. The purpose of existence itself is addressed in creation theology. These are not the questions of science. This does not mean that questions of human dignity and morality don't arise in the domain of science; just that when they do, the conversation has transcended its domain.

Creation theology is about who and why and to what end. The first three chapters of the Bible and the whole book of Genesis set the broad context for all that follows. It is a story of wonder and beauty, of tragedy and disappointment. It is a story. I do not believe it is a scientific description of "what happened" in space and time. A scientific description would read something like this: the universe came into being when a singularity exploded, sending hot gases out in every direction, more rapidly at first, and then after a short time, the expansion slowed and the gases began to cool, finally settling into the universe we observe today. In contrast, Genesis in the Bible is more like poetry—indeed some sections clearly are poetry—that tells a story. But like much poetry, it narrates a true story, in that it sets the foundation for understanding the world, our place in it as humans, and why so much of it seems at once noble and evil. As such, the Bible creates for us a worldview—a framework for understanding and interpreting the reality of our lives.

Now, one would think that embarking from this point would be dangerous for someone trying to argue for the acceptance of same-sex persons and the support of loving committed relationships between them. But I believe that the central teaching of the biblical story, as it is launched in the first three chapters, is where one must begin because the story it tells is of a loving creator God who makes a huge promise to creation.

Stories of Creation

A Big Story

Anyone who has read the first two chapters of Genesis realizes that it is two different creation stories. Most scholars believe Genesis 1 was written during the Babylonian exile. Genesis 2 is an older tradition in some form, perhaps dating back to the time of David. The Genesis story in the Bible was written and compiled against the beliefs of the surrounding areas. At the time it was compiled, however, Israel was living in exile in Babylon.

The question Israel was asking as they sat, held captive, in Babylon was: What had happened to Israel's God? If YHWH was all powerful, how come they were sitting in a foreign land? If they looked around, it sure looked like Marduk, the god of the Babylonians, was stronger than YHWH. To address these questions, Genesis 1 and the beginning of chapter 2 affirm:

- Creation is the work of one God, not the result of petty divine beings manipulating, copulating, or slaying.

20

- God made all that even the Babylonians worship; creation is good and orderly.

- Humanity is both male and female.

- To all humans was given regency, or the responsibility to govern the creation on God's behalf as good and faithful stewards.

- Humans, like the rest of creation, are to be fruitful and multiply.

- As such, it is a radical statement of monotheism against the pagan polytheism of Babylon and other world powers, such as Egypt. It was both reminder and warning to Israel of who her God was and therefore who Israel was.

An Intimate Story

The second creation story, beginning in Genesis 2:4, is older and more colorful. It puts the creation of humans at the center. Theologically it shares some of the ideas of Genesis 1. God is creator. Humans are created and given regency over the rest of creation, and a central problem for humans is resolved, that is, loneliness. It is in this text that the etiology of marriage is introduced. Clearly the text refers to the joining of a man and a woman. But the central issue is not marriage between a man and a woman, though that is obviously a key part of the story; it is that creation is incomplete until human community has been created. Humans were not meant to be alone. Humans were meant to live in community and to form new communities as they exercised their God-ordained regency over creation (e.g., naming the animals).

A Tragic Story

Genesis 3 introduces great tragedy into the story of creation. Humans as God's stewards were intended to enjoy close fellowship with God. As the story unfolds, we find humans in an idyllic garden and the creator God coming each day to walk with them, during the "breezy time of day." There is a moral innocence about them. They are given freedom to enjoy the garden and all its fruits except for one tree, the Tree of the Knowledge of Good and Evil. They are told that if they eat of the fruit of this tree, they will surely die.

21

Enter the wily serpent who suggests that God has not been quite honest with them, that God is holding out on them. Will they really die if they eat the fruit? The snake insinuates that they won't. Rather, if they will just act independently, they will discover knowledge that can only be gained by eating the tree's fruit. They believe the serpent, they eat the fruit, and they discover what they did not know before: that God was telling the truth. Humans can only "live" when they trust God and live in communion with God. When they choose to trust anything else, there is only loss. And so idolatry is introduced into the creation story as turning to someone or something other than God as the source of all life and meaning and purpose.

Eating from this particular tree was a statement of mistrust of the creator God. It meant humans did not trust God to be their source of life and that they had taken it upon themselves to determine their destiny. That destiny now included death, symbolized by exile from the garden. The way of exile and the end of it are themes that pass through the entire biblical story. Theologically, the Bible is the story of human exile and the hope of being reconciled with God and, consequently, with one another in the new and renewed creation.

Why Were These Stories Told?

There is one other theological idea that is important to understand before leaving these Genesis stories. Why are they told? Indeed, why was all of Genesis 1–11 told? Even from a conservative biblical perspective, these stories were prehistory. These stories were most likely told and passed on and compiled in some form after the Exodus. The stories look back to explain for Israel who she was, how she came into existence, and why. In fact, one could draw a line straight back to God from Abraham. And that was the point. (Luke does something similar by giving the genealogy of Jesus.) But that was only part of the point. Just as the line went back, it also extended into the future as well, the fulfillment of Israel's vocation. The Abraham stories tell us that he was called out of Ur of the Chaldeans by God and given a promise that he would be given a land, that he would be the father of an *ethnos*,² that is, a people, and that through him all the nations of the earth would be blessed:

> The LORD said to Abram, "Leave your land, your family, and your father's household for the land that I will show you. I will make of you a great nation and will bless you. I will make your name respected, and you will be a blessing. I will bless those who bless you, those who curse you I will curse; all the families of earth will be blessed because of you." (Gen 12:1-3)

Israel's identity as a people was tied to a calling. Later prophets would remind Israel that she was to be the light to the world, that through her all people would be set free from their captivity and darkness and come to know the one true God:

> God the LORD says—the one who created the heavens, the one who stretched them out, the one who spread out the earth and its offspring, the one who gave breath to its people and life to those who walk on it—I, the LORD, have called you for a good reason. I will grasp your hand and guard you, and *give you as a covenant to the people, as a light to the nations*, to open blind eyes, to lead the prisoners from prison, and those who sit in darkness from the dungeon. (Isa 42:5-7, emphasis added)

Note that the future is tied to the action of the creator God.

N. T. Wright explains that three ideas gave shape and form to Israel: monotheism, election, and eschatology. There is one God who has created all that is, and that God is YHWH. Humanity has turned against the one true God and has chased after other gods. *Election* means "calling"; Israel was called by God from among all people with a mission, and that mission is to be the people through whom the one true God heals creation. Eschatology is about endings. The one true God, who called a people and through whom creation would be healed and restored, would bring the story to completion.

Wright continues, two related ideas emerge and run through this three-fold structure: creation and covenant (1992; 1993). Creation affirms that God is the creator of all and the reason why everything exists and for whom everything exists. When creation departs from its creator, it begins to lose its proper being and place. Covenant focuses on the promise of the creator to fix it all, to bring things back into wholeness out of the great love that God has for creation. The relationships between these are illustrated in the following graphic. The three pillars run vertically while creation and covenant run horizontally through them.

Now why have I covered this biblical and theological ground? What does it have to do with homosexuality? The reason is simple, actually. First, everything is rooted in the idea that the God of creation has made a commitment to creation in the face of humanity's propensity to reject God and chase after other gods. Second, the root of human sin is idolatry. This is the consistent plotline from Genesis to Revelation. Without this understanding, it is hard to comprehend the core of the biblical story. As a result, and by way of example, we read a text like Romans 1 with Paul's list of vices and think it is those things that are the Sin. A better reading of Genesis 3 and following would have us understand that those particular things listed in Romans 1 are symptoms of the problem, not the problem itself. *The human tragedy is that we turn from trusting the living God to creations of our own making, and then we give ourselves to our creations as if they are gods.* We say to our idols, "You be for me all that I need for life!" And in reward for giving ourselves to them, we expect them to give us the life our own creations promise us. Nowhere is this clearer than in human sexuality. But as I will argue later, the problem is not about sexual orientation or behavior, it's that for which we pursue or use sex. It's about idolatry, which will be explored further in the section on Romans 1.

Love, Covenant, and Righteousness

Love, covenant, and righteousness all stand together in the biblical story. The entire narrative is about a loving creator who, while honoring the choices of God's created beings even as they "run themselves off the cliff" all of the time, still works to redeem them from their self-inflicted fate.

God's *Hesed*

After leading captive Israel out of Egypt, Moses goes up the mountain to meet with YHWH. On that mountain YHWH makes a covenant with Israel. A covenant is an enduring commitment to stay in a fruitful relationship. Most scholars think that this understanding of an enduring, committed, and fruitful relationship originates in Israel's family and clan structure. This understanding of covenant is seen through the promises to Noah or to Abraham. Covenant can also evoke similarities to the legal agreement made between two parties, such as the Sinai covenant, which stipulates obligations that God had for Israel. Each stipulation involves a promise to keep. God's promise is based upon God's "loyalty and faithfulness:"

The LORD passed in front of him and proclaimed: "The LORD! The LORD! a God who is compassionate and merciful, very patient, full of great *loyalty and faithfulness*, showing great loyalty to a thousand generations, forgiving every kind of sin and rebellion, yet by no means clearing the guilty, punishing for their parents' sins their children and their grandchildren, as well as the third and the fourth generation." (Exod 34:6-7, emphasis added)

It is difficult for us to grasp the meaning of the Hebrew word used to describe God's covenant commitment/promise. In Hebrew it is *hesed*, and it is often translated as "steadfast love" or "loyal love," "everlasting love," or "great loyalty and faithfulness," all trying to give some sense of the grandeur and magnitude of it. The word alone is not enough. It must be read in its context. Even after Israel has rebelled and Moses is fed up, YHWH reaffirms love for the people and expresses it in a covenant. If we read this language and keep it in the back of our minds, that is, God's promise-making love, we come close to the idea. It is not an abstract idea; it is concrete, made so in the covenant that reflects the kind of god YHWH is. Faithfulness is also part of this. God stays true to God's promise regardless of what creation does on the way. (Most of us bank on this characteristic of God!)

Psalm 136 is a celebration of YHWH's *hesed*, translated here as "faithful love." Notice also that it is rooted in creation.

Give thanks to the Lord of all lords—God's faithful love lasts forever.
Give thanks to the only one who makes great wonders—God's faithful love lasts forever.
Give thanks to the one who made the skies with skill—God's faithful love lasts forever.
Give thanks to the one who shaped the earth on the water—God's faithful love lasts forever.
Give thanks to the one who made the great lights—God's faithful love lasts forever.
The sun to rule the day—God's faithful love lasts forever.
The moon and the stars to rule the night—God's faithful love lasts forever! (vv. 3-9)

Hesed expresses God's faithfulness to divine creation and the blessings that come from the promise constituted in the covenant. Thus as creation and covenant run through all three pillars of Jewish/Christian faith, that which motivates it all—if I can put such a vast idea into words—is the loving commitment of the creator for the created.

25

Hesed and the New Testament?

The word *hesed* is linked to the New Testament word *agapē*. This is the word our Greek-writing authors primarily chose to use for the same covenant promising love of God. The idea of *hesed/agapē* is captured in many ways through stories and actions. I will explore this in the New Testament in the chapter titled "Constructing a Theology of Inclusion."

Love and Judgment

Anyone who reads the Bible knows there are two sides to the story—judgment and redemption—though I believe many Christians don't understand the relationship between these two properly. Because of God's love for creation, God cannot simply let it devolve into total chaos. God must make a judgment about creation. God's own "rightness" requires it. God would not be a loving God if God simply let creation dissipate, for that would not be "right." And so part of the loving covenant God has made with creation is that God would judge it.

Judgment is not about making sure the "bad guys get their just deserts." Judgment in the Bible begins with asking a simple question: Are things as they ought to be? If they are not, judgment is making that determination and restoring it. A court of law makes a judgment after being presented the evidence. The judge determines who or what is right and who or what is wrong.

The purpose of this process is to establish justice, to set things right, to restore things as they ought to be in God's eyes.

Some of us get a little weak in the stomach when the subject of judgment is raised, and I am a chief offender here. We must remember that there can be no peace until there is justice, until all things that have been spoiled are set right. This is the biblical meaning of *shalom*. *Shalom* comes from a word that means "a knitting of the bones." *Shalom* is restoration, a healing, a peace that puts things right. This is not the kind of peace that governments today constantly try to establish—that is, the lowest common denominator of agreement, so that the bullets will stop flying but injustices remain. The Treaty of Versailles after World War I is an example. The bullets stopped, but the underlying structure of the treaties imposed an unbearable burden on Germany and other nations that made up the Central Powers. This caused more anger to fester, bursting forth as World War II (Schmitt 1960).

In contrast, biblical shalom means all has been set right by the King, the Great Physician. Biblical shalom in a marriage is not the cessation of conflict, because you just wear each other out, rather it is dealing with the underlying wrong and bringing healing so that peace can prevail.

The Righteousness of God

When we look at Romans 1, we will consider again the notion of God's wrath and judgment, which are not so much God doing something to punish as God sadly letting humanity have its own way. This is unfortunately a way of saying: let people suffer the consequences of their own decisions—but not forever. Paul expounds how the promise of God to set it all right has finally been fully enacted in Jesus.

This thread then goes full circle back to an important phrase Paul uses in Romans, a phrase that was central to his Jewish faith and reflected God's *hesed*; the *righteousness of God* (in Greek *dikaiosynē theou*). N. T. Wright says about this important phrase in Paul's theology:

> There is no way that a modern English reader, faced with the word 'righteousness', or for that matter 'justice', will catch any glimpse of that warm-blooded, rich and tender, covenanted love of God for his people. Equally, if we translate the word as 'covenant faithfulness', we will miss the fact that it still carries plenty of meaning to do with 'justice', with things that are wrong being put right at last. We just do not have a single word, or even a single phrase, which will convey all that Paul meant when he wrote *dikaio-synē*. (2011)

The "righteousness of God" is "shorthand" for the central biblical theme of the loving covenant promise of God that God will judge the world; things are not as they ought to be. Therefore, God has made a promise that, without violating the freedom of creation, God will love it into healing, reconciliation, restoration, and peace. This takes us to the last piece of our creation theology.

Creation Is Not Finished

Remember that one of the three pillars of Jewish and Christian faith is eschatology. This means that the covenant-making, creator God will indeed finish the work of creation. What does this mean? To address this question, consider Romans 8 and Revelation 21–22.

Creation Groans

> I believe that the present suffering is nothing compared to the coming glory that is going to be revealed to us. The whole creation waits breathless with anticipation for the revelation of God's sons and daughters. Creation was subjected to frustration, not by its own choice—it was the choice of the one who subjected it—but in the hope that the creation itself will be set free from slavery to decay and brought into the glorious freedom of God's children. We know that the whole creation is groaning together and suffering labor pains up until now. And it's not only the creation. We ourselves who have the Spirit as the first crop of the harvest also groan inside as we wait to be adopted and for our bodies to be set free. (Rom 8:18-23)

Romans 8 is considered one of the most powerful texts in the New Testament. It is flooded with hope and promise and expectation all revolving around the righteousness of God, expressed through the faithfulness of Jesus and achieved by the power of the Holy Spirit. It looks forward to the day when what was initiated in the death and resurrection of Christ is made complete, when all things including human beings are finally as they ought to be. It is at that point that God will have completed creation. All will finally be set right, which is what the justice of God is about. God's creatures will have attained what is now their hope: the hope of glory. But until that point, Paul says all of creation groans longing for its completion; as do we.

It Is Done!

Revelation, in language that is at times beautiful, terrifying, and enigmatic, tells the story of how God, through the faithfulness of Jesus, is establishing God's reign on earth as it is in heaven. All of the (sometimes gory) battle detail is not to be taken literally. God does not need to ride in on a white horse and literally defeat enemies. Indeed resorting to such crude and violent means is antithetical to how God is, in fact, reclaiming divine creation. God's method is the enticement of love. Apocalyptic language, which is the literary style in which Revelation was written, was popular in the first century. Nobody reading it would have expected it to happen literally (Bauckham 1993). But what they did expect was that what Revelation described in highly symbolic language would in fact occur; the separation of the dominion of God (heaven) and the dominion of the Satan (earth) would finally be abolished and the two would become one under God's rule (Bauckham [1993] 2005, 185–98). That is the moment when the healing and restoration of creation will be complete. That is the moment when creation will be finished, and nothing describes that great moment that we all long for more than this text from Revelation:

> Then I saw a new heaven and a new earth, for the former heaven and the former earth had passed away, and the sea was no more. I saw the holy city, New Jerusalem, coming down out of heaven from God, made ready as a bride beautifully dressed for her husband. I heard a loud voice from the throne say, "Look! God's dwelling is here with humankind. He will dwell with them, and they will be his peoples. God himself will be with them as their God. He will wipe away every tear from their eyes. Death will be no more. There will be no mourning, crying, or pain anymore, for the former things have passed away." Then the one seated on the throne said, "Look! I'm making all things new." He also said, "Write this down, for these words are trustworthy and true." Then he said to me, "All is done." I am the Alpha and the Omega, the beginning and the end. To the thirsty I will freely give water from the life-giving spring. (21:1-6)

Summary

The biblical story is the all-encompassing narrative that shapes my life—not just my life, but all our lives as Christians. This story provides the contexts for my approach to any subject that has moral or social aspects. These days much is said about the Bible and homosexuality, most of it rather negative. The language used and judgments pronounced or implied simply do not square with this story. The God I find in the scriptures is a God who created in love and is committed to redeeming out of that same love. Justice is God setting things right that are not right. When I reflect on this story and the challenges of homosexuality, I simply cannot see the condemnation that is so often expressed. We will return to this later in the book. As a beginning point, creation theology establishes the framework within which we find our meaning, purpose, and future. Though each of us—straight or gay—is small within this framework, each of us—straight or gay—has a place in the story of creation and its loving creator God.

Notes

1. This does not mean "creationist." Creationists are people who believe in some kind of seven-day or seven-age creation scheme designed to construct a cosmology that they feel reflects and protects the "historical integrity" of Genesis 1.

2. *Ethos* in Greek; *goim* in Hebrew.

Chapter 3

Game Changer: Modern Science and Same-Sex Orientation

Science is a human enterprise seeking to understand the universe in which we live. To put it more directly, science tries to figure out how things work, with the assumption that if we can figure out how something works, we can predict how it will work in the future. There is no doubt—unless one is a total Luddite[1]—that, over the years, this enterprise has been exceedingly successful for good and for bad. So when science comes at the question of human sexual orientation and behavior and, specifically, same-sex orientation and behavior, it seeks to figure out why it occurs as a human phenomenon and the mechanics behind it. In its purest form science does not make value judgments about the objects of its inquiry. That is to say, it does not declare that a condition or behavior is right or wrong. It simply seeks to describe, categorize, and understand how the condition emerged or how the behaviors are practiced.

My goal in this chapter is to explore and outline the current scientific consensus on the origins of LGBT sexuality and the sexual behaviors that attend the various expressions. To set the context, I will briefly review the history of the development of the science that emerged to study the phenomenon. Because the current scientific consensus on the origins of homosexuality[2] departs from older beliefs about its origins, I will also explore the scientific theories and the therapies called upon to support what several conservative Christian groups believe to be traditional beliefs. This is important because many of these alternative theories and therapies are practiced by several conservative Christian groups, even though the science upon which they are based has mostly been discredited. In the next chapter, some of these practices will be explored.

But first, we must zoom way out and ask a fundamental question.

What Kind of Universe Do We Live in?

It may seem odd, but I want to begin by asking this question from the scientific domain: What kind of universe do we live in? In other words, how does the physical universe work? How does it unfold? At a detailed level, what are the mechanical processes at work, such that we are here, on this planet, at this moment in time, asking these questions?

At a macro level, modern physics explains that the universe unfolds through a continuous process of "chance and necessity." *Chance* is an unfortunate word because we associate chance with such things as throwing dice, but that is really not what is meant. Rather it means that physicists believe there is an element of contingency in how the deterministic rules of necessity work. This means that within every pattern, there is the possibility of newness and variation. Here is an example. Consider a red maple tree. Even though we categorize a maple as a type of tree, no one expects that any two will be exactly alike, because within each category there is a range of variation. If the variation becomes sufficient, the tree is then assigned to another category, perhaps a sugar maple. And even within the designation of red maple tree, each leaf will be slightly different from the others on that same tree. Also consider the pattern of snow as it melts down your car windshield. Watch the drops of water. They run in patterns, but there are always some drops that, for whatever reason, create a new path or stray from an existing path. The result is a remarkable diversity.

We live in an amazingly diverse universe. Nature is an unfolding process "bringing emergent novelty into being" (Polkinghorn 2000). The emphasis is on process, openness, and becoming. Cause and effect are foundational, but the scientific view of nature is shifting to see more subtlety and suppleness to its unfolding. There is now talk about "openness" in nature and that perhaps nature can be influenced. All is not the result of some uniformity of natural causes within an unbroken chain within a closed system. Rather, there is an openness in nature that allows diversity to emerge. A good example of this is identical twins. Any parent with twins will tell you that despite being genetically the same, twins are individual people. And although strangers may not be able to tell them apart at first glance, family and close friends clearly see defined differences. (We have twins, and though we never tested to discover if they were identical or not, in their young years and through high school, many could not tell them apart. But five minutes with them, and one knows they are two very different people.)

Perhaps a simple illustration will help clarify the difference between an open and closed system. Imagine living in a world we shall call Alpha, in which every action you take or even every thought you have is simply the result of something prior, and that something prior can be simply explained by what preceded it. At first glance, is this not the kind of world we live in, at least in theory? Well, yes, but now apply that to your future. Imagine that in this same world everything you will ever do and everything you ever think is simply the next step in a massive cause-and-effect chain. How do you feel about such a notion? Most of us would say, "Stop! That is not right! I have free will." But not in such a world as Alpha. Alpha is a closed system.

Now imagine a world that is similar to Alpha but one that we shall call Beta. In Beta, there is cause and effect, but it is not an unbroken chain. Causes and effects can be affected by alternative causes. In Beta, you can imagine three different decisions to make and freely choose one, making that one affect something else. This is an open system world.[3]

In Alpha, on the one hand, there is no real choice, genuine surprise, or accident. This world is more like dominoes lined up. Hit the first one, and the others all necessarily fall in a predictable pattern. In Beta, on the other hand, there can be choice, surprise, accidents, but also miracles—those things that happen against all odds. We may see patterns, but we also see the possibility for variation—individuality and novelty. In the real universe we know that things are not so simple. Real life is messy. We have freedom, but it is contingent. Existence is a matter of boundaries but with limits that can promise more.

The Vulnerability of Freedom

If our universe is an open system, similar to Beta in the illustration, then at a natural process level, there is a certain vulnerability in the freedom of nature to unfold in diverse ways. It means that sometimes the universe can be horribly destructive from the viewpoint of humans living. Tsunamis, earthquakes, volcanoes, tornados, asteroids, all the result of natural processes—while holding a certain beauty in them—can devastate human communities. At one level, this is the vulnerability of contingency.

It also means that nature may express diversity in how life emerges. I have red hair, a somewhat unusual human trait and one that caused me much suffering as child. Being different from the norm carries with it some danger.

Unfortunately sometimes nature's diverse unfolding will produce children with physical dysfunctions. And sometimes nature's diverse unfolding will produce people who are not heterosexual. Within the form and freedom of nature, there is always a range of expression with a diversity that can go in many directions. When thinking about homosexuality, this is intended not as a value judgment but as an observation. It is not intended to suggest that homosexuality is a mistake of nature but merely is part of the range of variation that emerges in nature. My point is simply that when process is open and, therefore, free, process will express itself in diverse ways. Indeed—and this is a value judgment—it is this freedom that is expressed in such diversity that creates so much beauty and wonder in our universe; it also gives us the possibility of individuality and a unique expression of humanity, which our culture values so highly.

A Theological Insertion

Although I want to avoid domain jumping, I cannot proceed without stepping out of a scientific description of how nature unfolds and stepping into my theological shoes. It seems to me that the wonder of chance and necessity, form and yet freedom in how nature unfolds is testimony to the creative love of God for creation. For the creation that God called into existence was a creation that was granted freedom to unfold as it will in all of its diversity. One could say that God took a great chance—made Godself vulnerable (speaking in human terms)—in creating such a universe. Not only could that universe manifest unbelievable creativity, but also it can manifest massive destruction. This means that life species can express an abundant diversity, and within that diversity, into existence may come some that are less likely to be able to reproduce due to their sexual orientation.[4] If we focus on human life, that chance means that the crown of God's creation may turn against God to other gods, but this is a discussion for later. The main point here is a God of love who, because of God's great love, granted creation tremendous freedom to unfold as it would and the result has been a manifold diversity cosmically, biologically and humanly. Now back to the science.

A Brief History of the Science on Homosexuality

That there have been persons who felt same-sex attraction and practiced same-sex behavior is well documented going back at least as far as Plato (and we assume way back into the beginnings of humans, but we don't know). But the term *homosexuality* is fairly recent, coined by a Hungarian named Karl

Maria Kertbeny (1824–82). Kertbeny was a late-nineteenth-century social activist who had a close friend who was gay. His friend committed suicide because someone was blackmailing him. This was an all-too-common occurrence at the time. There were still sodomy laws in most European (and American) law books. Being "outed" could ruin one's career, cause social ostracization, and even land you in prison and lead to execution. Kertbeny became an activist for many social causes in which injustice prevailed. In 1889, during one of his campaigns against antisodomy laws, he coined the term *homosexual* as a way of classifying sexual types. He also coined the word *heterosexual* as the word describing sexual attraction between men and women (Greenberg 2007; Burroway 2008). Prior to Kertbeny, same-sex attraction that resulted in a same-sex experience was called sodomy.[5] The first use of the term *homosexual* was in a letter to Karl Ulriches (Burroway 2008).

Letter to Karl Ulriches, May 6,1868

The general cultural assumption up to this time was that people chose to do sodomitic acts and thus to be a sodomist. This line of thought, of course, continues in some quarters even now. But Kertbeny and several others including Karl Heinrich Ulriches (1825–95)—to whom he wrote the letter—and Magnus Herschfeld (1868–1935) began to speak of homosexuality as a condition to which one was born. In conjunction with this, Herschfeld proposed that homosexuality was a third sex; male, female, and other.

This was a definite change in the fundamental assumption about homosexuality. For now the focus was not on behavior one did (i.e., sodomitic acts), it was on how one was born—an innate characteristic. The result of this shift of focus meant that homosexuality was now considered the result of

35

something that had not gone quite right in the formation of the person. Although the person may not have chosen to be a homosexual, there was something wrong nonetheless. Consequently many scientists of that period, who were sympathetic to the view that one was born gay, still considered it to be a condition that could be cured, and much of the science was driven by that objective.

While Herschfeld was promoting the view that homosexuality was a condition with which one was born, a second theory emerged. This view originated with Sigmund Freud. Freud proposed that homosexuality was a condition brought on by childhood trauma that interrupted the normal development process. Homosexuality was caused by an unhealthy reaction to one's thwarted development—a neurosis. These two alternative theories formed a fork in the scientific/medical road. Was the origin of homosexuality caused by *nature* (born that way by Herschfeld) or *nurture* (how one developed from birth to adulthood by Freud)? The two branches can be followed through the twentieth century and into the twenty-first. Herschfeld represented the biological or nature theory of homosexual origin, and Freud, a nonbiological or developmental nurture theory. Although there are variations and divergent opinions in each group, for a time the nurture side was dominant given the influence of Freud and his followers.

Nonbiological Scientific Theories of Sexual Orientation

Although a strict distinction between nature and nurture is more abstraction than real—Freud, for example, believed that human development was a natural process—the two do reflect two different paths down which science proceeded through the twentieth century and into the twenty-first. The primary distinction is between biological and nonbiological (or psychological) theories of sexual orientation—which are often thought of as nature versus nurture, though this is an oversimplified distinction. The nonbiological approach branches into at least two different schools; for the purpose of this book, those schools are psychoanalysis and behaviorism.

Psychoanalysis

The theory of the psychoanalytic school was that dynamics in one's family were responsible for the individual's sexual orientation. Although the developmental pattern was inherited, Freud thought that culture shaped the expression of instincts and that it gave preference to certain behaviors associated with the stages of development. Think for a moment about potty training. According to Freud, all children of a particular age naturally have to negotiate their bodily urges and find a culturally acceptable way to handle them. But if a child is traumatized in her efforts to become "trained," then that child's future development will not be optimal and a neurosis[6] will necessarily result. According to Freud, somewhere between the ages of three and five, boys go through their Oedipal phase. Sexual urges are directed toward their mothers but are later repressed for fear of their fathers. Sexual feelings are normal (and this was considered shocking at the time), but the body has to find a socially acceptable way of expressing instinctual feelings in order to keep a relationship with the mother and also with the father. Eventually those urges are redirected toward girls at puberty. According to Carl Jung, one of Freud's followers, girls go through something similar (called the Electra phase) wherein their sexual urges are directed toward their fathers until they are resolved and redirected toward boys. The popular term *Oedipal complex* simply means that the child did not completely or successfully negotiate the phase. The complex, then, becomes the nucleus around which a neurosis will emerge. The thing to remember with Freud is that no civilized person ever escapes suffering the effects of the Oedipal complex.

Homosexuality is the consequence of a neurosis resulting from failure to resolve the Oedipal phase, which in Freud's theory is a ubiquitous part of human development. Resolution occurs when the child is able to finally identify with the same-sex parent instead of feeling rage and undue competition with that parent for possessing the opposite-sex parent. The failure to resolve means that in some way the boy or girl is stuck and cannot move on to adulthood. Hence for Freud, homosexuality is stunted psychological growth and immaturity. The cure comes through insight, which "unsticks" development, leaving the person free to move forward. Although research has debunked many of Freud's theories, the influence is still evident in many people's assumptions about the origin of homosexuality. I suspect that the average person on the street still thinks that boys become gay because they had an overbearing mother who smothered them in femininity and a distant or removed father who did not help them develop masculine traits. These same assumptions continue to frame how many segments of the religious community understand homosexuality. Persistent in these ideas is the notion that homosexuality is in some manner a perversion of nature.

This is not to say that childhood experiences do not influence the psychosocial development of a child, for they certainly do. Most of us can reflect on significant events that shaped us growing up. But there is little research that supports the idea of such dynamics influencing or determining one's sexual orientation (Wilson and Rahman 2008, 30–31).

Behaviorism

Behaviorism, as articulated by B. F. Skinner, proposes that all human behavior is learned. In its more extreme versions, the child is born as a blank slate on which the world of his or her parents, teachers, playmates, and so on write. Casual observation would conclude that gendered traits are those behaviors that seem to follow gender lines. Boys like trucks and wrestling; girls like dolls and dressing up. But from a behaviorist's view of human behavior, boys like trucks and wrestling because they are *taught* that boys like such things. Girls like dolls because they are *taught* that girls like such things. Thus gendered traits, but also sexual orientation and even sexual behavior, are learned. If a child exhibits atypical behavior, such as a boy liking to play with dolls, this behavior is considered to have been learned. It is determined by nurture not nature.

Carrying this further, if, according to the behaviorist theory, sexual orientation, attraction, and gendered traits are learned behaviors, then classical and operant conditioning can be used to modify a person's orientation and sex-atypical behavior. Some extremely awful things have been done to gay and lesbian persons in an attempt to redirect their orientation and sexual behavior. (Some things still are done in quarters where this view is maintained, including some Christian counseling centers that use "conversion therapy" or "reparative therapy," which will be explored further in the next chapter.)

At the height of the behaviorist's influence, we were told that there was no difference between boys and girls (except sexually of course) and that if we just let a child play, he or she would develop whatever behavior he or she wanted. Additionally, it was argued—often by feminists of that era—that gendered traits were the result of socialization influences (Paglia 2013). It is pointed out by Simon LeVay that "the main difficulty with these ideas is that heterosexual parents don't seem to inculcate homosexuality or gender-nonconformity, in fact they often attempt to prevent these traits in children who nevertheless become gay" (2006, 1). It turns out that research has demonstrated there are gendered traits that children naturally express.

Today, these behaviorist ideas have been mostly dismissed as the primary reason for gendered traits, sexual orientation, and sexual behavior. Jacques Balthazart summarizes this well when he says, "though many popular books claim to explain homosexuality on the basis of educational or social factors, the currently available scientific studies show little or no influence of education on the development of sexual orientation" (2011, 8). Having said this, I must emphasize again that humans learn behavior through exposure to the world and that this is a given that all scientists and social scientists affirm.

Early Pleasure or Trauma and Sexual Orientation

One last theory explaining sexual orientation proposes that a person's early sexual experiences are determinant. A girl who suffers rape or other sexual abuse by a man may find future relationships with men repugnant and turn to same-sex relationships for intimacy and sexual expression. Conversely, a young person may have an early sexual experience that is pleasant and as a result wants to repeat the experience with the sex of the person who provided the initial experience. If a boy is seduced by a man or molested by his brother but enjoyed it, he may seek out future same-sex experiences.

While there is little doubt that such experiences do affect the psycho-social development of a person, there is not much evidence that they determine sexual orientation. Many people who have had such experiences go on to be heterosexual adults. One study looking into consensual same-sex behaviors in a single-sex boarding school where homosexual experiences were common found that such young people arriving at adulthood were no more likely to be homosexual than are children who do not attend these kinds of schools (LeVay 2006, 1–2). "If the early life experiences theory had some support, we should expect a higher incidence of homosexuality among adults raised in single-sex schools, which is absolutely not the case" (Balthazart 2011, 14).

The history I've provided is a general overview only. But there are alternate voices in both the nature and nurture camps. Freud and Eric Erikson (into the 1950s), in their human development scheme, postulated that a person's identity (including sexual identity) had to be solidified before intimacy was truly possible in a healthy way. However, Harry Stack Sullivan (in 1954) had a different view. He believed that intimacy was a prerequisite for identity. So he introduced what he called "chumship." This is a stage of development usually occurring from ages eight to eleven, during which a child begins to develop best friends of the same sex (chums). During this time same-sex sexual experimentation is frequent, normal, and healthy. Chums are needed so that a person's identity can solidify in the late teens but often into early young adulthood. For Sullivan, same-sex experimentation did not mean that the children are gay, but only that they are trying to find out who they are. In fact, he believed that without a chum, heterosexual love later

39

in life would be hampered and may even develop into a homosexual way of life.[7]

Biological Theories of Sexual Orientation

Recent research into the origin of homosexuality within the scientific and mental health research community has turned away from nonbiological origins as the primary force in determining a person's sexual orientation. That means it turns to biology—to nature. More specifically the disciplines involved in the research include neuroscience, genetics, endocrinology, and evolutionary biology. The field of psychology is involved on both sides of the discussion (nonbiological and biological), though mainstream psychology recognizes the biological element as a primary factor. Wilson and Rahman's book *Born Gay: The Psychobiology of Sex Orientation* explores how all of these fit together. In their introduction, they state the following about biology: "Biology in this case means at least either hormones or genes or both. Turns out, it is both and together they influence critical developmental processes of a fetus in utero. One element of that influence is that set of processes that shape the sex and gender of a person" (2008, 10).

Some Terms

Let's begin with some terms because conversations quickly can get sideways simply because of what people think these various terms mean. The definitions provided again come from the world of science. When discussing homosexuality, it is common to use the letters LGB or LGBT, which (again) stands for Lesbian, Gay, Bisexual, and Transgender.[8] I shall continue to use the abbreviations as shorthand.

Term	Definition
Gay	While often used as a generic term for homosexual persons, whether male or female, gay more specifically is a term describing male homosexual people. There is tremendous diversity within male homosexual expressions of sexuality.
Lesbian	Lesbians are homosexual women. Again there is great diversity in how lesbians experience and express their sexuality.
Bisexual	Bisexual persons find themselves attracted to both men and women but may prefer one in actual life experience and expression.

Transgender	Transgender persons are perhaps the most misunderstood due to the difference between biology and psychology. One's "sex" and one's "gender" can be different. A transgender person is one who is anatomically a male but whose gender identity is that of a woman. Or a person may have female genitalia but feel psychologically a male. In simpler terms, transgender people's sex is different than how they think of themselves. Anatomical boys usually think of themselves as boys, but boys who are transgender think of themselves as girls. Transgender persons will sometimes go through a sex change operation in order to align their "sex" with their "gender" and thus resolve the internal conflict in which they live. This internal conflict is different than that experienced by the LGB person.

Toward a Definition of Sexual Orientation

When is someone considered gay or lesbian? This is not a simple question, because as the old saying goes, "it depends on what you mean." There are three distinct ideas that inform our understanding; and each, while adding a dimension, is different though they often overlap in expression. The three ideas are: (1) sexual orientation, (2) same-sex sexual behavior, and (3) sexual identity.

There are four questions that will help bring each of these into better focus and hopefully lead to some clearer answers to the primary question: when is someone considered gay or lesbian?

Question	Has to Do with...
What does a person says he or she is?	Identity
What does a person do, that is, in his or her actual sexual behavior?	Behavior
What does a person feel, that is, fantasies and desires?	Orientation
What does a person's body do in response to various sexual stimuli?	Orientation

What Does a Person Say He or She Is? (Identity)

One way to answer the question is to ask a person: "Are you a heterosexual or a homosexual?" However, this is generally not considered to be a fruitful way to determine the orientation of a person. Most of us associate ourselves with a sexual identity. Someone may say, "I am a heterosexual." Another may say, "I am a homosexual." And others yet may say, "I am bisexual." But these statements of sexual identity—this is what I am—may or may not reflect one's actual orientation. For all kinds of reasons people may say they are a heterosexual when they are not. Cultural norms, religious beliefs, and economic interests all can affect what a person says his or her sexual identity is. Orientation is something else, though it may in fact align with one's sexual identity. That is, I may say I am a heterosexual and my orientation conforms to that. But I know of several people who, as young Christian adults, insisted that they were heterosexual only to finally come to terms with being gay years later and after much painful internal struggle—and in some cases, broken relationships and marriages.

What Does a Person Do, That Is, in Their Actual Sexual Behavior? (Behavior)

A second answer to the question of who is gay might be based upon the behavior of the person. But this surely is not a reliable determinant, because all kinds of people reveal that at some point in their life they had a same-sex experience. In our current youth culture it has become customary to "experiment" especially under the influence of too much alcohol or drugs. Prisons are notorious for same-sex behaviors, but most of the inmates—male or female—are not homosexuals. Likewise, same-sex boarding schools are also notorious for same-sex behavior among students who go on to heterosexual marriages. There is even a popular expression that goes with these behaviors, "gay for the stay." But most of these people are not gay.

What Does a Person Feel, That Is, in Their Fantasies and Desires? (Orientation)

A third answer to the question of who is gay actually gets closer to the mark. What does a person feel when he or she has sexual fantasies? What sex does the person desire? As stated in the first question above, it is possible for someone to be in a heterosexual relationship for cultural or religious or personal reasons (in the past, this was almost necessary to have children), but *inside* the person knows that he or she really prefers to be in a same-sex relationship in which he or she could express same-sex behavior. This internal feeling of attraction experienced often in fantasy life gets closer to indicating a person's sexual orientation. If you are a straight person reading this, and you can be honest with yourself, do you not have moments when you entertain sexual fantasies about another person? Are you a man? Do you look at women or men when they pass by you? Are you a woman? Do you look at men or women when they walk by you? What a straight person experiences in those fleeting moments of sexual fantasy, a gay or lesbian person does as well but only of the same sex. Such responses come from the center of who we are.

This is exactly the story of the Reverend Dr. Gene Robinson, bishop of the diocese of New Hampshire and the first openly gay bishop in the Episcopal Church. He was married for more than twenty years and has two children. But one day he simply could not do it anymore. What he "felt" inside was not consistent with an intimate relationship with a woman. He had tried many things to suppress feelings he had from his youth—not the least being constant prayer—but to no avail. One can read his story in two of his books, titled *In the Eye of the Storm: Swept to the Center by God* and *God Believes in Love: Straight Talk about Gay Marriage*. Bishop Robinson is an extremely controversial figure, but his personal story is the story of many LGBT people.

What Does a Person's Body Do in Response to Various Sexual Stimuli? (Orientation)

Researchers generally believe the best indicator of one's sexual orientation is how a person responds to sexual stimuli—that is, what the body does when shown sexually erotic images. There are testing instruments that can measure when a man is developing an erection and when a woman's vagina is engorging with blood—both telltale indicators of sexual arousal. Heterosexuals are more likely to be aroused by erotic images of the opposite anatomical sex. Homosexuals are more likely to show signs of arousal when shown images of their own anatomical sex. If honest with ourselves, most of us get this.

What Is Sexual Orientation?

Sexual orientation then is what a person sexually (erotically) desires in one's innermost self and is best confirmed by how one's body responds to sexual stimuli (LeVay 2010). Jacques Balthazart supports this definition when he explains that *sexual orientation* (a term that he prefers over *sexual preference*) "identifies the sex of persons to which an individual directs not only his or her behavior but also sexual fantasies" (2011, 4). Having said this, it is important to mention that the sexual orientation of men and women express somewhat different dimensions. To be perhaps overly simple, men's orientation is usually obvious by observing how they respond to sexually erotic images. Women are more complex, with relationship issues generally playing a greater role (LeVay 2010).

We can summarize our definition of *sexual orientation*. It is "an enduring pattern of emotional, romantic, and/or sexual attractions to men, women, or both sexes" (American Psychological Association 2008). It is intrinsically human to find oneself attracted to another. These attractions may be toward persons of the opposite sex, the same sex or both sexes. Regardless of the particulars, *sexual orientation describes how a person experiences attraction.*

The question then is how is this orientation shaped? This is the question we must address next.

Sex and Gender

A few additional definitions will help clear some definitional brush so that when certain words are used, we understand what is meant. Two words that are often interchanged are *sex* and *gender*.

Term	Definition
Sex	For most of us, the word sex means, well, sex! But from a biological perspective, sex has to do with "the anatomical, physiological, and genetic characteristics associated with being male or female" (American Psychological Association 2008). In other words, when one looks in a mirror at one's genitalia, does one see male or female reproductive organs? At a chromosomal level, does one have two X chromosomes or an X and a Y chromosome?
Gender	Gender is not quite so neat and tidy. Many of us assume gender and sex are the same thing. But from a psychological standpoint, they are quite different. Whereas sex refers to reproductive organs and genes, gender is a description of one's psychological sense of self, of identity. Gender has to do with whether a person senses he or she is male or female. For a large portion of the human population, sex and gender correspond—that is, a person with female sex organs also feels like a woman, her gender. It is also possible for the opposite to occur, which is essentially the core meaning of transgender, as was

	explained previously. Psychologists now call this gender dysphoria.[9] The emphasis of dysphoria is an experience of discontent with one's external sex vis-à-vis one's internal sense of gender. I remember a news magazine program in which a young person said, "I feel like a girl, but in the mirror, I look like a boy." Gender plays a role in our understanding of sexual orientation as discussed above because gender and sex may or may not correspond in an individual. If a person's sexual identity is that of a woman, but the individual biologically is a male, then "same-sex" attraction is not quite accurate. The anatomy may be the same but the sexual identity different.
Gender Role versus Identity	Gender role has to do with behaviors such as mannerisms, style of clothing, and activities one is inclined to prefer. Gender identity is similar to sexual identity as defined above.
Sexual Orientation versus Sexual Identity	As raised previously, depending upon the cultural norms of a society in which one lives, a person may have conflict between one's orientation and one's assumed identity (preference). That is, in a society in which homosexual expression is considered inappropriate or even sinful, a homosexually oriented person may define oneself as a heterosexual (one's preferred identity) and sexually behave as such. Psychologists note that in such cases the person is likely to experience internal "discordance" between one's orientation and one's identity.
Either/Or?	It is commonly thought that one is male or female, heterosexual or homosexual. That is generally a view that is disputed today. Rather research into sexual orientation and attraction has demonstrated that there is somewhat of a continuum. Some persons are exceedingly homosexual and some exceedingly heterosexual, with the bisexual person finding himself or herself variously attracted to the same sex or different sex. Recent studies have demonstrated that there is a difference between gay men and lesbians. There is less of a continuum for gay men. They are much more likely to be either heterosexual or homosexual, with few in the mid-range of bisexuality. Women, however, do not show such a bipolar profile. Rather, women tend to reflect a continuum with somewhat more on average being bisexual than wholly homosexual.

The Biological Basis: Current Research

Biological research into the origins of same-sex orientation has been developing at a rapid rate since the early 1980s. Many theories have been proposed, and much experimental research has been conducted. Numerous theories, once assumed to be true, have been upended. At this point in time the research appears to have narrowed to three areas that are considered to play the primary biological role in sexual orientation as well as a host of other sex- and gender-specific developments. Those three areas are all prenatal and include: (1) hormones, (2) brain structure, and (3) genes. In the introduction to their book, Wilson and Rahman summarize the position of current modern science: "Modern scientific research indicates that sexual orientation is largely determined by the time of birth, partly by genetics, but more specifically by hormonal activity in the womb arising from various sources" (Wilson and Rahman 2008, 10).

This is a complex conversation, and getting into detail here is beyond the scope of the study. There is a great deal of research material available either on the web or in some fairly recent books that delves into the specifics of how and why these conclusions are drawn. (Please see the bibliographic information at the end of this book.) I shall only attempt to summarize the "topline" findings, providing enough information to substantiate my belief that the science should challenge some of our more traditional attitudes toward same-sex attraction and behavior. This is not to preclude the moral discussion. I will engage the moral issue subsequently. But I believe the moral conversation must be informed by what modern science can tell us. In my seminary days I would often hear professors say, "'Is' comes before 'ought.'" That is the case here as well in my view. So what "is" the biological basis for same-sex orientation?

Exploring the Biological Causes

Hormone Exposure and Sexual Orientation and Anatomical Sex

There are multiple biological theories offered to explain how humans develop their sexual anatomy and orientation. Perhaps the strongest or at least most influential is that sexual orientation develops primarily during fetal neural development. Within this framework are models that include prenatal hormone exposure—which can include a genetic element, maternal immunological reactions, and an unstable prenatal development environment.

The prenatal hormone exposure theory proposes that sexual anatomy and orientation are determined by hormone exposure at two critical moments in fetal development. The first is the differentiation of the sexual organs, and the second occurs at a later date in the prenatal process wherein hormones affect brain structure. It is this latter process that is believed to be the origin of many differences, including sexual orientation (Garcia-Falgueras and Swaab 2010, 24; LeVay 2010). Sexual differentiation of the genitals takes place in the first couple of months of pregnancy. Sexual differentiation of the brain occurs in the second half of a pregnancy during a period of major and rapid brain development. This is significant because the gap means that the two processes can be influenced separately and influence development differently. In most of the human (and animal) population, the two processes are in synch. Male genitals align with typical male sexual behavior that prefers females due to the masculinization of the sexual behavior control areas of the brain. Conversely, the same is true for females. But it also means that sometimes they get out of synch. The result is "discrepancies between physical sex and aspects of sexual behavior that are sexually differentiated (orientation, gender identity)" (Balthazart 2011, 155). A fetus that develops male genitalia may not develop a masculinized brain. In some cases the result is a transgender person; in others, a gay, lesbian, or bisexual person.

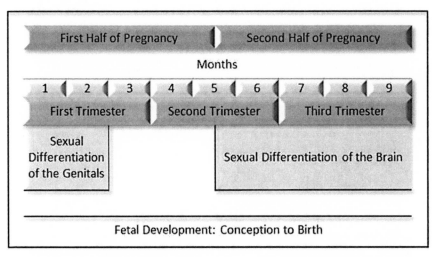

Recent evidence suggests that exposure to prenatal androgen (testosterone for males and estrogen for females) can influence later sexual orientation and behavior. It is proposed that hormone exposure works as a cofactor interacting with genes and environmental and social conditions (Wilson and Rahman 2008). Research also demonstrates that within the prenatal timeline, sexual differentiation and the development of the sexual centers of the brain (where orientation develops) occurring at different moments explains, in part, why some persons develop orientations that are different than their anatomical sex. A genetic male who develops male genitalia due to testosterone exposure may for some reason not experience the same testosterone exposure in the later brain development that would normally masculinize the brain. In other words depending upon the moment and extent of hormone exposure at two different points in the sexual development process, a fetus may emerge as straight, gay, bisexual, or transgender.

More about the Brain

Sex is in your head, it is often said. More accurately, a person's sexual orientation and behavior originate in the brain. Research into prenatal development proposes that the brains of males develop differently than those of females due to hormone exposure or lack thereof, as stated above. In the second half of prenatal development, the fetal brain develops in a male direction (masculinization) through a surge in testosterone on the forming nerve cells. A brain develops in the female direction (feminization) through the absence of the hormone surge. The default pattern of fetal development is female unless exposed to testosterone. This surge can be seen in the following graphic that compares the development of male versus female mice. Notice that the male has a spike before birth and for a little time after. Females do not have a hormonal spike until puberty.

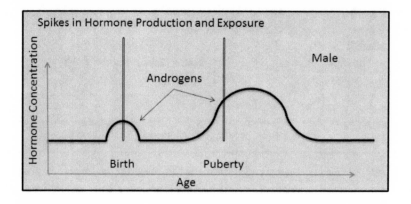

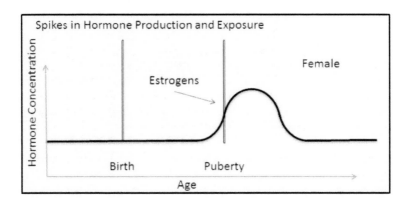

Males typically experience two spikes in fetal hormone exposure whereas females experience only one (Vandenbergh 2003, 220).[10]

The research into hormone exposure also found that some mice exhibit same-sex preferences. In these cases, at some point the brains of female mice were exposed to androgen hormones, which masculinized the brain. This can be seen in the following graph in which a female (XX chromosomes) is exposed to androgens just prior to birth and as a result exhibits same-sex behaviors. Though females anatomically, the mice were sexually attracted to other female mice (Vandenbergh 2003, 220).

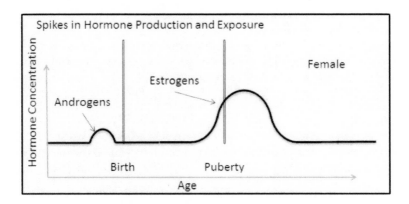

A similar pattern occurs in humans. A 2010 study by Garcia-Falgueras and Swaab of the Netherlands Institute for Neuroscience, at the Royal Netherlands Academy of Arts and Sciences, concluded:

The fetal brain develops during the intrauterine period in the male direction through a direct action of testosterone on the developing nerve cells, or in the female direction through the absence of this hormone surge. In this way, our gender identity (the conviction of belonging to the male or female gender) and sexual orientation are programmed or organized into our brain structures when we are still in the womb. There is no indication that social environment after birth has an effect on gender identity or sexual orientation. (2010, 22–35)

Garcia-Falgueras and Swaab believe the effects of hormones are permanent.

Balthazart reports the same, namely, that during ontogeny—the process of development of an organism to maturity—the effects of the hormone exposure is permanent: "We now know that these sexually differentiated behavioral responses to steroids (i.e., testosterone or estrogen) are the result of early actions of these steroids and that during ontogeny the brain differentiates into a male or female brain. These differentiating effects occur during the embryonic period or just after birth and are completely irreversible" (2011, 40).

Garcia-Falgueras and Swaab explain that the main mechanism determining sexual identity and orientation is the effect of exposure to testosterone on an intrauterine developing brain. Sexual organs develop first, and following that, the brain is differentiated "under the influence, mainly, of sex hormones such as testosterone, estrogen, and progesterone on the developing brain cells and under the presence of different genes as well" (2010, 23–24). During fetal development, gay, lesbian, and bisexual people experience a different hormone exposure affecting how certain areas of the brain that determine one's sexual orientation and gender identity develop. A gay man may develop male genitalia, which form first, but when the brain is ready to develop, a change in hormone exposure—little or no testosterone—results in the sexual part of the brain forming in a way that is more typical of a straight female brain resulting in an orientation that is attracted to other males. This is referred to as the "masculinization" of the brain. The converse is true for a lesbian wherein she experiences a surge in testosterone. Put simply, because of a change in hormone exposure, the sexual part of the brain that is the source of sexual attraction and behavior can develop such that a woman is attracted to a woman and a man is attracted to a man. The shape and development of the brain sets the gender identity and sexual orientation; that is their pattern of attraction. That is their natural state just as is the case for a straight person.

Other research shows that there are parts of the straight male brain that are differently shaped than the straight female brain. Those areas having to do with sex and gender are called sexually dimorphic areas, meaning "different forms." (In other words, they have different shapes.) Some studies have demonstrated, however, that these same areas of the brain in gay men are more likely to be the same shape as heterosexual females. Conversely, these specific areas in a lesbian brain are similar in shape to a heterosexual male (Balthazart 2011).

A Homosexual Gene?

With the advent of gene science, there has been an effort to find a gene or genes that are the "cause" of homosexuality. As noted earlier, from an evolutionary perspective, the frequency of homosexuality should decrease unless there is some evolutionary advantage. A decrease in the incidence of homosexuality among many species is clearly not the case. (Nor has it increased as a percentage of the population.) Theorists propose that there is some genetic predisposition that creates a positive adaptation and thus the maintenance of a certain percentage of populations that are LGBT. For example, a study conducted by Dean Hammer found that gay men had more gay uncles and cousins on their mother's side than on their father's side. The theory is that there is some genetic phenomenon at work that results in the persistence of a nonstraight percentage of the population. More specifically, the theory is that at least some portion of male homosexuality is an inherited trait through the mother's side. Research has identified a location on the X chromosome (that comes from the mother) that is associated with sexual orientation, though no specific gene or genes have been identified. Studies attempting to discover if there is a genetic origin of male homosexuality found certain "markers" transmitted on the X chromosome (from the mother) in the Xq28 region (Balthazart 2011, 156).

The sexual orientation of women is more complex. Nonetheless Balthazart notes that several studies "have identified an increased rate of nonheterosexuality (the term used to group homosexual and bisexual women) in girls, nieces, and cousins of the paternal lineage of lesbians" (2011, 145). Balthazart explains that this transmission could be linked to the X chromosome or it could come from either the father or the mother. More research is needed on female sexual orientation in general because the actual genetic mechanisms are not clearly understood at this time. (New work in the field of epigenetics may shed light on the heritability of sexual orientation. See the discussion on epigenetics later in this chapter.)

Another suspected genetically influenced source of male homosexuality (only) is referred to as the "Older Brothers Effect." It has been statistically demonstrated that with each brother born to a mother, there is an increasing likelihood that next brother will be gay. "An analysis of 14 independent studies representing more than 10,000 subjects found that for each additional older brother an experimental subject has, his probability of being gay increases by 33%" (Balthazart 2011, 148–50). The current hypothesis—having disproved others—is that there is an immune response in the mother. With each boy born, the mother develops an immune system response to the foreign body (the male embryo) by forming antibodies, and these antibodies affect parts of the brain involved in the determination of sexual orientation. It is possible that the origin of this phenomenon is genetic, though how is yet to be determined. It is also possible it is just an immune system response (LeVay 2010).

Just how genes affect sexual orientation—either heterosexual or homosexual (or anywhere along a spectrum in between)—is still being explored. As Wilson and Rahman somewhat humorously write, "Clearly, the proteins that make up genes do not literally spell out 'gay' and 'lesbian' or 'straight'" (2008, 54). Rather, as they continue to explain, genes affect the development of the brain and, specifically relative to sexual orientation, the sexual areas of the brain that determine gender. How the mechanics of gene control mechanisms work is beyond this study, so I will leave it here. But I would highly recommend reading the chapter in Wilson and Rahman's *Born Gay* in which these processes are explained, if for no other reason than to appreciate the wonder of how it all happens with the result that little people are born and grow up and become adults. It is an amazing process!

It is expected that future research into how genetics influence human development will also shed more light on the mechanics of that influence.

Gender- and Sex-Related Traits

As noted previously, hormones activated based upon some cluster of genes shape the sexual parts of the brain in terms of size and organization, with the result being an immutable trait of sexual orientation (Balthazart 2011; LeVay 2010). But these same processes are also involved in a larger cluster of traits that are referred to in the literature as *gender-typical* or *gender-*

atypical. Sometimes these terms appear to be used interchangeably with the phrases *sex-typical* and *sex-atypical traits.* At other times they do not seem to be interchangeable. For the purposes of this study, gender-typical/atypical focuses on sexual or gender identity whereas sex-typical/atypical focuses on physical traits.

The phrases *gender-typical* and *gender-atypical* refer to behavior preferences that on average align with "boys" or "girls," men or women. Boys like trucks and cars, are more aggressive in play, and tend to be more competitive. Girls are more likely to prefer to play with dolls and exhibit nurturing behaviors. Adult males mostly still like trucks and cars and competitive sports. Adult females are more likely to prefer nurturing, fashion, and shopping. Even though the feminist movement of the 1960s through the 1980s worked hard to dispute such behavior as intrinsic, the research supports it on average (LeVay 2010).

Research has also found that gay and lesbian children often exhibit gender-atypical preferences and behaviors. Boys, who later grow up gay, may prefer to play with girls and dolls, and as adults, gay men are more likely to enjoy fashion and clothes. Girls, who later grow up to be lesbians, may show gender-atypical aggressiveness as children and as adults are more inclined to participate in activities often preferred by men. This is not absolute, however, and the trouble with averages is that a particular person may be quite distinct from the average. Some gay men actually show super-masculinized behaviors as children that continue into adulthood, such as bodybuilding. Conversely some girls may show completely gender-typical behaviors and grow up to be lesbians whose super-feminine preferences continue. This difference in lesbians is often referred to as "butch" versus "femme," though these should not be understood as either/or but as two poles on a continuum. The same continuum is described for gay men as "top" for the more masculine and "bottom" for the more feminine (LeVay 2010, 288).

There are also anatomical differences between men and women beyond the obvious differences of sexual genitalia, especially those related to brain structure and function. These differences can be physical, functional, or cognitive—none of which are part of sexual orientation but are affected by the same sex hormonal exposure processes that occur at the point the sexual parts of the brain are being influenced. LeVay as well as Wilson and Rahman describe these differences along with the research behind them. LeVay speaks of these as a "package of traits": "The association between sexual orientation and a 'package' of gendered traits arises, according to this idea, because several brain systems that mediate such traits develop in the same developmental time period and are all sensitive to circulating testosterone level" (2010, 127).

Causation does not have to be definitively established. It is likely the case that genetic factors come into play influencing typical or atypical sex hormone exposure. But it is also possible that such a factor is simply part of the randomness of the universe in which we live or can be attributed to other factors yet to be discovered. Studies of identical twins, who most assume to have the same genetic code, have shown that in some cases, one twin is gay and one is straight. Research designed to ascertain the concordance of sexual orientation of identical twins (i.e., both have the same sexual orientation) has not given a clear finding, with percentages ranging from a dubious 100 percent to a questionable less than 10 percent with the mean around 60 percent (Balthazart 2011, 143–44). This is compared to between 10 and 20 percent in fraternal twins. But why would identical twins not have the same sexual orientation always? It is actually not the case that identical twins have exactly the same DNA. Recent studies have shown that identical twins acquire many genetic differences in early fetal development. Mutations or code copy errors occur after the initial splitting of the single fertilized egg. These small changes can result is small differences over time (Ghose 2012). Additionally, "Other studies have shown that chemical modifications, or epigenetic effects, can change which genes are expressed over the years, one factor that renders twins not completely identical" (Ghose 2012). Epigenetics, in very simple terms, describes the processes whereby a gene is turned on or off, resulting in a gene being expressed at one moment or another or not at all.[11] (We will return to epigenetic effects below.) These data point to a consistent conclusion; for whatever reason, from a random event (LeVay 2010) to a small change in genetic code replication, exposure to higher levels of testosterone while in the womb is differentially experienced by identical twins with the result that they may not have the same sexual orientation.

Research on these issues continues apace with genetics leading the way. Our understanding of humans via our genome continually opens new doors and closes many old doors as well. Craig Venter and Daniel Cohen, two of the world's leading genetic scientists, made the following prediction in 2004: "If the 20th century was the century of physics, the 21st century will be the century of biology. While combustion, electricity, and nuclear power defined scientific advance in the last century, the new biology of genome research—

which will provide the complete genetic blueprint of a species, including the human species—will define the next" (73).

One area of emerging research is the impact of epigenetics on sexual orientation. As stated above, epigenetics focuses on how genes are switched on or off, a process that can be influenced by environment—in this case the fetal environment (Rice, Friberg, and Gavrilets 2012). As of this writing, this research is quite new and is yet to be tested but if confirmed would blur the nature/nurture distinction, but only within a biological theory of sexual orientation. (For example, it may shed light on what otherwise looks in some cases to be random.)

Summary

This simplified explanation of the biological origins of sexual orientation is intended to make the point that the science leans heavily in the direction of a prenatal biological determination of a whole cluster of gender- and sex-related traits. If this is true, and the evidence certainly would appear to support this theory over other theories, then one's sexual orientation is the result of genetic and hormonal processes that shape one's orientation as well as a host of other gender and sex traits such as gender-conforming preferences and behaviors, some physical characteristics, and size and structure of sex-related areas of the brain. LeVay provides the following illustration that attempts to demonstrate how all of these factors interact.

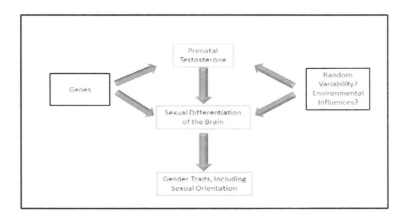

Development of Sexual Orientation: Basic Elements of a Prenatal Hormone Theory (LeVay 2010, 64)

What our adult sexual orientation will be is largely determined in our mother's womb.[12] We are born the way we are.

Symmetry Breaking and Sexual Orientation

I want to tie the current science on the origins of sexual orientation to the prior discussion about the kind of universe we live in. It was pointed out under the discussion about chance and necessity that chance, as we normally think of it, does not mean "anything" can happen. In reality, in our universe there is a range of options available, and chance means any one of them may in fact occur. But the laws of nature persist, so there is not much "chance" that if you step off the edge of a building that you will go up instead of down! Chance then means historical contingency—many possible happenings, one single selection. But not everything is possible. Perhaps a simple illustration will make this somewhat clearer. Consider the first image below. It is a table fully dressed for a banquet. The question is: With which place setting do the glasses go?

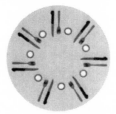

There are many *potential* options but no certainty. But there are not an infinite number of options. There are a finite number of options that can become *actual*. At the point a glass is chosen by a guest, potentiality becomes actuality. Each glass becomes uniquely tied to a particular place setting. This is called "symmetry breaking."

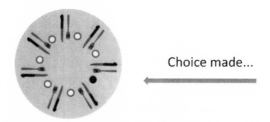

Choice made...

Chance is a way of suggesting there is contingency in nature—there are potential options that, in time, are made actual. Not all is reduced to a linear cause-effect chain. If this is true, then the universe is not quite so deterministic after all—there is an openness to it.

Now what does this have to do with a discussion on the origins of nonheterosexual orientation? In the beginning a fetus is given a specific genetic inheritance. As the prenatal development process unfolds, potential becomes actual through the interaction of genes and hormones and the uterine environment. However those mechanical dynamics work, the science points to a symmetry breaking, a point when organizational hormones have their effect on the sexual parts of the brain that determine gender and on the development of sexual anatomy. First, hormones direct the formation of the sexual organs and they take shape, and sometimes that taking shape becomes mixed or ambiguous. Somewhat later, parts of the brain that manage human sexuality take shape, and gender is established. Regardless of what occurs, the process establishes a set of traits that make up the sexuality of a person at birth. Once the symmetry is broken, the path for the human person is set. As the person grows and develops, environmental factors will of course give further shape to who he or she becomes as an adult and the kinds of choices the person makes. But at this point, science would say that, for most people, their orientation has been set and what will unfold in their adult life will follow within those bounds.

Impact of Psychosocial Dynamics

Although most current science supports a biological origin of sexual orientation and other gendered traits, there is agreement that there are in fact psychosocial dynamics that affect the development of the person who is born with a particular set of gender traits. What do I mean? We go back to the concept of nature versus nurture. We have seen that gendered or cross-gendered traits are mostly the result of the processes of nature. However, once we are born, we enter into a social environment in which we are (hopefully) nurtured; and in that environment, our psyches develop through to adulthood and beyond. We are in fact affected by our environment, and that environment can and does have an effect on how we are able to take advantage of or not take advantage of those traits. In fact the environment can affect how our genes are expressed, and science is still working to understand how and to what extent this happens.

A couple of illustrations will make this more concrete. Many in my generation (childhood and adolescence in the 1950s to the mid-1970s) were raised in a culture shaped in large part by religious moral values vis-à-vis one's sexuality and proper sexual behavior. As I suggested in the introduction, when I was a singles pastor, I encountered several young men whose struggle revolved around the conflict between their sexual desires and their upbring-ing. In two tragic cases that I personally know of, this ended in suicide.

But it was not just the gay men in my group who seemed to have sexual conflicts between desire and moral upbringing. I found in counseling both men and women who were afraid of their sexual desires. The hormones were raging, but so also were the voices of Sunday school teachers who taught them that sex was bad and, worse, in some cases, dirty. This form of teaching, I fear, still occurs in some religious traditions. The objective of such teaching of course is to control the raging "tiger" before it can pounce. But the effect on many was to think of sex as unseemly and for some women, in particular, to even think of their female genitalia as dirty. Although I have not actually seen the full play, I did watch a couple of scenes from *The Vagina Monologues* on HBO. From what I could tell, much of the message of that otherwise, in my estimation, vulgar play was to give women the freedom to feel good about their anatomy. (This is not to say that men do not have issues with their body image.) Where I encountered the problem as a pastor was not before mar-riage but after, when women found (surprisingly) that it was tough to think, "Yesterday I wasn't married and sex was dirty, but today I'm married and sex is suddenly OK!" Indeed, how often in some traditional societies are young brides-to-be pulled aside by their mothers and told what their husbands will need and their responsibility to provide it (Burke 2012)?

We find our problem with sex going back (at least) to the period in Chris-tian history when Saint Augustine lived. For Augustine, human desires were what kept him from God. He was especially active sexually (he kept a con-cubine) before he became a Christian, and in his *Confessions* he states that it was sexual desire above all other sin that was the obstacle. But it was not just Augustine. Asceticism was an exceptionally popular conceptualization of faithful Christian life in the early fifth century CE. (We will find that the origin of this sexual asceticism was emerging even in the Corinth of Paul's time when we look at the text from 1 Corinthians.) Many were giving up all sex, even married people, to seek a higher level of spirituality. Sex was consid-ered inimical to one's relationship with God. But Augustine actually created a context in which "sex was good." How did he do that? Sex was good because through sex came procreation: "The union, then, of male and female for the purpose of procreation is the natural good of marriage. But he makes a bad use of this good who uses it bestially, so that his intention is on the gratifica-tion of lust, instead of the desire of offspring" (Augustine 1887, 265).

This fixed association between sex and procreation continues even today. We have of course made great strides, and even during my own young adult years, there were voices affirming the God-given gift of our sexual desires and sexual experiences. (I still love the idea I first encountered in C. S. Lewis that we humans don't desire too much; we desire too little. I will pursue this idea more when discussing idolatry under the interpretation of Romans 1 below.) But for some young women of that time (most likely this is still true in some contexts), this "nurturing" simply created more confusion because now the message was "dirty" until "not dirty, then fun!"

The dynamic at work here is the interplay between nature and nurture in the domain of one's sexuality. So returning to our primary topic, how children and adolescents are nurtured will play a large role in how they feel about themselves and their identity and the sexual behaviors they will (or will not) express as they enter young adulthood. For a boy whose father observes less gender-typical behaviors (less aggressive, more feminine) in his son and who then withdraws or who expresses other forms of rejection, the boy will find it harder to arrive at adulthood with a healthy identity and sense of self-worth. (Note here it is not the distant father who is responsible for the emergence of a homosexual son; it is the reality of gender-atypical behaviors in the son that results in the withdrawal of the father.)

Some young women who are somewhat gender-atypical in behavior (who love sports more than average young girls, are more aggressive, are more tomboyish, and so on) may find mothers trying to "feminize" them, making them dress more "girlish" and behave more feminine. Such nurturing activities, though presumably well intentioned, may have the effect of creating tremendous identity confusion as the child progresses toward full sexual self-awareness. Science suggests that orientation is biologically fixed, but science also suggests that there may be a range of expression from strongly heterosexual on one end to strongly homosexual on the other and with bisexual falling in between. How children develop and understand who they are is greatly influenced by the kind of environment they experience growing up.

This brings us then to the thoughts in the next chapter. What we believe about the origins and reality of homosexuality will determine how we respond to gay people. In the next chapter using a Q&A format, I look at some of the different ways Christians have approached this. Their assumptions about origins determine their environmental and therapeutic strategies for dealing with LGBT people.

Some Summary Thoughts on the Biology

At this point in my study of the biology of human sexual orientation and how it develops, I conclude three things.

First, it is clear that current scientific research has found that one is born with a particular sexual orientation, and therefore it is not a choice. This being the case, people's sexual orientations are "natural" to them for that is the way they developed in their mothers' wombs.

Second, while the research into the causes and sources of sexual orientation has provided significant understanding, there is much still to research for a full understanding of human sexual behavior, if that is even possible.

Third, I do not know how people can continue to subscribe to the traditional and scientifically unsupported views of sexual orientation and same-sex attraction if they give the findings of modern science any credence.

In my mind these data are a game changer in the discussion about homosexuality. The clear direction of the research points mostly to factors beyond the control of the person and, further, mostly to events that happen while in utero. But the same research also indicates that there is no single factor that can be traced as the originating source and that influences range from prenatal hormones to genetics and to environmental factors within the womb. These data then, I believe, ought to inform our reflections theologically. Much of the later chapters will be my attempt to do just that.

Notes

1. A Luddite is a person who does not like new technology and opposes using technological advances.

2. Within the review of the historical development of the science of LGBT sexuality, I use the term *homosexuality* as a banner. This is because this was the word coined as the science began to develop. I fully recognize that the term is inadequate as a single banner for the LGBT phenomenon.

3. This illustration of open and closed systems is agreeably simplistic. But it works for my purpose, which is to introduce the idea of a universe in which contingency can happen and therefore diversity will emerge.

4. I am not saying LGBT persons should not be parents and raise children. In fact, I believe the opposite. But that is a moral question not under consideration at this point. Rather, I am simply saying that from a biological standpoint, same-sex expressions within a species are less likely to reproduce.

5. *Sodomy* was the term used to describe sexual acts of any kind that were not male-female. It is a term based upon behavior, not an innate condition. The term will be explored in more detail when looking into the biblical texts.

6. *Neurosis* is a term no longer used to describe a psychological state. *Mosby's Medical Dictionary* gives this definition: "former name for a category of mental disorders in which the symptoms are distressing to the person, reality testing is intact, behavior does not violate gross social norms, and there is no apparent organic cause. Classified in DSM-IV under anxiety disorders, dissociative disorders, mood disorders, sexual disorders, and somatoform disorders."

7. Sullivan considered homosexuality to be a social dilemma in need of a solution. He was rumored to have been a homosexual himself. "Whatever may be the truth regarding his sexuality, Sullivan was, by all accounts, an unmarried and lonely individual, who saw 'homosexuality as a developmental mistake, dictated by the culture as substitutive behavior in those instances in which the person cannot do what is the simplest thing to do'" (Evans 1996, 17).

8. More recently the gay, lesbian, bisexual, and transgender community has added the word *queer*, and thus the short-hand becomes *LGBTQ*. This additional word reflects the somewhat fluid understanding of this whole range of sexual orientation, preference, and behavior descriptions. *Q* can stand for *Queer* or *Questioning*.

9. There is some controversy in the medical and psychological community over how to classify the transgender phenomenon. In 1973, homosexuality was removed from the DMS III and replaced by the category "Sexual Orientation Disorder." After homosexuality was removed from the DSM, this diagnosis was added to describe transgender persons. It was called gender identity disorder (GID). That has now been changed to gender dysphoria, which is defined as "cognitive discontent with the assigned gender" or the roles associated with that gender (American Psychiatric Association 2013). The change has been promoted because it is felt that GID stigmatizes a person. Dysphoria attempts to focus on the individual's own sense of contentment.

10. These three graphics were recreated from the original article by Vandenbergh (2003).

11. The epigenome wraps around the genome and therefore makes genes accessible or inaccessible; or perhaps put another way, the epigenome makes the genome readable or unreadable. If made inaccessible, the genome cannot be expressed. Environmental factors can be the triggers on the epigenome that makes the genome accessible. The following graphic illustrates a portion of the DNA sequence that is bound tightly and therefore unreadable and another portion that is loosely bound and therefore readable (Bonetta 2008).

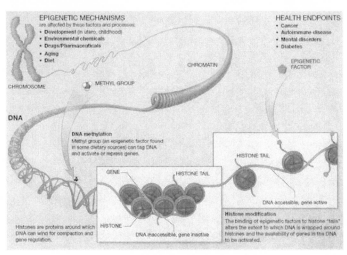

Epigenetic mechanisms are affected by several factors and processes including development in utero and in childhood, environmental chemicals, drugs and pharmaceuticals, aging, and diet. DNA methylation is what occurs when methyl groups, an epigenetic factor found in some dietary sources, can tag DNA and activate or repress genes. Histone modification occurs when the binding of epigenetic factors to histone "tails" alters the extent to which DNA is wrapped around histones and the availability of genes in the DNA to be activated. All of these factors and processes may result in cancer, autoimmune disease, mental disorders, or diabetes, among other illnesses." Courtesy of National Institutes of Health.

12. The research data available on female homosexuality is significantly less than on male homosexuality. There is enough information to know that female homosexuality (like, I suppose, female heterosexuality) is different than male homosexuality, though the basic prenatal mechanisms are assumed to be similar. It does leave one a tad frustrated when trying to understand how this is expressed and what the potential mechanisms are in half the human population.

Chapter 4

Questions

It is probably self-evident, but I will state my reason for exploring in some detail the biological research into the origins of homosexuality. Quite simply, my hope is that if it can be demonstrated by science that one does not choose one's sexual orientation, then to treat LGBT people as inherently deviant or perverted or sinful is no longer tolerable. In addition, efforts to try to change the orientation of a LGBT person are questionable endeavors and may even cause harm. Being gay is not a moral issue any more than my having red hair is a moral issue. It is a human trait or perhaps more accurately, as Simon LeVay, Qazi Rahman, and others would say, "a package of traits" that is determined in the womb.

With the biology of homosexuality increasingly established, I shall pose a series of questions and provide answers derived from the science reviewed in the previous chapter. First the list of questions:

- Is sexual orientation a choice?

- Is homosexuality the result of childhood experiences?

- Is homosexuality a disease that can be cured?

- Can sexual orientation be changed?

- Are same-sex desires unnatural?

- Are same-sex behaviors unnatural?

63

- Are same-sex orientation and behaviors unique to humans?

- If the science points to a biological source of homosexuality, why are many conservatives opposed?

- What about the LGBT person who is also religiously conservative and believes that acting upon one's same-sex attractions is contrary to their faith?

Is Sexual Orientation a Choice?

The current evidence, as presented in the prior chapter (and the extensive research on homosexuality that stands behind it), would propose that one's orientation is not a choice but rather an innate trait with which one is born, regardless of where on the sexual-orientation continuum between heterosexual and homosexual one falls. Most gay and lesbian people will, like straight folk, tell you there was never a point when they "made a choice." Rather one hears stories of LGBT people who always sensed they were different and were attracted differently than most around them. Their memories of differences in interests and attractions are often from an early age.

However, there are people for whom there is a misalignment between their orientation and their identity. We must remember that orientation and identity are not always the same. One's identity can express itself in a range of options, which clearly implies some level of choice. But even this may not be quite so clear as it seems. I am a heterosexual. It is my orientation, and it is also my identity. I am not aware of any time in my life when I chose to be a heterosexual, and I suspect that this is the case with most heterosexuals. For me, my orientation and my identity are in alignment. Yet as pointed out earlier, many people raised in a conservative Christian environment, in which homosexuality is not considered a moral and faith life option, think of themselves as heterosexuals even though their underlying orientation is not. This misalignment is likely to create discordance between their biological orientation that was imprinted in utero and their environmental experience that shapes their identity. For these people, as they begin to realize their same-sex attraction, there is a choice, even if at first it is not a clear choice due to confusion and internal turmoil. The choice is whether they can embrace their orientation, resolve the discordance, and allow their identity to align with their orientation.

There is one other case we must consider under the question of choice. For those persons who fall in the bisexual range on the orientation continuum (and among women, this is a larger group than the "same-sex only" group) there usually is a choice involved. Although these people may have attractions in both directions, it is often the case that there is a leaning. More often than not, they will choose in one direction. This was the case for a man I know. He eventually chose to marry a woman and have children. In contrast, there are bisexual women who due to environmental factors—such as an abusive father or other man in her life—may choose to embrace her romantic attraction toward women, whom she perceives to be safer.

In summary, current research, much of which has been completed in the last twenty years across the domains of science—psychology and biology—points to sexual orientation as an innate trait imprinted prenatally, not as a choice. Future research will hopefully continue to clarify the specific mechanics of orientation formation. Additionally, future research will continue to explore how environment affects the prenatal and postnatal development of sexual orientation and the expression of that orientation as child becomes mature adult.

Is Homosexuality the Result of Childhood Experiences?

There are really two questions that we must consider—and keep distinct. The first is the question of this section. Is homosexuality the *result* of childhood experiences? But a second question is also important to consider. Is homosexuality *affected* by childhood experiences? The distinction is important because one points to the cause or origin of nonheterosexual attraction and the other explores whether a child's growing-up experience in some way influenced his or her sexual orientation and identity. Some who oppose same-sex expression mix the two up and I fear confuse those trying to make sense of this human phenomenon.

This is the case with the work of Dr. Joseph Nicolosi, one of the founders of the National Association for Research & Therapy of Homosexuality (NARTH). He will sometimes acknowledge a biological influence, but then he will work hard to discredit the biological origins and press for a different etiology that is the result of childhood experiences. Dr. James Dobson of Focus on the Family is highly respected among conservative Christians. He holds similar views as Nicolosi that homosexuality is a condition whose origins are in childhood and that there are behaviors to watch for and interventions to implement to avoid its full development. He wrote the following endorsement of Nicolosi's book *A Parent's Guide to Preventing Homosexuality*:

To get to the issue of sexual-identity disorder and what can be done to help, we will turn to the very best resource for parents and teachers I have found. It is provided in an outstanding book entitled *A Parent's Guide to Preventing Homosexuality*, written by clinical psychologist Joseph Nicolosi, Ph.D. Nicolosi is, I believe, the foremost authority on the prevention and treatment of homosexuality today. His book offers practical advice and a *clear-eyed perspective on the antecedents of homosexuality*. I wish every parent would read it, especially those who have reason to be concerned about their sons. Its purpose is not to condemn but to educate and encourage moms and dads. (Dobson 2001, 118, emphasis added)

Note that Dobson refers to same-sex orientation as a "sexual-identity disorder" that has clear antecedents that Dobson believes Nicolosi can explain and prevent. What is the origin of the "disorder"? Nicolosi outlines his theory of the "framework fostering the development of homosexuality" in the book endorsed by Dobson (Nicolosi 2002, 59). The following is straight from *A Parent's Guide to Preventing Homosexuality*:

- "The first level is a temperamental predisposition. A boy is born with a tendency to be sensitive and easily hurt and to avoid the rough-and-tumble play through which most males compete and develop a sense of themselves.

- "Such a child is particularly sensitive to parental moods due to a 'constitutional vulnerability to high arousal in stressful or challenging situations.' (This is probably the same temperamental variable that makes the boy avoid rough-and-tumble play.) This child has difficulty in bouncing back from physical and emotional hurts and in persevering against aggression.

- "Take a boy with that particular type of temperament (or with a physical problem, like asthma, that similarly handicaps him) and put him in an environment where the father is unavailable or unattractive as an identification object, and where the mother is very emotionally attractive or too available, and you have a strong potential for a homosexual outcome."

Here is the classic model for explaining why a boy is a homosexual with a little twist. He acknowledges the boy's "temperamental disposition," which would appear to be a nod to natural development, and then proceeds to explain that this makes him vulnerable to an unavailable father and a too-available mother. He concludes with this statement: "He is usually the sensitive, relational son who suffers deeply from his father's disinterest or criticism and who easily becomes enmeshed in a mother's protection" (Nicolosi 2002, 59). Does this automatically make him gay? Of course not. A tender and vulnerable boy can grow up and be a straight man just as a tomboyish girl can grow up to be a straight woman. Nicolosi says as much and even quotes, what he calls, a gay-activist psychiatrist who agrees. But most in the science community would agree as well. Gender nonconforming behaviors in childhood do not destine one to be gay.

But does Nicolosi even believe it is possible to be born LGB? No. Does he believe that everyone is heterosexual but somewhere things got messed up? Yes, that is what he believes. In the same book, advising parents, he says:

> Perhaps you are concerned about your child and his or her sexual development. Maybe your son or daughter is saying things like "I must be gay" or "I'm bisexual." You have found same-sex porn in his room. You have found intimate journal entries about another girl in your daughter's diary. *The most important message we can offer is that there is no such thing as a "gay child" or a "gay teen."* We are all designed to be heterosexual. Confusion about gender is primarily a psychological condition, and to some extent, it can be modified. (Nicolosi 2002, 16, emphasis added)

Nicolosi likes to describe children with gender nonconforming behaviors as *"prehomosexual, gender-conflicted, gender-confused, and gender-disturbed"* (2002, 13). He denies that people are gay or, more specifically, have a same-sex orientation. For him, same-sex attraction is a disorder that originated in childhood that needs to be fixed for a person to be whole. The banner from Nicolosi's website says it all pretty clearly (2013).

You don't have to be gay.

Diminish your unwanted homosexuality

Develop your heterosexual potential

During the research for this book, I came across a website that provided a list of reasons why someone has same-sex attractions and homosexual leanings. Curiously, the web page has been taken down, but the list can still be found on secondary sites that have copied it.[1] It is consistent with the views held by Nicolosi and Dobson and, sadly, many Christian people:

- Peer pressure created by the propaganda of sexualization in media and school

- A distant, hostile, abusive, or alcoholic father

- Parents who failed in some significant ways to encourage same-sex identification (i.e., failed to encourage boys to identify with father and other male role models, and girls to identify with mother and other female role models)

- An overprotective, needy, or demanding mother

- Rejection and mocking by peers in childhood because of poor hand-eye coordination, incompetence in sports, and reluctance to engage in roughhousing and team sports

- Sexual abuse or rape

- Separation from parent during key developmental years

- Loss of parent by death or divorce

- Extreme shyness and social phobia

None of the items in this list reference a biological origin of homosexuality. None of them subscribe to the science that asserts that sexual orientation is an innate trait that is the result of prenatal process. In fact the views expressed above are fairly stereotypical of those who are either ignorant of or reject the science of human sexual orientation development. Is it possible that a person might experience some of these? Certainly! In fact, it is likely that some will and some will be gay or lesbian and even more will be straight, and all of it is horribly sad and wrong. But the science simply does not see in any of these the origin of sexual orientation.

So we return to the questions. First, is homosexuality the *result* of such childhood experiences? Are Nicolosi and those who subscribe to his viewpoint right? Not if the science is accurate—as we explored in the prior chapter—that indicates same-sex orientation is an innate trait established in the womb. Thus theories and therapies that persist in propagating childhood experiences as the origin are, to say the least, not helpful—no matter how well intentioned they are. And often they are even harmful.

Second, can childhood experiences *affect* how a child with a same-sex orientation matures as an adult? Clearly that is the case. We have already seen that the "classic dynamic" of distant father and overbearing mother can be the *result* of orientation, not the cause. The father may withdraw from a son who exhibits gender nonconforming behaviors, and the mother may intervene. Mothers may work overtime trying to make their tomboy girls more girlish. These experiences will affect the psychological development of a child and ultimately how they experience and express their sexuality as adults. There is no doubt that some LGBT persons did not feel accepted by their same-sex parent, but there are many more straight people who have also had that experience.

Is Homosexuality a Disease That Can Be Cured?

To ask this question is to still fail to understand the science. Qazi Rahman was asked in an interview if homosexuality is the result, in part, of genetics. Does that mean it is a disease? His response is important and points back to the prior discussion. He said, "It is a trait not a disease" (*The Biology of Sexual Attraction*). *As a trait, it just is.* But behind the disease question is the real question: if it were a disease, could it be cured? Again, the answer is obvious. If it is not a disease, there is nothing to cure. But it was considered to be a disease, and diseases need cures. Consequently for many years in the twentieth century there were proposed "therapies" that would "cure" the homosexual of same-sex attraction so that he or she could live as a healthy heterosexual—or at least not as a homosexual.

Please note that this part of the discussion focuses primarily on the LGB population. The transgender population must be given special consideration due to the person's experience of internal dissonance between physical sex and mental/emotional gender.

At least two different therapeutic approaches were developed to address the question of homosexuality as a disease to be cured. One approach comes out of the psychoanalytic world of times past and another from the behaviorist world. Often the approaches are mixed in some way. Within a religious context, additional practices associated with religious beliefs are included, such as prayer and Bible study.

Psychoanalytic school approach: The psychoanalytic school took the "talk therapy" approach, which grew out of Freudian theory. Unhealthy behaviors are the result of some disruption of normal childhood development.

Talk therapy is intended to help the person dig into the unconscious and discover the repressed material that is manifesting itself. Homosexuality was considered a form of neurosis in the first half of the twentieth century by many psychoanalysts. As such it was a treatable condition. This view has been repudiated by the mainstream psychiatric community, which includes today's doctors who practice psychoanalysis. See statements below from the American Psychiatric Association.

One psychiatrist and psychoanalyst who continued to see homosexuality as a neurosis was Dr. Charles Socarides (1922–2005). He claimed to have treated over a thousand homosexual patients, a third of whom he insists were cured. Socarides (like Nicolosi) continued the long-dismissed notion that the cause of homosexuality was an overbearing mother and absent father. Ironically, or perhaps sadly, Socarides had an openly gay son. Socarides was also one of the founders, along with Dr. Joseph Nicolosi, of the National Association for Research and Therapy of Homosexuality (NARTH) in 1992.

Behaviorist school approach: The behaviorists' approach was to "unlearn" the same-sex attraction and "learn" a hetero-sex attraction. Under this umbrella fell some pretty awful approaches that included shock treatments and other therapies designed to create a revulsion to same-sex attraction. The behaviorist approach uses a "classical conditioning" methodology to create an aversion to same-sex attraction followed with "operant conditioning" methods to reinforce the "positive" (i.e., opposite-sex attraction) response and negatively reinforce the "wrong" (i.e., same-sex attraction) response.

Behaviorism, like psychoanalysis, has also progressed in its thinking in the last century. But looking back, beginning in the 1960s, a primary expression of the behaviorist approach in treating homosexuality was "aversion therapy," which usually employs some or all of the following strategies. A gay man is shown a sexually provocative picture of another man. This stimulates a sexual response. To this is added an additional stimulus. In one case the client is attached to a machine that shocks his hands or his genitals at the same time that he begins to sexually respond. In other cases an emetic (that causes one to vomit) is paired with the provocative picture, inducing vomiting whenever a sexual response occurs (Haldeman 2002). A second stimulus is presented of a sexually provocative picture of a woman. In this case, no negative stimulus is added.

In the 1960s, aversion therapy was considered a great therapeutic tool in dealing with homosexuality. Initial results suggested that up to 50 percent of clients stopped acting on their homosexual urges. But the findings were found to be flawed. Most of the men treated were bisexual, and the treatment simply discouraged pursuing their homosexual urges. Most of these therapies only reduced the homosexual urge; they did not induce heterosexual desires (Seligman 2007). Today, aversion therapies are considered a dangerous practice by mainline mental health professionals and are even considered unethical. (See the statement from the American Psychiatric Association in the text below.)

Reparative therapy: Reparative therapy (also known as "conversion therapy") is the heading under which a range of aversion therapy and psychiatric and (sometimes) religious practices are found. *Reparative* obviously means that something needs to be repaired, and *conversion* means that something is in a state that needs to be converted to another state. Clearly the assumption again is that sexual orientation is a disorder than can (and should) be cured. Conversion therapies were popular in the United States into the 1980s but had already begun to fall out of favor in the 1970s. Once the psychiatric, medical, and psychological communities no longer considered homosexual orientation to be a disorder, there was nothing to be cured. In 2001, the US Surgeon General's office under Dr. David Satcher released a report, in which it said, "there is no valid scientific evidence that sexual orientation can be changed" (4).

Nonetheless, advocates of conversion therapy have persisted primarily in conservative religious circles (Roman Catholic and Protestant). In 2001, Dr. Robert Spitzer, a respected psychiatrist, published a paper that claimed, based upon a study he had conducted, that a homosexual person could be "cured," in other words, that their orientation could be changed. Dr. Spitzer has had a long career and was active in the development of the American Psychiatric Association's *Diagnostic and Statistical Manual of Mental Disorders* (DSM-III), which was released in 1980 (2003). So a study attached to him was considered a green light for those whose views were that homosexual orientation was something to change. In fact, it energized the development of "reparative therapy." Eleven years later he completely repudiated his claim, insisting that it was based upon a small sample size that was not randomized. In a letter to Dr. Ken Zucker, editor of the *Archives of Sexual Behavior*, he wrote:

> I believe I owe the gay community an apology for my study making unproven claims of the efficacy of reparative therapy. I also apologize to any gay person who wasted time and energy undergoing some form of reparative therapy because they believed that I had proven that reparative therapy works with some 'highly motivated' individuals. (Mustanski 2012)

He had struggled to find enough individuals who claimed to have been cured through conversion therapy. Most of the people in the sample were referred to him by either "ex-gay ministries" or NARTH. Spitzer's claims had been criticized by the American Psychiatric Association, who said, "There is no published scientific evidence supporting the efficacy of 'reparative therapy' as a treatment to change one's sexual orientation" (2014).

Though he has disavowed those initial claims, they were taken as scientific support for conversion therapies by NARTH and the conservative religious community who claimed that it "shows some people can change from gay to straight, and we ought to acknowledge that" (M. Ritter 2001). In fact, remarkably, NARTH actually repudiates Spitzer's retraction. They go so far as to parse the language of retraction to explain that he really did not retract his research conclusions but that he only apologized for them. But if one reads any of the reports on Spitzer's statement, they all make it clear that he repudiates the research because it was flawed by a sample size that was too small and a sample that was referred by organizations that were trying to cure homosexuality and had a vested interest in anything that would support their work. For more information on NARTH and their reaction to Spitzer, go to their website (Rosik 2012).

Mental health communities discredit reparative/conversion therapies: There are many mental health associations for mental health professionals, and the overwhelming majority—if not all of them—have made such statements as: (1) homosexuality is not a disease, and (2) they do not support efforts to try to change a person's sexual orientation. Of special focus in the literature is reparative therapy or conversion therapy. Reparative/conversion therapy is considered pseudoscientific. Following are just a few of the statements from the medical and health services communities:

- **American Academy of Pediatrics:** "Therapy directed specifically at changing sexual orientation is contraindicated, since it can provoke guilt and anxiety while having little or no potential for achieving changes in orientation" (Just the Facts Coalition 2008). This organization is not to be confused with the American College of Pediatrics, which is a conservative break-off group.

- **The American Psychiatric Association** issued a position statement on reparative or conversion therapies. It said in part:

  The validity, efficacy and ethics of clinical attempts to change an individual's sexual orientation have been challenged. To date, there are no scientifically rigorous outcome studies to determine either the actual efficacy or harm of "reparative" treatments. There is sparse scientific data about selection criteria, risks versus benefits of the treatment, and long-term outcomes of "reparative" therapies. The literature consists of anecdotal reports of individuals who have claimed to change, people who claim that attempts to change were harmful to them, and others who claimed to have changed and then later recanted those claims.

Even though there are little data about patients, it is still possible to evaluate the theories which rationalize the conduct of "reparative" and conversion therapies. Firstly, they are at odds with the scientific position of the American Psychiatric Association which has maintained, since 1973, that homosexuality per se, is not a mental disorder. The theories of "reparative" therapists define homosexuality as either a developmental arrest, a severe form of psychopathology, or some combination of both. In recent years, noted practitioners of "reparative" therapy have openly integrated older psychoanalytic theories that pathologize homosexuality with traditional religious beliefs condemning homosexuality.

The earliest scientific criticisms of the early theories and religious beliefs informing "reparative" or "conversion" therapies came primarily from sexology researchers. Later, criticisms emerged from psychoanalytic sources as well. There has also been an increasing body of religious thought arguing against traditional, biblical interpretations that condemn homosexuality and which underlie religious types of "reparative" therapy. (2000, 1)

In short, they see no scientific evidence to support claims of efficacy of these therapies, but even so they do believe that what is known can be and has been evaluated and found not only unsuccessful but in many cases harmful.

• **The American Psychological Association** established the Task Force on Appropriate Therapeutic Responses to Sexual Orientation in 2007. The abstract of their report says:

The American Psychological Association Task Force on Appropriate Therapeutic Responses to Sexual Orientation conducted a systematic review of the peer-reviewed journal literature on sexual orientation change efforts (SOCE) and concluded that efforts to change sexual orientation are unlikely to be successful and involve some risk of harm, contrary to the claims of SOCE practitioners and advocates. Even though the research and clinical literature demonstrate that same-sex sexual and romantic attractions, feelings, and behaviors are normal and positive variations of human sexuality, regardless of sexual orientation identity, the task force concluded that the population that undergoes SOCE tends to have strongly conservative religious views that lead them to seek to change their sexual orientation. Thus, the appropriate application of affirmative therapeutic interventions for those who seek SOCE involves therapist acceptance, support, and understanding of clients and the facilitation of clients' active coping, social support, and identity exploration and development, without imposing a specific sexual orientation identity outcome. (APA Task Force on Appropriate Therapeutic Responses to Sexual Orientation 2009, v)

- **The Governing Council of the American Counseling Association (ACA)** adopted a motion that "opposes portrayals of lesbian, gay, and bisexual youth and adults as mentally ill due to their sexual orientation; and supports the dissemination of accurate information about sexual orientation, mental health, and appropriate interventions in order to counteract bias that is based in ignorance or unfounded beliefs about same-gender orientation" (ACA 1998, 15).

- The American Counseling Association also developed "Competencies for Counseling with Lesbian, Gay, Bisexual, Queer, Questioning, Inter-sex and Ally Individuals." In a section specifically addressing the issue of reparative therapy as a viable therapeutic strategy, the association said the following:

The authors feel it important to be clear about our perspectives regarding the issues of reparative therapy, physiological changes forced on Intersex individu-als and the relative dearth of empirical and qualitative data regarding effectively serving this population. Reparative therapy (also known as conversion therapy, reorientation therapy, Sexual Orientation Change Efforts) is the practice of attempting to change or alter the affectional orientation of an individual from lesbian, gay, bisexual, queer, or questioning to that of heterosexual. Consistent with the stance taken by both the ACA and the American Psychological Asso-ciation (APA), the authors hold that attempts to alter ones' affectional orienta-tion (reparative therapy) "are unlikely to be successful and involve some risk of harm" (APA 2010, p. v). Additionally, the authors believe reparative therapy poses serious ethical concerns because of the risks to clients.

Understand that attempts to "alter," "repair," "convert," or "change" the affectional orientations or gender identities/expressions of LGBQQ individu-als are detrimental or may even be life-threatening, are repudiated by empirical and qualitative findings, and must not be undertaken. (Association for Lesbian, Gay, Bisexual, and Transgender Issues in Counseling Competencies Taskforce 2012)

• **The National Association of Social Workers** followed the American Psychological Association: "NCLGB believes that such treatment potentially can lead to severe emotional damage.... No data demonstrate that reparative or conversion therapies are effective, and in fact they may be harmful" (National Committee on Lesbian, Gay, and Bisexual Issues 2000).

• **The American Association of Pastoral Counselors (AAPC)** is inclusive of pastor-counselors from many traditions, some of whom are more supportive of the LGBT community than others. But even so, in their code of ethics members agree, "To avoid discriminating against or refusing employment, educational opportunity or professional assistance to anyone on the basis of race, ethnicity, gender identity, sexual orientation, religion, health status, age, disabilities or national origin; provided that nothing herein shall limit a member or center from utilizing religious requirements or exercising a religious preference in employment decisions." Additionally, in their code of ethics they state, "Anti-racist multiculturally competent pastoral counselors are committed to pursuing social justice and democratic ideals in which all persons are regarded as having equal worth regardless of identity markers, including but not limited to race, gender, age, sexual orientation, difference in ability, religion, language, and cultural or national origins" (AAPC 2012).

• **The American Association of Marriage and Family Counselors (AAMFT)** provides therapeutic guidelines for counseling with same-sex couples. The guidelines assume the propriety of same-sex couples and seek to provide wisdom on how to help them navigate the kinds of issues common to all couples but especially those that a same-sex couple may face (K. Ritter 2014).

This has been a somewhat long way of answering the question of whether homosexuality can be cured. A simple yes/no answer will not do, because the question comes from a specific assumption. That assumption—that homosexual orientation is a disorder to repair—has been repudiated by the vast majority of the mental health community. Unfortunately, within particular conservative Christian circles, it is still the dominant assumption. But I believe this assumption persists in the face of the science due to a particular approach to biblical interpretation and specific ways of thinking about what the Bible says on the subject. In this regard it is an issue of biblical authority and exegesis. See chapters 6 and 7.

Can Sexual Orientation Be Changed?

The prevailing science today would say no. If it is not a disorder, as discussed under the prior question, there is little need of a change. But in addition, if sexual orientation is part of the fetal development process, it cannot be changed. It is an immutable trait (or cluster of traits, per LeVay). Sexual behavior certainly can be changed as sexual behavior is a choice. To choose to sexually act contrary to one's orientation, however, can create psychological issues, and current mental health professionals (as demonstrated above) consider encouragement in this direction to be dangerous and harmful.

Why would this question even be raised, especially if it has already been demonstrated that it is not a disease to cure? There are those in the religious community who may accept that a person is gay as a result of natural biological process but who still believe being gay and pursuing same-sex experiences are wrong biblically. So for these religious people the question then becomes: How do we change someone's orientation? But the answer is the same; if it is innate, it most likely cannot be changed. The American Psychological Association task force's paper, titled "Appropriate Therapeutic Responses to Sexual Orientation," again provides insight into the effectiveness of "sexual orientation change efforts" (SOCE):

> These studies show that enduring change to an individual's sexual orientation is uncommon. The participants in this body of research continued to experience same-sex attractions following SOCE and did not report significant change to other-sex attractions that could be empirically validated, though some showed lessened physiological arousal to all sexual stimuli. Compelling evidence of decreased same-sex sexual behavior and of engagement in sexual behavior with the other sex was rare. (APA Task Force on Appropriate Therapeutic Responses to Sexual Orientation 2009, 2)

Are Same-Sex Desires Unnatural?

To address this question, we must first be clear about the domains within which we are asking the question. Is this a theological or moral question or a scientific question? If the biological science referenced earlier is true, then the notion of same-sex desires being unnatural makes no sense. The biological process that results in a person with a same-sex orientation *is* a natural process. That being the case, to have same-sex attraction or desires is "natural" to the LGBT person. This statement is within the domain of science, and nature here means natural process.

However, there persists in some communities, especially in conservative faith communities, the idea that homosexual desires are unnatural and therefore sinful. In these communities, the definition blurs between psychobiology and morality, making the discussion more difficult. When it is suggested that to have same-sex desires is unnatural, what is really being said is that it's not "natural" to the process of reproductive success. It is true that same-sex persons are less likely to reproduce; this is a statement of science.[2] However, a moral judgment is mixed with the statement, namely, it is not natural to reproductive success and therefore is wrong.

So where does this "unnatural" argument really come from? It is one vestige of the natural law theory that argues that observable nature reflects the way things ought to be (i.e., morality). Some propose that the observable phenomenon of male sexual biology and female sexual biology is complementary. Most of us would agree with this as an observation. However, natural law folks press this further so that what we observe in nature becomes a moral law (Gagnon 2001). In simple terms, because nature's way to reproduce for many species is through sexual reproduction, then that is the way all sexual intimacy expression "ought" to be. To act otherwise is "unnatural." To this basic thesis is added the reproductive argument that obviously the way God intended for the world to be populated was by heterosexual reproduction—observable nature = moral law. (A brief discussion on natural law and theology will also follow in a subsequent chapter along with a rebuttal.) There has been a subtle shift here. The discussion is no longer about the science. It is about morality and theology. Unfortunately the same word *nature* is used in both domains of conversation, but the meaning is different. These are different domains of inquiry. What science means by *nature* is not the same as what is meant by natural law or any who absolutize nature's typical form and reproductive function as moral law.

Are Same-Sex Behaviors Unnatural?

Although some who oppose same-sex relationships are willing to acknowledge that one does not choose one's orientation and the desires that come with it, they nonetheless hold to a view that homosexual behavior is unnatural. Strictly speaking, from a scientific standpoint, homosexual behaviors are the natural and normal consequence of same-sex orientation and desire. This reflects a viewpoint from the domain of science. However, there is a moral question that still must be addressed vis-à-vis same-sex behaviors. While same-sex behavior per se is not unnatural, not all same-sex behaviors are moral. This is precisely the same case with other-sex behaviors. They are intrinsically natural, but not all expressions are moral. This will be discussed in a subsequent chapter as well.

Are Same-Sex Orientation and Behaviors Unique to Humans?

It is well documented that same-sex attraction and behavior are present in multiple animal species. Behaviors that have been observed include "courtship, affection, sex, pair bonding, and parenting" among same-sex animals (Bagemihl 2000, 12). Like all things having to do with sexuality, there is a spectrum of explanations, but that same-sex sexual behavior occurs in nature beyond humans is undisputed. One specific species that has been observed is that of rams. Of the male population of sheep, around 8 percent of rams prefer other rams (Balthazart 2011, 57).

If the Science Points to a Biological Source of Homosexuality, Why Are Many Conservatives Opposed?

A wave has been building toward this question from the beginning of this chapter—perhaps from the beginning of the book. In one way or another, answers have been given throughout. But this is such an important question reflecting a great deal of pressure for LGBT people and their families and conflict within some churches that it needs a direct answer.

If we step back from all of the rhetoric, we can see that two factors give shape to the conservative view of homosexuality in light of the findings of the scientific domain. First, this view begins from a presupposition that homosexuality or, at least, same-sex behaviors are, at the very least, a psychological disorder or, worse, a sexual deviance/perversion and therefore a moral sin. It cannot be overlooked that almost all of the groups who embrace this position are also deeply religious. The following graphic illustrates how the mainstream scientific community differs from the conservative (and often religious) community.[3] The vertical axis reflects the level of influence of biological factors on orientation and identity development. The horizontal axis reflects the level of influence of environmental factors.

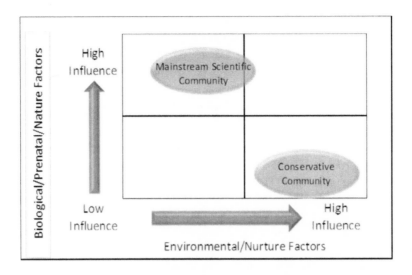

As was discussed in the prior chapter, most mainstream science leans toward the biological as the primary origin of orientation but recognizes that environmental factors are influential in at least how sexual identity is shaped. Conversely the conservative world continues to maintain a position that is opposite of that of mainstream science. It places more emphasis on environmental factors with little room for biological factors. It is this emphasis that also allows them to maintain the position that orientation and identity are choices.

Second, because of this first assumption, conservatives cannot accept the paradigmatic shift that occurred in the 1970s, which culminated in the removal of homosexuality as a disorder in the 1973 DSM-II and further changes in subsequent DSM editions. Those comfortable with their sexual orientation were no longer considered to be mentally ill, and the stigma associated with it by the medical and mental health community was removed. Through the 1980s, the medical and mental health community increasingly moved toward the view that "homosexuality per se is a normal variant of human sexuality and that lesbian, gay, and bisexual (LGB) people deserve to be affirmed and supported in their sexual orientation, relationships, and social opportunities" (APA Task Force on Appropriate Therapeutic Responses to Sexual Orientation 2009, 11). Therapeutic efforts that focused on changing sexual orientation that had been common mid-century were increasingly abandoned, rejected, and even considered potentially harmful.

This shift was dramatic and, as I said, paradigmatic. A paradigm is like a pair of glasses; it provides the lenses through which the world is mediated to us. If we are used to glasses that have a green tint and we suddenly put on a pair that has a rose tint, we immediately see our world differently. Of course there are many things that are familiar. But there are things noticed that were not noticed before. Additionally, some things that we thought were certainly one way look different with the different color of tinting. Some things seem clearer while others fade into the background. So the color of glasses—the paradigm through which we see the world—will influence what one sees and what one believes to be true about the real world.

We all have paradigms (and in some ways they operate like a worldview) of which we are mostly unconscious. In any fields of knowledge and inquiry, paradigms frame the questions asked and the answers expected. In the classic book *The Structure of Scientific Revolutions*, Thomas Kuhn wrote about how science (the pursuit of understanding about reality) advances. It is not a steady climb to enlightenment in an evolutionary sort of way. Rather science lives within a particular paradigm—conceptual world of theory—for a period of time, and then suddenly the paradigm is stood on its head by some new insight that replaces what was the existing conceptual world with a new one. The change from one to the next, he explains, is not peaceful but rather (sometimes) violently revolutionary. The most classic example is the radical shift that occurred when relativity and quantum physics superseded Newtonian physics. Kuhn explained that a paradigm change is preceded by an anomaly in the standard understanding—a problem or problems that the current paradigm cannot address. This problem begins to create a crisis around the currently standard conceptual model. Out of the crisis a new insight emerges that resolves one or more of the anomalies, and a new conceptual model—paradigm—is born (Kuhn 1996). This, I believe, is at the center of why conservatives have maintained their resistance to a modern science and mental health view of homosexuality. The paradigm has shifted, but they have not gone with it.

It was a paradigmatic shift when in the late nineteenth and early twentieth centuries, homosexuality emerged as a field of study and was soon classified as a "disorder" instead of a sexual perversion (though the distinctions between these two were often blurred in the religious community). The assumption of the newly developing psychological paradigm was that as a disorder, perhaps a cure could be found. (We have seen this already.) But increasingly this paradigm—this conceptual model of homosexuality—began to fail to address many of the problems the medical and mental health communities were encountering in the day-to-day treatment of LGBT people.

Curiously, many in these fields began to "come out of the closet" themselves. Were they deviants? Did they suffer from a disorder? Additionally, it became increasingly clear that orientation-change efforts were mostly failing. Finally, in the last twenty years, the biological origins of homosexuality began to take center stage. The result is that the older psychological paradigm of "disorder" broke under the weight of the new information. And in true Kuhnian style, the biological discoveries were a jolt, and it has all been quite revolutionary. But as the "smoke cleared," what emerged was a view of same-sex attraction, orientation, and behavior as normal expressions of a diverse human sexuality.

But not everyone has accepted the new paradigm. The NARTH organization was founded in reaction to the paradigmatic shift in the mental health community when it no longer considered homosexuality to be a disorder. Nicolosi and many others in the conservative (and usually religious) community insist on maintaining the older paradigm, which sees homosexuality and homosexual behaviors as a disorder—and in some cases, a perversion. Because they hold this position, they also sustain the belief that orientation, or at least behavior, can be changed. To support this, they still cling to the almost universally dismissed notions of the origin of homosexuality and that it is a choice one makes.

This was clearly illustrated in a document available on the Family Research Council's website. It is the first chapter from *Getting It Straight*, although the document is unattributed here. It simply starts, "Chapter 1: What Causes Homosexuality?" (Sprigg and Dailey 2014). The first eighteen pages of the chapter review much of the research current as of 2004 that would point to biological origins of homosexuality. Much of this research was published after the 1970s, and curiously, it is this post-1970s research that the authors mostly dismiss. The final sixteen pages review older, pre-1970s research that was still working on the "disorder" paradigm. Much of this research the authors embrace. In the second paragraph of the chapter, the authors acknowledge that there are two paradigms and that the more recent paradigm is displacing the older:

> There are two main theories as to what causes homosexual attractions. One is that a homosexual orientation is essentially dictated by genetic and or biological factors—put simply, that people are "born gay." The other theory is that homosexual attractions develop primarily as a result of psychological and environmental influences and early experiences. In the public square, the latter theory has appeared to be in decline and the former gaining favor in recent decades. But what does the research show? Let's look at these two theories in turn. (Sprigg and Dailey 2014, 1)

Why do they hold on to what is now considered to be contrary to all of the sciences working this problem? Simply, it comes down to religious beliefs—though some, like the Family Research Council, will try to insist that their views do not (Sprigg and Dailey 2004, v). The pair of glasses they cannot remove is the pair that sees homosexuality or same-sex behavior as sinful, immoral living, and a lifestyle choice. But here is an example of domain jumping. They hold what looks like scientific viewpoints that really jump over from the domain of a particular theological/philosophical viewpoint. The apriority is that all same-sex behavior is evil and that to be homosexual is the result of a choice because all people are born heterosexual. This view trumps the new scientific conceptual model—paradigm—about nonheterosexual attraction and its origins and its expressions.

Is this valid? Well, of course that depends upon who one asks. But from my standpoint, as a Christian, I want to understand God's creation and what each domain of inquiry contributes to that. As I said in an earlier chapter, we must let each domain speak from within its field. Science helps us understand how the physical universe works. This includes ourselves as biological creatures. The Bible reveals to us a God who has covenanted with creation to complete it and to heal us of our many faces of brokenness by calling us to a certain moral life. What that looks like is the subject of subsequent chapters. But for now, the answer to the question of why conservative people reject much of the current science on homosexuality is that the new paradigm clashes with their pre-held beliefs about homosexuality. They cannot see a way of reconciling the two so they continue to pursue courses of action that science and the mental health communities have demonstrated to be false.

I have one last comment. Although one can find and read a great deal on the web from these groups and organizations that is hateful and alarming, I also personally know many good, kind Christian people who sincerely believe they are holding on to what their Bibles teach against the rising tide of unchristian culture. These dear folk are naive when they insist that they want to be open to homosexual persons and invite them into their faith communities but do not understand how their assumptions make this extremely unlikely. How do LGBT people and their families, given the new paradigm understandings, join a congregation that rejects these and expects them to change if they are to be true disciples? As the research will demonstrate in the next chapter, at least among those born since 1980, they are voicing their opposition by largely rejecting the church and its message.

What about the LGBT Person Who Is Also Religiously Conservative and Believes That Acting upon One's Same-Sex Attractions Is Contrary to Their Faith?

Between those who are pressing hard for full acceptance of LGBT persons and same-sex expression and those who oppose it are some real people who are gay and also religiously conservative. They believe that to be faithful to their beliefs they cannot give way to their same-sex attractions. (In the gay Christian world, these persons are referred to as "Side B." Side A Christians support gay marriage.)[4] What do we say to these people? This is a difficult question and one the APA Task Force on Appropriate Therapeutic Responses to Sexual Orientation was tasked with addressing. While probably somewhat simplistic, there are two kinds of person that fit this description:

- Those who are convinced that there is something wrong with them and are looking for a way to change their same-sex orientation.

- Those who accept that their sexual orientation is most likely fixed but believe that acting upon it is wrong and consequently suffer some psychological distress.

Research across many mental health care providers corresponds to what the APA Task Force recommends: that persons in the first category should at least be informed that sexual orientation change efforts seldom are successful and may even be harmful, regardless of what some practitioners advocate. Beyond this, and encompassing both types of LGBT person, the task force proposes that the goals for treatment focus, not on sexual orientation, but on sexual identity (they call it sexual orientation identity). Even though sexual orientation, as we have observed, is generally considered to be fixed, the identity one has vis-à-vis his or her orientation is more fluid. Given this fluidity, the task force proposes "an affirmative approach [that] is supportive of clients' identity development without an a priori treatment goal concerning how clients identify or live out their sexual orientation or spiritual beliefs" (APA Task Force on Appropriate Therapeutic Responses to Sexual Orientation 2009, 4). It believes that such an approach provides a "safe space" wherein clients can explore the identity that they hope to shape informed by their faith and within a therapeutic environment.

This is a middle ground. Many of us would want more for these folk, but respect for them and their beliefs trump what we might want. The real goal must be the flourishing of these individuals so that they can hopefully find peace with themselves within their religious tradition. Not everyone will be able to fully embrace a place for same-sex behavior and religious faith.

The Game Has Changed

What is the significance of these data? It is argued by some who oppose LGBT people that they have chosen this life. But if we begin with the earlier assumptions about the way the universe unfolds and the diversity it creates, then the fact that same-sex behaviors can be observed in nature would suggest that nature is behind the incidence of human nonheterosexuality—that is, it is the outcome of a natural process. This is significant.

In the simplest of terms, as already indicated, I believe the science is a game changer for the religious community. With the science leaning so heavily in the direction of sexual orientation and attraction being a set of innate traits, I do not believe it is tenable to continue to hold to certain positions about same-sex orientation. If it is not a choice, then same-sex attraction is natural to those whose sex and gender-specific brain and physiological development has resulted in a person with a same-sex orientation. It is in fact no different than some people's brain development resulting in being right-handed or left-handed. We are first the products of our genes and prenatal hormonal processes. This new knowledge from the domain of science—the new paradigm—therefore must inform how the religious community looks at the exceptionally human phenomenon of nonheterosexuality. To continue to debate and in some cases express hostility toward LGBT persons as morally reprobate can no longer be sustained. We need to move on from this. There is still a moral question to discuss, which will be done below. But we must move beyond the idea that LGBT persons have chosen to be gay or that they are broken in some way that needs to be fixed. The science simply does not support such positions.

Addendum to This Chapter

Writing about a current issue carries with it the challenge of issue fluidity. That is to say that a written text is fixed at a moment in time, but the issue the text writes about continues to evolve. That is the case on this issue. The first draft of this book was written in the fall of 2012 and winter and spring of 2013. On June 20, 2013, I was reading the morning news as I do most days. Two articles jumped out at me. The first was from the *Huffington Post*:[5]

Exodus International Shuts Down: Christian Ministry Apologizes to LGBT Community And Halts Operations (2013)

The second article was in the *New York Times*:

Strategist Out of Closet and Into Fray, This Time for Gay Marriage (Stolberg 2013)

Why are these significant? Because they show how much this issue is evolving within our culture, including in the conservative community. This includes the conservative Christian community that has traditionally stood hard against the LGBT community and same-sex marriage. The first is a story about Exodus International, a Christian ministry that has focused on changing same-sex orientation to other-sex orientation. That organization's primary methodology revolved around a form of reparative therapy discussed earlier that also included intensive prayer and Bible study.

At its 38th Annual Exodus Freedom Conference in June of 2013, the board of directors announced that it was closing down Exodus International and initiating a new ministry. Its president, Alan Chambers, said, "For quite some time we've been imprisoned in a worldview that's neither honoring toward our fellow human beings, nor biblical." He continues, "From a Judeo-Christian perspective, gay, straight or otherwise, we're all prodigal sons and daughters. Exodus International is the prodigal's older brother, trying to impose its will on God's promises, and make judgments on who's worthy of His Kingdom. God is calling us to be the Father—to welcome everyone, to love unhindered." These are the reasons given for closing Exodus and starting a "new season of ministry, to a new generation," said Chambers. "Our goals are to reduce fear..., and come alongside churches to become safe, welcoming, and mutually transforming communities" (Steffan 2013).

This announcement followed an earlier public apology by Chambers. Below are his comments taken from the Exodus International blog post of June 19, 2013, titled "Exodus Int'l President to the Gay Community: 'We're Sorry'": "It is strange to be someone who has both been hurt by the Church's treatment of the LGBT community, and also to be someone who must apologize for being part of the very system of ignorance that perpetuated that hurt," said Chambers. "Today it is as if I've just woken up to a greater sense of how painful it is to be a sinner in the hands of an angry church" (Chambers 2013). Chambers also said:

I am sorry for the pain and hurt that many of you have experienced. I am sorry some of you spent years working through the shame and guilt when your attractions didn't change. I am sorry we promoted sexual orientation change efforts and reparative theories about sexual orientation that stigmatized parents.

I am sorry I didn't stand up to people publicly "on my side" who called you names like sodomite—or worse. I am sorry that I, knowing some of you so well, failed to share publicly that the gay and lesbian people I know were every bit as capable of being amazing parents as the straight people that I know. I am sorry that when I celebrated a person coming to Christ and surrendering their sexuality to Him, I callously celebrated the end of relationships that broke your heart. I am sorry I have communicated that you and your families are less than me and mine.

More than anything, I am sorry that so many have interpreted this religious rejection by Christians as God's rejection. I am profoundly sorry that many have walked away from their faith and that some have chosen to end their lives. (Steffan 2013)

The second article was about Ken Mehlman, who "orchestrated President George Bush's 2004 re-election on a platform that included opposition to same-sex marriage." He also served for two years as the Chairman of the Republican National Committee. Mehlman "came out" in 2010 after years of denying that he was gay. "It's taken me 43 years to get comfortable with this part of my life," says Mehlman, now an executive vice president with the New York City–based private equity firm KKR. He continues: "Everybody has their own path to travel, their own journey, and for me, over the past few months, I've told my family, friends, former colleagues, and current colleagues, and they've been wonderful and supportive. The process has been something that's made me a happier and better person. It's something I wish I had done years ago" (Ambinder 2010).

Mehlman is now actively advocating for same-sex marriage. Not surprising, his change of focus has created some consternation among Republicans. Some now vilify him as embracing the evil he used to fight against, and others have embraced him. Mehlman's inspiration to admit that he was gay and then to embrace LGBT causes was largely the result of meetings he had with Theodore B. Olson who served as solicitor general in the Bush administration from 2001 to 2004 and who was one of two attorneys challenging California's Proposition 8 before the Supreme Court. Now Mehlman is working hard to convince Republicans that support of same-sex marriage reflects conservative values such as freedom and liberty (Stolberg 2013).

In addition to these two articles, on June 26, 2013, the Supreme Court released its rulings on both the challenge to Prop 8 and the Defense of Marriage Act (DOMA). Proposition 8 was a California initiative designed to ban same-sex marriage in the state of California by amending the state constitution. The proposition was challenged in court immediately. Subsequently "United States District Court Judge Vaughn Walker overturned Proposition 8 on August 4, 2010 in the case Perry v. Schwarzenegger, ruling that it violated both the Due Process and Equal Protection clauses of the United States Constitution" (Wildermuth 2008). The Ninth Circuit Court affirmed Judge Walker's ruling that Prop 8 was unconstitutional. The ruling was appealed to the Supreme Court and on June 26, 2013, the Supreme Court ruled in Hollingsworth v. Perry that the lower court's decision would stand. Proposition 8 will not go into effect. Same-sex marriages will be able to proceed in the state of California.

On this same day the court also issued its ruling that Section 3 of DOMA, which was enacted on September 21, 1996, was not constitutional. DOMA allowed states not to recognize same-sex marriages performed in other states. That portion of DOMA that restricted federal marriage benefits was the focus of the Supreme Court case. It was this portion that the justices ruled as unconstitutional on June 26, 2013. It is no small irony to me that my wife and I were married on June 26, 1976. And now my daughter, if she wanted to, could also get married in our home state.

Notes

1. Originally the web page was on the website questions.org, which is part of RBC Ministries (Radio Bible Class).

2. Although it is true that gay folk are less likely to reproduce, many have reproduced throughout history because getting married and having children was the only acceptable path for a person. But in these cases it could be argued, standing the other argument on its head, that these persons chose a path that was "unnatural" to them.

3. The graphic is intended to illustrate how different emphases of the source of impact on orientation and identity development result in an incredibly different view of homosexuality. It is not a graphic based upon numerical data.

4. See the Gay Christian Network website for a further discussion on these two sides of the debate in the gay Christian world: www.gaychristian.net.

5. *The Huffington Post* is a source that not all appreciate. It has a younger audience orientation and its political and social leanings are clearly not conservative. But it excels in being in touch with happenings around the world—trends that are occurring and challenges to those trends. It is important, however, to always search beyond *HP* to get a more balanced view.

Chapter 5

A Changing Cultural Tide

There is no question that the cultural tide is changing relative to views on homosexuality and same-sex marriage. My reading would suggest that there are three reasons for this. First, in 1973, in the publication of the DSM-II, the American Psychiatric Association removed homosexuality as a pathologic mental illness and instead described it as a normal expression of human sexuality. Even though, as we saw in the previous chapter, there are still some who want to hold on to the older paradigm, most in the medical, mental health, and behavioral health sciences have rejected the idea that homosexuality is a disorder or abnormality.

The second reason is the result of biological science that has been briefly reviewed above. If in the course of prenatal development certain hormonal and genetic factors occur, a person may develop same-sex attraction. From a biological standpoint, this just happens. It is one of many "normal" paths of development that may occur. (The exception here would appear to be for the transgender person. The discordance this biologically based development creates presents challenges for the transgender person that he or she will confront in his or her life as it develops.)

The third reason most likely flows out of the first two; the younger generation has grown up in the post-1973 world. They simply were not raised in the same social-norm environment that was once dominant (LeVay 1997). None of these are necessarily reasons why the church ought to change its views (indeed, I would insist the church should not change its views just because the culture does), but they do have a great deal to do with why the issue simply will not go away in religious communities and why increasingly there are those in religious communities who are supportive of same-sex relationships and marriage and the ordination to ministry of LGBT persons.

89

In this chapter the focus will be on the current demographic statistics of the LGBT community mostly in the United States and current national views on homosexuality based upon national research, some of which was conducted by my company, MissionInsite. The chapter will close with current views on the topic within the religious community. What ties it all together is the intent to portray the changing cultural tide toward openness and inclusion in some quarters but continued exclusion in others.

The Demographics of LGBT

Demographic research is the study of population, households, and characteristics about each. I have spent most of my professional career providing and analyzing demographic data—a strange fact given that my graduate degree is in theology! There are some real questions in this study that pertain to demographics. Before jumping into the specifics and some of the difficulties this particular topic presents for demographic research, I want to state the large question that is germane to this study. How many LGBT people are there in the United States? Is it a large number? Or is it not so large? Given the amount of attention given to homosexuality today in our culture, one would be inclined to think it large. But is it? Getting a right answer to this question is not as easy as one might think.[1] So, how do we go about answering our primary question?

The Percentage of the US Population That Is LGBT

It would be nice and certainly tidier if one could obtain a demographic count of LGBT persons and what percentage of the total US population they represent by going to some single source, such as the US Census Bureau. But it is neither nice nor tidy because the research findings are influenced by so many factors. For example, in the classic study done by Alfred Kinsey, a figure was released and repeated for decades. They claimed that 10 percent of the American population was homosexual. This same percentage is still repeated today. Another study done in 1990 claimed that 10 percent of men and 8.6 percent of women "had at one point in their life experienced some form of homosexuality" (Laumann 1994, 299). A study by Samuel and Cynthia Janus reported on a survey comprised of 2,765 adults—male and female over the age of eighteen. Of the men, 9 percent reported frequent or ongoing homosexual experiences and women, 5 percent (Janus and Janus 1993). But what do these numbers mean? Are they all homosexuals, or have they just had a same-sex sexual experience at some moment in their life?

Getting the Questions Right

A 2011 poll by the Gallup organization asked Americans what percentage of the population *they* believed were gay or lesbian. Surprisingly, on average respondents said 25 percent (Morales 2011)! Is this true? Is every fourth person you see gay? Or is it one in ten as Kinsey suggested? What is the actual percentage? The LGBT community tends to inflate the number. It works in their favor to do so politically. But inflation does little to bring truth to the question. Furthermore even with data the analysis is complicated by several factors. What is being counted? Sexual orientation? Same-sex attraction? A homosexual encounter at some moment in life? There is the issue of what a person's sexual identity is versus his or her orientation, all of which has already been discussed. Additionally, when it comes to surveys or the census, there is still some reticence to "come out" even on a confidential survey. This discretion likely tamps down the percentage but how much is unknown. It is the case that with a more open and accepting social environment, LGBT people are more likely to disclose than in the past. But researchers are sure that there are still many who resist "coming out." All of this makes counting murky. Consequently it is important to get the questions as clear as possible. We begin with the four distinctive groups: lesbian, gay, bisexual, and transgender persons. Once we have these numbers, they can be aggregated to give a total percentage. Sometimes that total will be the entire LGBT community and sometimes just the LGB community.[2]

- What percent of the total US population is gay (i.e., gay men)?

- What percentage is lesbian?

- What percentage is bisexual?

- What percentage is transgender?

It is necessary to define these questions tightly. This is in part because some of the larger percentages published (such as 10 percent of the population) often conflate orientation with those who have at some point had a same-sex experience such as in a same-sex boarding school or prison where "gay for the stay" is not unusual. There are two sources that appear to have a pretty good picture of the LGBT population as of this writing. The first comes from the Williams Institute of UCLA and the second from the Gallup polling organization.

The Numbers

The Williams Institute conducted a comparative analysis of nine surveys in the United States and other nations and in a report released in 2011 provided a good summation of LGBT demographics. (In some cases, the numbers reported here are broader than in just the United States.) The following are some of the bullet points listed in the executive summary (Gates 2011, 1):

- "An estimated 3.5% of adults in the United States identify as lesbian, gay, or bisexual and an estimated 0.3% of adults are transgender.

- "This implies that there are approximately 9 million LGBT Americans" at the time of the report.

- "Among adults who identify as LGB, bisexuals comprise a slight majority (1.8% compared to 1.7% who identify as lesbian or gay).

- "Women are substantially more likely than men to identify as bisexual. Bisexuals comprise more than half of the lesbian and bisexual population among women in eight of the nine surveys considered in the brief. Conversely, gay men comprise substantially more than half of gay and bisexual men in seven of the nine surveys.

- "Estimates of those who report any lifetime same-sex sexual behavior and any same-sex sexual attraction are substantially higher than estimates of those who identify as LGB. An estimated 19 million Americans (8.2%) report that they have engaged in same-sex sexual behavior and nearly 25.6 million Americans (11%) acknowledge at least some same-sex sexual attraction."

The following two graphs derived from the Williams Institute data summarize some of these findings graphically. The first graph shows percentages across the nine surveys. It illustrates how difficult it is to get a clear read on the LGB population. Note that for each survey, there is a total of those adults who identify as lesbian or gay or bisexual at the right of the graph bar. Percentages range from 1.2 percent to 5.6 percent. More specifically, it shows the split between exclusively gay or lesbian (G/L) versus bisexual persons.

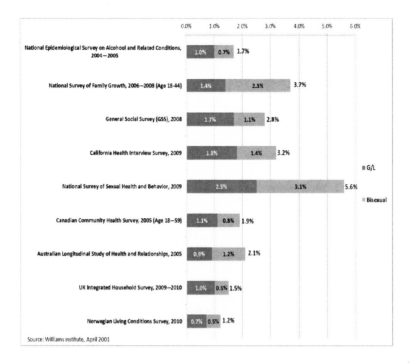

Percent of adults who identify as lesbian, gay, or bisexual (information from Gates 2011, 3)

In many of the surveys, the bisexual percentages are higher than the G/L percentages. The second graph portrays those who at some point have experienced same-sex attraction. In two of three surveys the percentage of persons who indicated some same-sex attraction who also identify themselves as LGB is smaller than those who admitted to having same-sex attraction at some point.

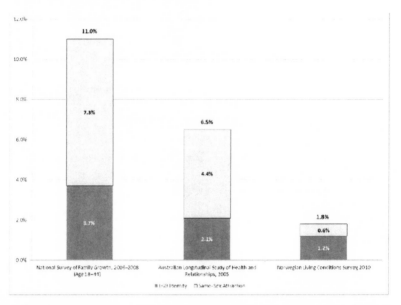

Percent of adults who report any same-sex attraction (information from Gates 2011, 5)

The third graph reveals those who at one or more points in their life had a same-sex experience. In all three cases, the percentage identifying as LGB is smaller than those who admitted to a same-sex encounter.

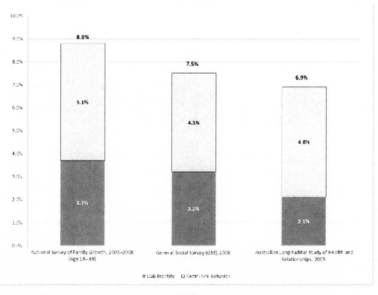

Percent of adults who report any behavior (information from Gates 2011, 5)

These data do help to distinguish between those who have imagined or acted upon same-sex attraction at a moment in time and those who consider themselves gay, lesbian, or bisexual. The percentages of the latter category track pretty closely with the estimated total percentages for LGB people, though they are somewhat lower.

A Gallup report released in 2012 estimates that 3.4 percent of the US population is LGBT. Gallup introduced a new question to 121,290 US adults. This is by far the largest study to date that focuses on just this question. They asked, "Do you, personally, identify as lesbian, gay, bisexual, or transgender?" Note that the question is not quite as clean as we might like it but is exceedingly valuable nonetheless for its sheer size, allowing multiple valid cross-tabulations. The graph that follows takes several slices of the data of those who answered yes to the question.

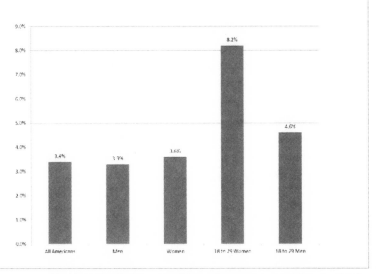

Do you, personally, identify as lesbian, gay, bisexual or transgender? Answer "Yes"

Overall the survey conforms to much prior research that consistently places the percentage between 3.3 percent and 3.8 percent. (The working figure reported by Wilson and Rahman is about 3.5 percent (2008, 22–23). Perhaps the most remarkable result reflected in this chart is the high percentage of women between the ages of eighteen and twenty-nine. Over 8 percent answered yes to the question. Caution is called for in the interpretation of this percentage. Although in times past it would have been shocking to admit to any aspect of same-sex attraction, due to the shift in our culture especially among young people, experimentation seems to be more socially acceptable. One hears anecdotal stories of same-sex encounters, often under the influence of drugs or alcohol. What will be true over time is yet to be seen, but one wonders if it is not a new version of "gay for the stay." Perhaps more aptly named "gay for the play." It seems unlikely women would jump 4.6 percentage points within a single age band, especially given that men are closer to the overall male population percentage. Time will of course tell.

Changing or Stable over Time?

Public perception most likely is that the number of persons identifying themselves as LGBT is growing in the United States. But is that really the case? If we have enough trouble getting a firm grip on percentages within our own moment in time, looking back over time is even more difficult.

Research suggests that the percentage of the population that is LGBT has been fairly stable over time. In other words, the LGBT population is not growing as a percentage of the total population. Nature would appear to be fairly constant in spinning out LGBT persons. There is a cultural perception, perhaps due to some group's efforts to bring the LGBT community out into the open (some are the LGBT community, and some are those trying to create some discomfort about same-sex issues), that it is growing or, as in the Gallup poll referenced above, larger than it really is. But it does not appear to be growing as a percentage, and it certainly is not as large as the "person on the street" thinks.

Where LGBT People Live

A national percentage is helpful in identifying the overall total of LGBT people in the United States. But in reality, no population group is evenly spread across the country. Same-sex people are far more likely to gravitate to large urban areas, to the coasts, and to regions that are more accepting. This concentration of LGBT people in cities contributes to the perception of a large, growing population. But demographically it is another example of "birds of a feather, flock together." So where are LGBT folk more likely to flock? The following tables provide estimates based upon the American Community Survey by the US Census Bureau in 2005. The first is by state, and the second is by major US city (information from Gates 2006, 5–7).

LGB Population Top States Ranked by LGB Population: ACS

Rank	State	Percentage of State Pop	Population
1	California	5.20%	1,338,164
2	Florida	4.60%	609,219
3	New York	4.20%	592,337
4	Texas	3.60%	579,968
5	Illinois	3.80%	345,395
6	Ohio	4.00%	335,110
7	Pennsylvania	3.50%	323,454
8	Georgia	4.30%	278,943
9	Massachusetts	5.70%	269,074
10	Washington	5.70%	266,983

LGB Population Top Cities Ranked by LGB Population: ACS

Rank	State	Percentage of State Pop	Population
1	New York City	4.50%	272,493
2	Los Angeles	5.60%	154,270
3	Chicago	5.70%	114,449
4	San Francisco	15.40%	94,234
5	Phoenix	6.40%	63,222
6	Houston	4.40%	61,976
7	San Diego	6.80%	61,945
8	Dallas	7.00%	58,473
9	Seattle	12.90%	57,993
10	Boston	12.30%	50,540

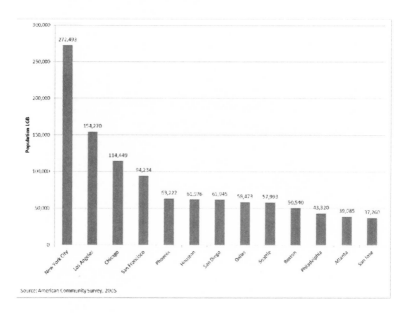

Source: American Community Survey, 2005

Population LGB by US City

Same-Sex Couples

Of the population that is LGBT, a certain percentage are couples. There are problems in providing demographic data on couples. The first problem is how we think about a couple. When the census data is collected, respondents are asked questions about persons in their household. Two specific questions become the source of Census Bureau reporting: relationship to householder and the sex of each person (US Census Bureau 2011). Within this reporting are couples who have been together a short time but happen to be together at the time of the census, couples who have been together a long time, and couples who are married. The first table shows the total number of unmarried partner households. Opposite-sex unmarried households make up 5.2 percent of all households, but same-sex unmarried partner households make up a mere half of a percent.

2011 American Community Survey 5 Year Estimates		
Unmarried Partner Households	**Percent of HH**	**Est. HH**
Same Sex	0.5%	573,807
Opposite Sex	5.2%	5,967,591

At the level of same-sex couples, the following data have been released by the Census Bureau following a correction made in the 2010 census data due to data capture errors (O'Connell and Feliz 2011; see also Cohn 2011).

Same-Sex Couples: US House-holds	All		Unmarried		Spouses	
	2010 Census	ACS 2010	2010 Census	ACS 2010	2010 Census	ACS 2010
Percent of Households	0.554%	0.518%	0.441%	0.385%	0.113%	0.133%
Estimated Households	646,464	593,324	514,735	440,989	131,729	152,335

As a percentage of the total US households, same-sex couples make up a fairly small group, barely a half of one percent. These data are in flux because of the rapidly changing nature of US households and families.

The Williams Institute completed an analysis of the 2010 census. Two maps are provided from their report that show: (1) the number of same-sex households per 1,000 households by county and (2) the percent of same-sex couples raising their own children[3] by county. Displaying the data by county clarifies where greater and lesser concentrations of same-sex couples and same-sex couples with children are more likely to reside (Gates and Cooke 2014, 1, 3). Note that the darker the area on the map, the greater the concentration. Look for patterns. For example, same-sex couples per one thousand households are more concentrated in the Northeast and coastal Northern California.

Same-sex couples per 1,000 households
by county (adjusted)

0 - 2.7
2.8 - 5.5
5.6 - 6.8
6.9 - 30.9

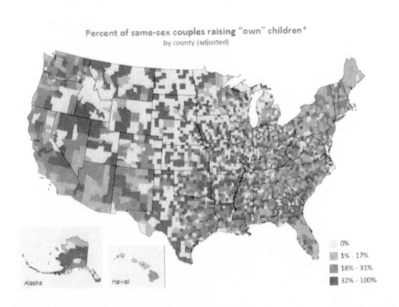

Percent of same-sex couples raising "own" children*
by county (adjusted)

0%
1% - 17%
18% - 31%
32% - 100%

What Americans Think

Recent polls have shown a shift in views in the US population vis-à-vis acceptance of LGBT people and same-sex marriage. One of my companies provides demographic research services to churches and church denominations. As part of that service we launched the Quadrennium Project. The Quadrennium Project was conceived to provide clients insight into the likely religious preferences, practices, and beliefs of the American population (MissionInsite 2012).[4] It is intentionally designed to assist churches in understanding these dynamics in their communities.

One section of the questionnaire was designed to measure where the American public stood on a series of current social and moral issues. Given that LGBT issues are presently debated, especially same-sex marriage, we asked for attitudinal responses to four statements of belief that indicated to what extent they agreed or disagreed with each. These are listed below.

Of the following statements of personal belief, please indicate your level of agreement or disagreement.	Strongly disagree	Somewhat disagree	No opinion	Somewhat agree	Strongly agree
I believe religious communities should fully embrace LGBT persons (lesbian, gay, bisexual, transgender).	1	2	3	4	5
I believe same-sex marriage should be legalized.	1	2	3	4	5
I believe marriage is only a relationship between one man and one woman.	1	2	3	4	5
I believe children ought to be raised in two-parent, mother and father families if possible.	1	2	3	4	5

What makes our survey somewhat different than others is our sample size. With more than fifteen thousand respondents, who are demographically and geographically balanced across the entire United States, we are able to cross-tabulate by other items in the survey such as sex, age, religious affiliation if any, and so on, and derive reliable findings. For the purposes of this study, the focus will be on specific questions that the survey addresses that are germane to this topic. I have said before that just because the culture attitudes swing in a certain direction in no way means the church should as well. However, not to understand what the culture thinks on social issues is to fail to effectively engage the culture with the gospel. In my years of working in churches across the United States I have seen Christian groups "take stands" on various issues and lose a voice among the people they are called to reach with the good news. Instead what the culture hears are condemning, judgmental, and too often angry and self-inflated preachers playing more to their religious audiences than to the people who need to see Jesus. Some within these same audiences then launch nonprofit or political organizations with the intent of "saving Christian America." But saving it for whom? Saving it from what? Instead of effectively communicating with the culture, they go to war with the culture. It is Jesus's message that is then lost or completely misrepresented.

All of these speak to why we must look at what the culture thinks. Even if we believe the culture is wrongheaded, from the perspective of the church, it is not the enemy. So then what does US society think about these four questions from the survey? For the purposes of this study we shall look at the following results:

- what the United States thinks about each of the four belief statements

- what the data reveals when dividing the respondents between those who are thirty-nine and under and those who are forty and older

- how data on each statement distributes when segmented by the larger Christian traditions (These data are aggregated Baptists, Episcopalians, Lutherans, Methodists, nondenominational/independent, Pentecostals/Holiness, and Presbyterians/Reformed.)

- how the data distributes when the larger Christian traditions are segmented by those who are thirty-nine and under and those who are forty and older

- what those with no religious preference think across the four statements in total and segmented by the two age groups

Some interesting stories are to be found in these data. But if this kind of data is "not your thing," please feel free to skip to the next section.

The United States as a Whole

We begin with the national results. The following graph portrays how Americans responded when asked to indicate their level of agreement or disagreement with each statement. We have aggregated them into three response categories; disagree, no opinion, and agree.

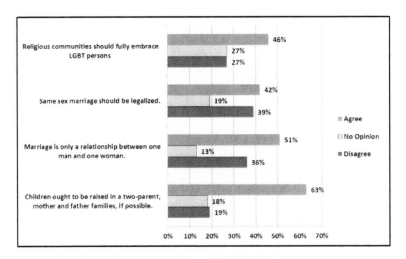

Source: The Quadrennium Project, 2012 by MissionInsite, LLC

Americans, by nearly two to one, believe religious communities should embrace LGBT people (46 percent to 27 percent). But there is also a solid 27 percent that, as of the time the survey was taken, do not have an opinion. A similar percentage believe same-sex marriage should be legalized, but those disagreeing increases by 12 percentage points, the increase coming from a smaller percentage with no opinion. People were far more likely to have an opinion on the legalization of same-sex marriage. This percentage continues to move around. In a 2011 Gallup Poll, it was estimated that 53 percent supported same-sex marriage, but that number fell to 50 percent by 2012, the same year that MissionInsite conducted its survey and found the percentage to be 43 percent (Newport 2012a). Positive support has been increasing overall for years, however, according to the annual tracking of the Gallup organization as represented in the following graph.

Do You Think Marriages between Same-Sex Couples Should or Should Not Be Recognized by the Law as Valid, with the Same Rights as Traditional Marriages?

Note: Trend shown for polls in which same-sex marriage question followed questions on gay/lesbian rights and relations. 1996–2005 wording: "Do you think marriages between homosexuals..." (Newport 2012a).

The positive support for LGBT issues begins to shift, however, when we get to what marriage is. Fifty-one percent believe marriage is between a man and woman only. The percentage who disagree and who would more likely support LGBT aspirations for same-sex marriage drops to 36 percent. People were far more likely to have an opinion about what a marriage is than whether it should be legalized for homosexuals, revealing a more conservative shift of attitude within the data. This same shift toward the conservative is presented in the kind of family structure in which children should ideally be raised. More than 63 percent believe they ought to be raised in the traditional two-parent, mother and father family if possible.

So what do we take from this? These data reflect the general national mood as of this writing. There is an overall shift toward support for LGBT people but at the same time a holding on to traditional understandings of marriage and family. It does indicate that things are fluid yet moving in the direction of full inclusion and rights for the LGBT person. However, it also indicates that there is an internal struggle within Americans as well. This apparent double-mindedness most likely contributes to the ongoing struggles to give LGBT persons the same marriage and family opportunities as straight people.

US Population Forty Years of Age and Older Grouping

When the respondents forty years of age and older are segmented out of the data, the profile moves more conservative. The percentage that believe religious communities should embrace LGBT people drops from 46 percent to 44 percent. Similarly legalization of same-sex marriage drops significantly to only 39 percent, and the opposed percentage is higher than the support. Continuing the more conservative shift, 55 percent believe in the traditional definition of marriage, and two out of three believe children should be raised in the traditional two-parent, mother and father family structure.

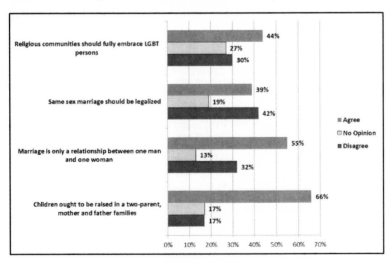

Source: The Quadrennium Project, 2012 by MissionInsite, LLC

US Population Thirty-Nine Years of Age and Younger Grouping

The picture changes when the profile is of the adult respondents thirty-nine years of age and younger.

Aggregated Results of US Adult Population Thirty-Nine Years of Age and Younger on LGBT

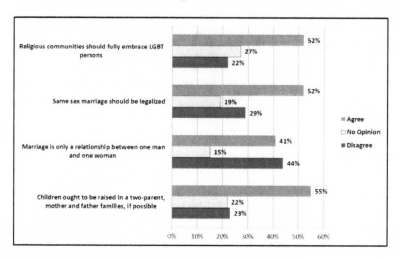

Source: The Quadrennium Project, 2012 by MissionInsite, LLC

At 52 percent, a clear majority of people under forty believe religious communities should embrace LGBT people, and the same percentage believe same-sex marriage should be legalized. Both of these are higher than the national profile, and the legalization percentage is ten points higher. On the definition of marriage and the context in which children ought to be raised, the under-forty group also moves to more traditional. Unlike the national or forty-plus group, more disagree with a traditional definition than agree, but the difference is fairly evenly split. Relative to households for raising children, they are close to the national profile. They agree just a little bit less and disagree a little bit more but otherwise look similar.

No Religious Preference

What do people who have no religious preference believe about these four issues? One segment of people that is watched by the media and to some extent (though not enough!) by the religious community is the group often referred to as the "Nones." This is short for "no religious preference." This group comprises 22 percent of the American population. I have tracked this group for over twenty years. In that period it has increased from 11 percent of the US population to 22 percent. In that period, a whole generation has arrived at adulthood. These are people to watch and to understand. What they think about these issues, I believe, is informative of where people's views are headed. So, what do they think about the LGBT issues? In the following analysis, the total profile of Nones is presented. Following that, the Nones profile is age segmented.

No Religious Preference Results on LGBT Social Issues

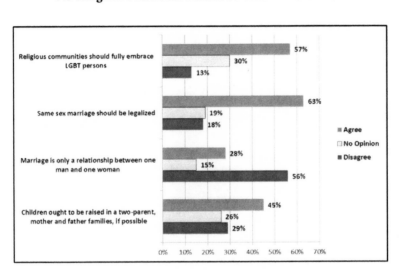

Source: The Quadrennium Project, 2012 by MissionInsite, LLC

Those with no religious preference mostly lean toward the progressive side of a conservative-progressive continuum with significant strength. Nearly 57 percent (ironically!) believe religious communities should embrace LGBT people, this compared to 39 percent from within the religious groups. More than 63 percent believe that marriage should be legalized, compared to 49 percent from within the religious groups. And while 62 percent of those from the religious groups hold to the traditional view of marriage, only 28 percent of the no preference group does.

They do turn more conservative, however, when it comes to families in which children are raised. Here 45 percent believe they should be raised in the traditional mother and father family structure. However, this is a much lower percentage than the religious groups or even the total national profile.

Now if we segment this group by age, does the story change? The first chart presents the beliefs of "nones" who are forty and older. This segment is still more progressive than the national profile but less so than the total "nones" profile. For example, nearly half still believe that children should be raised in the traditional family.

No Religious Preference Results on LGBT Social Issues: Age Forty and Over

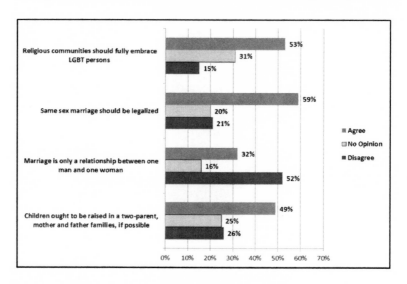

Source: The Quadrennium Project, 2012 by MissionInsite, LLC

The second chart presents the beliefs of "nones" who are thirty-nine and under. There is little of a conservative view for those with no religious preference who are under forty. On religious communities embracing LGBT people, legalization of same-sex marriage, and traditional marriage, these people fall significantly on the progressive side of the continuum, more so than any other grouping. Nearly three out of four believe that same-sex marriage should be legalized, and a clear two-thirds reject the belief that marriage is between one man and one woman. The only place they become more conservative is the context for raising children, and even there it is only 38 percent who believe they should be reared in a traditional family structure.

**No Religious Preference Results on LGBT Social Issues:
Age Thirty-Nine and Under**

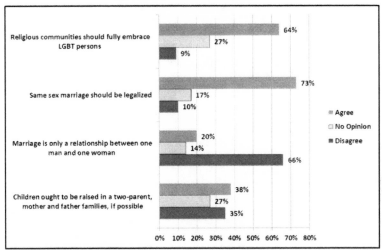

Source: The Quadrennium Project, 2012 by MissionInsite, LLC

Religious Preference Grouping

How do the different major religious traditions respond to each of the four statements? The graph displays the aggregate views of the major religious traditions by each statement (Baptist, Catholic, Episcopalian, Lutheran, Methodist, nondenominational, Presbyterian/Reformed, and Pentecostal/Holiness. Please note that these are not specific denominations but people's religious preferences.). We notice immediately a more conservative movement. For example, whereas 46 percent of the national profile indicated that religious communities should fully support LGBT people, this percentage among the religious people drops to 39 percent. Legalization of same-sex marriage also shifts conservative with the national profile at 42 percent but dropping to 31 percent among the religious traditions. Not surprising then, the religious profile is much more conservative on the definition of marriage and the optimal family structure for raising children. (For detail results by religious preference, please see the appendix.)

Aggregated Results of Major Religious Traditions on LGBT Social Issues

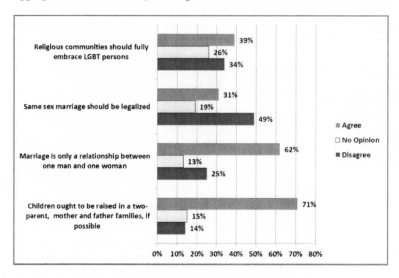

Source: The Quadrennium Project, 2012 by MissionInsite, LLC

Same-Sex Marriage Trends

In November of 2012, the Gallup organization fielded a phone survey of 1,015 adults between the ages of eighteen and fifty.[5] Their findings tracked with the Quadrennium results. Those with religious beliefs were asked why they opposed same-sex marriage. Almost half of those who oppose same-sex marriage do so because they believe the Bible says it is wrong. The second and third reasons are probably different versions of the first. They believe it is between a man and a woman because that is what they believe the Bible teaches. They think it is morally wrong or they have traditional beliefs because those beliefs are based upon what they believe the Bible and their religious tradition teaches.

The following table provides the general reasons by percentage.

(Asked of those opposed to same-sex marriage:) What are some of the reasons why you oppose legal same-sex marriages? [OPEN-ENDED}	
Religion/Bible says it's wrong	47%
Marriage should be between a man and a woman	20%
Morally wrong/Have traditional beliefs	16%
Civil unions are sufficient	6%
Unnatural/Against laws of nature	5%
Undermines traditional family structure/Mother and father	5%
Other	7%
No opinion	4%

Source: Newport 2012b

Summary

The changing social perspectives on homosexuality that are evolving in the larger culture are also reflected within the religious community. The research (details found in the appendix) demonstrates that depending on the particular religious tradition, views tend to fall along a conservative to progressive continuum, with different religious traditions or groups falling somewhere along it. This is no surprise to those who follow such things. But it does translate what we think is the case to real numbers.

These data suggest two things. First, the younger generation does not share the same social issue space as the older generation. Second, if this continues over time and the younger generation carries these beliefs into their older years and if the generation coming after them continues the trend, the social structures and institutions that have shaped the lives of those over forty will look different in the not-too-distant future. If we keep in mind that the "nones" are a growing group, the churches will look extremely different— possibly old and empty.

Continuum of Religious Views

With all of the demographic information provided in this chapter in mind, where do religious institutions and religious people go from here? In large part it depends upon what they believe the Bible says. As the Gallup poll indicated for religious people, the Bible is the main opposition they have to embracing the LGBT community and their desires to marry and have families.

We will look at the Bible and what I think it teaches in the following three chapters. But first, I want to explore further this spectrum of religious views along the conservative-progressive continuum. I developed a typology that is designed to sort through how different people and religious traditions are likely to respond to five statements. The five statements are derived from the primary issues that are at the center of the scientific, medical, and cultural debate about homosexuality. Each statement calls for one of two completions. Each religious type is associated with how traditions or groups within a type are likely to respond to the statement. The four types are (1) fundamentalist, (2) conservative, (3) moderate conservative and (4) post-Evangelical/emergent/progressive. Definitions will follow the Statement Response table.

The Statements

- Sexual orientation is (1) a choice or (2) innate?

- Same-sex desires are (1) evil or (2) natural?

- Same-sex behaviors are/can be (1) immoral or (2) moral?

- Same-sex marriage is a (1) moral issue or (2) justice issue?

- Ordination of active same-sex persons is a (1) moral issue or (2) justice issue?

Statement Response Table by Type Code		
Statements about Homosexuality	Response Options	
Sexual orientation is . . .	a choice or	innate
	Fundamentalist	Moderate Conservative
	Conservative	Post-Evangelical, Emergent, or Progressive

112

Same-sex desires are . . .	evil	or	natural
	Fundamentalist		Moderate Conservative
	Conservative		Post-Evangelical, Emergent, or Progressive
Same-sex behaviors are/can be . . .	immoral	or	moral
	Fundamentalist		Post-Evangelical, Emergent, or Progressive
	Conservative		
	Moderate Conservative		
Same-sex marriage is a . . .	moral issue	or	justice issue
	Fundamentalist		Post-Evangelical, Emergent, or Progressive
	Moderate Conservative[6]		
	Conservative		
Ordination of active same-sex persons is a . . .	moral issue	or	justice issue
	Fundamentalist		Post-Evangelical, Emergent, or Progressive
	Conservative		
	Moderate Conservative		

The Four Types

The four types are intended to reflect common worldviews across religious traditions. No typology is perfect and most likely could be constructed differently. But for the purposes of this study, each of these types represents what people believe about each of the five statements. Any religious affiliation, denomination, or group may have people in any one of the types. The types are:

113

Type	Description
Fundamentalist	• See homosexuality, orientation, and behaviors as a willful rejection of God's plan for humans and an evil. • Think same-sex marriage and ordination of practicing homosexuals must be rejected on moral/biblical (or some other authoritative text) grounds. • See homosexuality as a moral scourge on human society. • Are likely to encourage therapies to change desires. • Show little empathy for homosexual people.
Conservative	• See homosexual orientation as a choice but provoked by some kind of childhood trauma. • See a homosexual as a victim who must be helped to fight their same-sex desires and choose a heterosexual lifestyle. • Are likely to encourage therapies to change desires. • Think same-sex marriage and ordination of practicing homosexuals must be rejected on moral/biblical (or some other authoritative text) grounds. • Show some empathy toward homosexual people as long as committed to change.
Moderate Conservative	• See homosexual orientation as possibly the result of biological processes, and desires are therefore part of the natural result. • Think, however, that homosexual behavior is immoral and must not be practiced. • May want to try therapies to deal with same-sex attraction and encourage homosexuals to live a celibate life. • Think same-sex marriage and ordination of practicing homosexuals must be rejected on moral/biblical (or some other authoritative text) grounds within the church. • May accept the inevitability of same-sex marriage within the larger culture and even appreciate it as a legitimate civil rights issue but say no within the church.[7] • Have some empathy and little hostility toward homosexual persons.

Post-Evangelical, Emergent, or Progressive	• See homosexuality as a part of natural process, and therefore orientation is innate.
	• Think the resulting desires are part of that process of development and therefore are natural.
	• Think same-sex behaviors can be moral within certain relational frameworks that are informed by core beliefs.
	• Are likely to support same-sex marriage and the ordination of practicing homosexuals.
	• Support same-sex marriage, and believe the lack of ordination is an injustice that must be corrected.

The fourth category looks to be somewhat of a catchall. For the purposes of the typology, what distinguishes one type from another is their views on the five statements. As a result on the nonconservative side fall three somewhat overlapping but distinct groups. Progressives reflect the traditional "liberal" side of the church. Post-evangelicals reflects a group that would have been solidly in the evangelical community in the past but have begun to find themselves at odds with some evangelical values and beliefs, such as the homosexuality issue. But when it comes to core, traditional evangelical beliefs, such as the death and resurrection of Jesus, they are still much in agreement. Emergent is a category that is difficult to define and could share much with both the progressives and the post-evangelicals. I find myself in the post-evangelical/ emergent mix. In this mix will be leaders such as Brian McLaren and Rob Bell. Phyllis Tickle provides an especially helpful overview of all of this in her book *The Great Emergence: How Christianity Is Changing and Why* (2008). See also Diana Butler Bass's *Christianity after Religion* (2012). For a good book that captures McLaren as an emergent, see *A Generous Orthodoxy* (2004).

Conclusions

What conclusions can we draw from the demographic data? The LGBT community is not the large growing menace to society that some would have us believe. Neither is the community as large as some in the LGBT community would have us believe. Rather consistent with the science, the demographic data suggests that there is a percentage of the US population that identifies with some group within the LGBT community. The percentage is not large, with many estimates hovering around 3.5 percent. If we assume some level of undercount, then it would not be unreasonable to consider a 5 percent number, though this is admittedly an estimate. Men, on the one hand, are more likely to be either strictly gay or strictly straight. Women, on the other hand, are more likely to be bisexual than strictly lesbian.

The amount of data available for analysis is directly related to the changing American attitudes toward homosexuality. These data also tell us that attitudes toward the LGBT community are changing, with more than 40 percent believing that religious communities ought to be open to them as well as grant the right to same-sex marriage. Overall Americans are not yet as comfortable with redefining marriage away from the traditional man-woman relationship, nor are they as comfortable with nontraditional families with children. But it would seem to be the case in the research that attitudes are shifting and are shifting more in the direction of inclusion. Based upon the historical data from the Gallup organization, the percentage of people supporting same-sex marriage has increased from 27 percent in 1996 to around 50 percent as of this writing (Newport 2012a). Add to this the fact that the younger generations are significantly more favorable and it seems unlikely that the social movement toward full inclusion of LGBT people in American society including same-sex marriage and even families will abate.

These changes will continue to put pressure on religious communities. All but the post-evangelicals, emergent, or progressives maintain some level of exclusion of LGBT people. I know that many in their hearts, especially among the "moderate conservatives," believe that they are accepting of LGBT people, and I personally do not doubt the sincerity of those sentiments. But the reality for the LGBT person is that the exclusions are barriers. The message received is that they are second-class citizens. Not unlike women or black people in the past, they cannot rise to leadership in many denominations and churches. Thus the message that they are welcome is perceived as a shallow invitation. There is a "You are welcome, but..." in the message. In times past, LGBT people lived by the now infamous phrase, "Don't ask, don't tell," but no longer. The emergence of solid science and social acceptance means that they are living more consistently with who they are in their public life as well as in their private life.

If the Bible, as reported by Gallup, is one of the main reasons Christians cannot accept homosexuality and all that comes with it, then the next step in my reflection is to look at the biblical texts that are believed to oppose it.

Notes

1. There are many other questions that could be asked under the heading of demographics, such as ethnicity, education level, incomes, and so on. Although these are important data to know, they do not serve the more focused purpose of this study.

2. Numbers for the transgender population were not as easily available and so will not be reported as fully.

3. The term *own children* means never-married children under the age of eighteen who are sons or daughters of one partner or spouse by birth, marriage, or adoption.

4. For more information on the Quadrennium Project, go to www.missioninsite .com.

5. Results for this *USA Today*/Gallup poll are based on telephone interviews conducted November 26–29, 2012, with a random sample of 1,015 adults, aged eighteen and older, living in all fifty US states and the District of Columbia. For results based on the total sample of national adults, one can say with 95 percent confidence that the maximum margin of sampling error is ±4 percentage points.

6. As of the writing of this book, there is a subtle shift occurring among those whom I would consider moderate conservatives. They are still adamant about shutting the door to same-sex marriage and partnered ordained gay persons, but they are less oppositional to the civil rights issue of same-sex marriage.

7. An *LA Times* article dated June 7, 2013, makes this point. The headline says it all: "Even most foes say gay marriage rights are inevitable, poll finds" (Lauter 2013).

Chapter 6

The Old Testament and
Same-Sex Behavior

My son is a professor of engineering and as such he is constantly doing research and presenting and publishing his findings. As his father, I have observed from close proximity some of the ways that scientists in academia behave, especially when considering whom to add to their ranks. These very smart people can have extremely large egos, and those egos can be expressed in many ways, even as they do their science and they increase the field of knowledge. In the sciences, in spite of cranky professors and sensitive egos, the data they explore and the conclusions they draw can be verified by replication studies. As a result the scientific enterprise generally proceeds—regardless of the crankiness and egos.

But once we cross over into the humanities and biblical studies, in particular, it's not so easy. There are still large egos and cranky scholars, but getting to a single definitive description, solution, or explanation is seldom accomplished. In fact, it appears to a person outside this world that some write papers to counter someone else only to provoke that someone else to write a counter to the original counter, ad infinitum.[1] This phenomenon is especially true when it comes to what the Bible teaches about homosexuality. Much of the conversation revolves around how to translate certain Hebrew or Greek words, ancient stories, and laws or communications, such as Paul's letters. It also revolves around traditional translations of these that are anachronistic. I begin with these comments because no matter what conclusion I might draw, there is at least one if not multiple counterarguments. I have no expectation—like my son would have as a research scientist through peer review and reproducible results—that I am going to review the data and give it an interpretation that settles anything other than my own desire to make sense out of these texts. Perhaps the best I can hope for is that others will understand that it is not as simple as "the Bible teaches" when it comes to what we can say about homosexuality.

Several biblical texts are used to support the view that the Bible condemns homosexuality. There are other stories that some writers will explore but that are not clearly and explicitly about same-sex behaviors, so I will not cover those.[2]

Old Testament	New Testament
Genesis 19:1-11	Romans 1:18-32
Leviticus 18:22-24	1 Corinthians 6:9-10
Leviticus 20:13	1 Timothy 1:10
	Jude 1:7

It is disconcerting how little context is provided when quoting these verses in condemnation of homosexuality or homosexuals.[3] Too often it is assumed that a reader or listener just knows that the references are about practices that are equivalent to modern-day homosexuality and same-sex relationships, which can then be denounced as morally revolting. It is especially troublesome when statements are made about how "clear" the Bible is on homosexuality by simply reading the isolated verse. To counter these practices of proof-texting, I will look at each one of these texts in some depth—while trying to avoid the "shock and awe" approach of many proponents and opponents of homosexuality.[4] The analysis is split over two chapters. The first will deal with texts from the Hebrew Bible, called the Old Testament (OT) by Christians. The second will turn to the New Testament (NT) and first-century Greco-Roman culture. At the end of the second chapter, I will summarize what the Bible does teach from my perspective. But prior to that, I will also deal with one text that no discussion on homosexuality in the church can avoid: Mark 10:2-12, in which Jesus makes a statement about marriage between a man and a woman.

If you, the reader, do not want to go into the detail that I must cover to treat the texts fairly, please feel free to jump to the summary at the end of chapter seven where you will find conclusions for both chapters.

Genesis 19:1-11: The Sodom Story

The first text is found in the book of Genesis. To set the context, we must ask ourselves: What is the purpose of the book of Genesis in the Bible? Israel's formative events were the exodus out of Egypt (Bauckham 1993) and the exile from the promised land. These events determined her identity, but our focus is the exodus.

In the exodus, Israel's God had come to her[5] rescue and defeated the most powerful man in the world at that time, Pharaoh. YHWH had demonstrated God's sovereignty over the earth by going head-to-head with Pharaoh and defeating him in his own land. The exodus was a crucial event in Israel's history. Everything worked its way back to that event. But what led up to that event? Why the exodus?

Israel had many stories that spoke to this question, starting with what we call the book of Genesis. *Genesis*, which means "beginning," covers much ground, telling the story of Israel up to the exodus. The following graphic illustrates this.

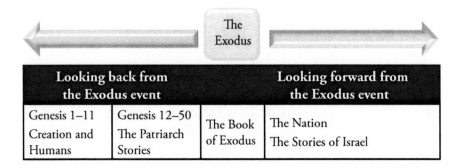

Looking back from the Exodus event		Looking forward from the Exodus event	
Genesis 1–11 Creation and Humans	Genesis 12–50 The Patriarch Stories	The Book of Exodus	The Nation The Stories of Israel

The Book of Beginnings

Genesis 1–11 is the story of primeval beginnings. It speaks of how God created the earth and sky and great waters. It speaks of how God created all life including humans. Genesis 1–11 also tells the sad tale of how humans turned against their creator.

Genesis 1–11 also establishes another important dynamic. Going all the way back to the first three children of Adam and Eve, there are two threads running through humans. Cain murders his first brother, Abel. For that he is exiled. A third brother named Seth is born. Seth and Cain represent two lines in the human family: one of faith and one of faithlessness, one of promise and one of desolation, one of hope and one of desperation, one of righteousness and one of evil. Chapter 11 ends with Terah, the father of Abraham in the line of Seth. The promise of God to heal and renew will come through the line of Seth, which will be the line through which Cain also will be redeemed.

Genesis 12–50 covers the ancient ancestors, the founders of the clan. The story of Genesis ends with Israel in Egypt, and then it works backward to the founding patriarch and matriarch, Abraham and Sarah. To them was given a promise that they would be the founders of a great nation and that through that nation all nations would be blessed; their clan would be the vehicle through which God would redeem creation and specifically human-ity. While Genesis 12–50 explains Israel's origin in Abraham and Sarah and the covenant that YHWH made with them, it also explains why they were in Egypt but, more important, why they were redeemed out of Egypt—the exodus event: "Then the Lord said to Abram, 'Have no doubt that your de-scendants will live as immigrants in a land that isn't their own, where they will be oppressed slaves for four hundred years. But after I punish the nation they serve, they will leave it with great wealth'" (Gen 15:13-14).

It was fundamental to the Israelite's identity that she had a special voca-tion (which we looked at earlier). The stories of the patriarchs and the gene-alogies tied them back to the beginning with the first parents. Through that Israel was able to find that she was in the line of faith, the line through which her God was going to save the world.

This overview of Genesis is important for properly setting the story of Sodom in its appropriate context. The people of Sodom represented the line of unfaithfulness, the line of Cain. They were the line of humans that had rejected the true God and were pursuing all manner of other things that were contrary to the world God intended.

Who Are the Righteous?

We first encounter the term *righteous* in the Bible in the story preceding the story of Sodom. Abraham has been told by two emissaries from God that they have two messages for Abraham. First, his wife Sarah will conceive and bear a son in her old age, and it is through him that the promise of a great nation will come: "Is anything too difficult for the Lord? When I return to you about this time next year, Sarah will have a son" (Gen 18:14).

But the second message is that they intend to destroy Sodom for its evil:

> The Lord said, "Will I keep from Abraham what I'm about to do? Abraham
> will certainly become a great populous nation, and all the earth's nations
> will be blessed because of him. I have formed a relationship with him so

that he will oversee his children and his household after him. And they will keep to the Lord's path, being moral [righteous][6] and just so that the Lord can do for Abraham everything he said he would." Then the Lord said, *"The cries of injustice from Sodom and Gomorrah are countless, and their sin is very serious!* I will go down now to examine the cries of injustice that have reached me. Have they really done all this? If not, I want to know." (Gen 18:17-21, emphasis added)

Two lines then—the line of faith that will run through Abraham and the line of unfaithfulness—are on full display in Sodom. Abraham will keep the way of YHWH by following the "Lord's path, being moral and just." This is in contrast to what is happening in Sodom. Against Sodom comes an outcry because of its sin. So what does this mean? YHWH is a God of justice. Injustice cries out to YHWH demanding that what is wrong be set right. Israel's own story of slavery and rescue includes just such a response from God.

This is the backdrop for the story of Sodom. Whatever was going on in Sodom (the so-called sin of Sodom), it was unjust. The cries of the victims of injustice have reached the ears of God, and in response, God intends to set things right by destroying the wickedness. Abraham pleads with the messengers not to destroy Sodom. Abraham makes a bargain with God. If just ten righteous people can be found, the messengers promise they will not destroy the city of Sodom.

So what would a righteous person look like? Briefly, it is one who does the right thing and is faithful to God alone. But we too often emphasize the moral side of this word in English and miss the side that is more prominent in the biblical story. Those who are righteous are those who trust God and who do not go after other gods and all of the behaviors that attend such—what is called idolatry. A righteous person is in a right relationship with God. It is faith that is the central concern, and morality follows that. In the Bible, faith is something that you do, that you act on in response to a proper recognition of the God of creation.[7] This is critical to understanding the Sodom story. *I contend that it is critical to understanding the entire biblical story.* Paul the apostle clearly understands it that way when he declares that it is Abraham's *trust* that is reckoned (counted) as righteousness:

What does the scripture say? Abraham had faith in [trusted] God, and it was credited to him as righteousness. Workers' salaries aren't credited to them on the basis of an employer's grace but rather on the basis of what they deserve. But faith [trust] is credited as righteousness to those who don't work, because they have faith [trust] in God who makes the ungodly righteous. (Rom 4:3-5)

So the messengers will look for ten people in Sodom who trust in God and are not chasing after other gods and how those gods call them to behave.

What Is the Story About?

Let's begin then with the story itself. The full text is provided so that we keep in mind that it is a story and that pulling a verse out of it is inimical to the story's purpose for inclusion in Genesis:

> The two messengers entered Sodom in the evening. Lot, who was sitting at the gate of Sodom, saw them, got up to greet them, and bowed low. He said, "Come to your servant's house, spend the night, and wash your feet. Then you can get up early and go on your way."
>
> But they said, "No, we will spend the night in the town square." He pleaded earnestly with them, so they went with him and entered his house. He made a big meal for them, even baking unleavened bread, and they ate.
>
> Before they went to bed, the men of the city of Sodom—everyone from the youngest to the oldest—surrounded the house and called to Lot, "Where are the men who arrived tonight? Bring them out to us so that we may know them intimately."
>
> Lot went out toward the entrance, closed the door behind him, and said, "My brothers, don't do such an evil thing. I've got two daughters who are virgins. Let me bring them out to you, and you may do to them whatever you wish. But don't do anything to these men because they are now under the protection of my roof."
>
> They said, "Get out of the way!" And they continued, "Does this immigrant want to judge us? Now we will hurt you more than we will hurt them." They pushed Lot back and came close to breaking down the door. The men inside reached out and pulled Lot back into the house with them and slammed the door. Then the messengers blinded the men near the entrance of the house, from the youngest to the oldest, so that they groped around trying to find the entrance. (Gen 19:1-11)

The two messengers from God approach the city of Sodom at evening. Lot is sitting at the gate and was most likely accompanied by the important men of the city. During the day the gate was a marketplace and the seat of the court where matters related to the city were conducted. In the evening the men would gather for a social time. The appearance of the two messengers should have provoked a response from them all, but only Lot stands to greet them. He invites them to stay with him. At first they demur, insisting that they would just spend the time in the town square. But Lot presses his hospitality for them to accept his invitation, which they finally agree to do. Lot is acting according to the rules of hospitality. Before we proceed, we need to consider this in more detail because it is central to the narrative.

Hospitality in the Ancient Near East

Hospitality in the ancient Near East was an essential social practice (de Vaux 1965, 4). Calling it a social practice misses the magnitude of the tradition. Hospitality was indispensable to agrarian and pastoral life. Because travelers knew that they could not survive without assistance, hosts made sure that any stranger who came to their dwelling must be taken in and cared for. Roland de Vaux describes hospitality in ancient Israel: "The guest is sacred: the honor of providing for him was disputed [among the clan or tribe as to who would provide it] but generally falls to the sheikh" (1965, 10). The provision of hospitality became the basis of a moral virtue of ancient Near Eastern life.

Hospitality was about the stranger. The Greek word found in the Septuagint and when used in the New Testament is *philoxenia,* and it means "love" (*philo*) and "the stranger" (*xenia*)—love the stranger. *Baker's Evangelical Dictionary of the Bible* provides this helpful definition:

> Hospitality in the ancient world focused on the alien or stranger in need. The plight of aliens was desperate. They lacked membership in the community, be it tribe, city-state, or nation. As an alienated person, the traveler often needed immediate food and lodging. Widows, orphans, the poor, or sojourners from other lands lacked the familial or community status that provided a landed inheritance, the means of making a living, and protection. In the ancient world the practice of hospitality meant graciously receiving an alienated person into one's land, home, or community and providing directly for that person's needs. (Duke 1996)

Hospitality was not about how one treats friends and family or even neighbors. Our concept of hospitality is so tied to social gatherings that it is hard for us to truly grasp its significance when we read about it in scripture. We think of hospitality and think of an optional event that we may host and that will be judged by how well we execute the event.

Jesus apparently draws on this practice when he speaks about how the Human One (or Son of Man) would be received:

> "Now when the Human One [Son of Man] comes in his majesty and all his angels are with him, he will sit on his majestic throne. All the nations will be gathered in front of him. He will separate them from each other, just as a shepherd separates the sheep from the goats. He will put the sheep on his right side. But the goats he will put on his left.

125

"Then the king will say to those on his right, 'Come, you who will receive good things from my Father. Inherit the kingdom that was prepared for you before the world began. I was hungry and you gave me food to eat. I was thirsty and you gave me a drink. I was a stranger and you welcomed me. I was naked and you gave me clothes to wear. I was sick and you took care of me. I was in prison and you visited me.'

"Then those who are righteous will reply to him, 'Lord, when did we see you hungry and feed you, or thirsty and give you a drink? When did we see you as a stranger and welcome you, or naked and give you clothes to wear? When did we see you sick or in prison and visit you?'

"Then the king will reply to them, 'I assure you that when you have done it for one of the least of these brothers and sisters of mine, you have done it for me.'" (Matt 25:31-40)

We know the story. Jesus then turns to those on his left and says that they failed to do this simple act of kindness of welcoming the stranger: "Then he will answer, 'I assure you that when you haven't done it for one of the least of these, you haven't done it for me.' And they will go away into eternal punishment. But the righteous ones will go into eternal life" (Matt 25:45-46).[8]

Jesus was a stranger; some welcomed him, and some did not. But Jesus welcomed all strangers to the chagrin of the religious leaders. They in part plotted against him because he hung out with outsiders—with strangers.

In Genesis, Lot had seen the strangers coming and ran to them and bowed low. He then prepared a feast for them. Lot is portrayed as the quintessential host. Sodom is portrayed as the exact opposite. The two messengers from YHWH approach the city gate, and nobody moves. The offense of this behavior for ancient Near Eastern people is almost incomprehensible. Those who heard this story or read it in the text would gasp! They would understand how insulting it was not to offer the strangers hospitality for the night.

Lot alone—the immigrant living among them—jumps up (and then bows low) to greet the visitors in a manner that should have been the behavior of everyone sitting at the gate. In offering them hospitality, he was committing to their protection. Such a commitment was a pledge of his own life and everything that was his. We must keep this in mind as we read this text. We read it through our twenty-first-century eyes and sensibilities, and we are horrified by his offer of his daughters. But this is no act of cowardice. In fact it's anything but cowardice because the first thing Lot does is step outside and shut the door behind him. He was totally exposed at that point. The crowd could (and most likely would have) moved first against him and then on to the strangers and his daughters.

But how could Lot offer his daughters? Women in ancient Near Eastern cultures were considered the property of their husbands if married or their fathers if not married. Even though this practice runs counter to our twenty-first-century sensibilities, even the last of the Ten Commandments assumes this: "Do not desire your neighbor's house. Do not desire and try to take your neighbor's wife, male or female servant, ox, donkey, or anything else that belongs to your neighbor" (Exod 20:17). This does not mean necessarily that women were treated as slaves, but it does mean they were considered property that was the man's to dispose of as he felt necessary. When confronted with the dilemma of how to protect his guests from a drunk, crazed, lust-filled mob, Lot chose to give up his daughters over his other possessions. Von Rad explains, "Lot intends under no circumstances to violate his hospitality; that his guests were for him more untouchable than his own daughters must have gripped the ancient reader, who knew whom Lot intended to protect in this way" (1995, 218).

What Were the Sodomites Intending?

What were the Sodomites intending to do? Some interpreters at this point focus on the sexual act they wanted, which would obviously have been a male-on-male sexual act on the visitors. But by focusing on the intended sexual act, the reader misses the point. Lot confronted a crazed mob set on rape. The fact that the messengers were male and that it would have therefore been a homosexual act is not what the story is really about. Walter Brueggemann says: "It is possible that the offense of Sodom is understood with specific reference to sexuality. But if such a reading is accepted, the turbulent mood of the narrative suggests gang-rape rather than a private act of either 'sodomy' or any specific homosexual act" (1982, 164).

The violence intended, which is in violation of the rules of hospitality, is the offense. These people did not like strangers, which is made obvious by what they say to Lot: "They said, 'Get out of the way!' And they continued, 'Does this immigrant want to judge us? Now we will hurt you more than we will hurt them'" (Gen 19:9). So instead of welcoming the strangers, they intended to savagely humiliate them.[9] While same-sex behavior was practiced in the ancient Near East, as it was among the Greeks and later the Romans, gang rape was not tolerated. Nonetheless gang rape was practiced as a demeaning punishment for prisoners and especially against those defeated in war. As we will find when we look at the sexual practices of Rome, the issue was not what sex one had intercourse with, so much as the physical position one took in the sex act. Being the forced passive receiver was a dehumanizing act intended to debase the prisoner and to demonstrate who had the real power. The mob had only one intent: to demean and perhaps kill these strangers through gang rape.

What was behind the mob's actions? Clearly it had to do with the immigrant, Lot, who received the strangers in their city. They took his action as a judgment on them. It wouldn't be the last time an offender does violence to an innocent caregiver.

What Was the Sin of Sodom?

So, what was the sin of Sodom? Many traditional interpreters conclude that the sin of Sodom was homosexual behavior (Gagnon 2001, 75). But this conclusion does not fit the story. The story is about a gross violation of the rules of hospitality through the violent act of gang rape. This does get closer to the intent of the story, for it portrays a depraved people who demonstrate wanton disregard for a well-established social norm at the time. This also fits with the statement of the messengers as to their reason for coming to judge Sodom: "Then the LORD said, 'The cries of injustice from Sodom and Gomorrah are countless, and their sin is very serious!'" (Gen 18:20).

As demonstrated by their intent and threats, the men of the city were flagrant perpetrators of moral injustice toward others. This would fit with the various ways their sin is referred to by the prophets. Walter Brueggemann observes:

> The Bible gives considerable evidence that the sin of Sodom was not specifically sexual, but a general disorder of society organized against God....It is likely that interpreters will disagree about the "sin of Sodom" but the evidence in any case shows that the Bible itself did not agree that the sin was homosexuality. The use of the term "outcry" in 18:20-21; 19:13 argues in the direction of a general abuse of justice. (1982, 164)

That it is about justice is demonstrated in several prophetic allusions. The first comes from Isaiah. In the opening verses the prophet condemns Israel for her sin against YHWH. She has forsaken her God and has suffered miserably for doing so: "Doom! Sinful nation, people weighed down with crimes, evildoing offspring, corrupt children! They have abandoned the LORD, despised the holy one of Israel; they turned their backs on God. Why do you invite further beatings? Why continue to rebel? Everyone's head throbs, and everyone's heart fails" (Isa 1:4-5).

It is only the grace of YHWH that has stopped the bleeding; else Israel would be like Sodom and Gomorrah. The prophet pleads with Israel, unlike Sodom, to listen. Sodom was the exemplar of moral depravity for Israel, and so to be compared to Sodom meant she had really hit a low point: "If the

LORD of heavenly forces had not spared a few of us, we would be like Sodom; we would resemble Gomorrah. Hear the LORD's word, you leaders of Sodom. Listen to our God's teaching, people of Gomorrah!" (Isa 1:9-10).

Within the larger context of this initial prophecy, the central issue is Israel's idolatry and consequent injustice. This is reinforced in another allusion by Isaiah to Sodom: "Yes, Jerusalem has stumbled and Judah has fallen, because the way they talk and act in word and deed insults the LORD, defying his brilliant glory. Their bias in judgment gives them away; like Sodom, they display their sins in public. Doom to them, for they have done themselves in!" (Isa 3:8-9).

Continuing in the same prophecy, the injustice of Israel is revealed along with YHWH's intent to set things right. It is Israel's leaders who are the one's leading Israel astray and profiting from the weak and the poor—who are YHWH's people:

> As for my people—oppressors strip them and swindlers rule them. My people—your leaders mislead you and confuse your paths. The LORD arises to accuse; he stands to judge the peoples. The LORD will enter into judgment with the elders and princes of his people: You yourselves have devoured the vineyard; the goods stolen from the poor are in your houses. How dare you crush my people and grind the faces of the poor? says the LORD God of heavenly forces. (Isa 3:12-15)

It is this way in which they are like Sodom, for Sodom's leaders failed to show hospitality at the gate but instead led the mob in their rapacious plans against Lot's visitors.

Jeremiah 23:13-14 follows a similar theme. The prophets of Jerusalem are more wicked even than the prophets of Samaria who led Israel away to follow Baal: "In the prophets of Samaria I saw something shocking: They prophesied by Baal and led astray my people Israel. In the prophets of Jerusalem I saw something horrible: They commit adultery and tell lies. They encourage evildoers so that no one turns from their wickedness. In my eyes, they are no better than Sodom; its people are like Gomorrah."

The prophets of Jerusalem had exceeded the prophets of Samaria in their evil. They are unfaithful to YHWH (they committed adultery). Instead of standing in the way of those who would do evil to others, they support their injustice and corruption.

Ezekiel 16:49-50 defines the sin of Sodom more explicitly. Sodom was filled with pride over her prosperity, though it was gained at the expense of the poor and needy. She lazed about in her plenty and showed no care for the needy in her midst: "This is the sin of your sister Sodom: She and her daughters were proud, had plenty to eat, and enjoyed peace and prosperity; but she didn't help the poor and the needy. They became haughty and did detestable things in front of me, and I turned away from them as soon as I saw it."

Here the connection between idolatry and injustice is drawn. "Detestable things" throughout Ezekiel would be worship of idols. Here we have the core issue. *The sin of Sodom is idolatry.* In this case, idolatry is to treat God's image, bound up in a human life, as worthless. The unjust and uncaring behavior toward the stranger or the poor or the needy among God's people is a form of idolatry:

> Commentators will no doubt continue to debate the sin of Sodom but the "'outcry' in 18:20-21 and 19:13 argues in the direction of a general abuse of justice. It may be that sexual disorder is one aspect of a general disorder. But that issue is presented in a way scarcely pertinent to contemporary discussions of homosexuality. (Brueggemann 1982, 164)

Robert Gagnon acknowledges that idolatry is the issue for Ezekiel, who compares Judah to Sodom for her failure to do justice by the poor: "Thus, on the level of allegory, Jerusalem's 'abominations' are sexual sins; on the level of reality, Jerusalem's 'abominations' are idolatrous practices" (2001, 80). Gagnon continues:

> Ezekiel thought that the inhabitants of the city became "prideful" and "haughty" as a result of the city's prosperity, and in their prosperity they both neglected the poor and committed a particularly abominable act of sexual immorality. The two evils are linked by a flagrant disregard of God's own priorities, putting the human self at the center of the cosmos. In Ezekiel's view, the overarching rubric for the sin of Sodom is not inhospitality or homosexual behavior but human arrogance in relation to God. The focus is theocentric. (2001, 85)

The core of human arrogance in relation to God is the essence of what idolatry is.[10] And sadly with it comes human tragedy of all sorts.

We conclude then that Genesis 19 has little to contribute to the issue of homosexual behavior in general and specifically between two committed same-sex partners. It does have much to say about cultures in which the rich and powerful use their riches and power for their own ends and at the expense of the poor and needy or the strangers among them.

What Is a Sodomite?

There is one last question that needs to be addressed before we leave this passage. What is a Sodomite? In simple terms, in the Bible, a Sodomite is a person who dwells in Sodom just as a Moabite is a person who lives in Moab. The association of Sodomite with homosexual behavior is not in the Bible. It is an association made based upon the assumption that the sin of Sodom was homosexuality and that homosexuality is unnatural.

Leviticus 18:22-24 and 20:13: The Abomination

Least Read Biblical Book

The book of Leviticus must be one of the least read books of the Bible, at least among Christians. It seems like a book of rules. It is painfully detailed in its stipulations, and Christians wonder which parts of this book are supposed to provide them with a reliable guide for faith and practice. Unfortunately, Leviticus becomes a "pick-and-choose" book. People of faith use it to pick and choose verses that support their view on some topic or that oppose someone else's. Perhaps we ought to begin by asking what the book of Leviticus is about. What role does it play in the life of Israel? It is part of the Torah, the core religious and sacred text of historic Judaism. Christians, having been grafted into the people of God, have adopted the Torah as inspired scripture as well.

The primary focus of Leviticus is on priestly practices and Israelite faithfulness to the covenant through proper ritual and life in the land. In our culture, and even among Christians, we have separated religious life from secular life. But in ancient cultures, such a bifurcation of life was never imagined. Everything they did had worship or sacred significance. This was especially the case with Israel. Her identity was grounded, as we have seen, in her calling and election as God's chosen people who are given an eschatological purpose. That calling meant separation, a coming forth from the surrounding cultures and their religious practices. But this separation was not just to make Israel different. The religious and worship practices of many of Israel's neighbors, and at times among the Israelite's own rulers, were oppressive, tyrannical, corrupt, exploitive, and ultimately unjust. We would call many of the practices immoral and discriminatory. Yet they were practices that formed part of the entire sacred and ritual life of the people groups who surrounded Israel.

131

Israel's call to separation then was a call to turn away from those practices, and Leviticus, along with other parts of the Torah, sets out how that was to look for Israel in practice. As we approach our reading of Leviticus, we must keep this religious context in mind. The prohibitions were proscriptions against the worship and sacred practices that YHWH found offensive in the surrounding cultures. Such practices were offensive because they were not the way humans were to live together and worship in God's world. They were offensive because they were harmful to people, and that harm was opposed to what is right and good in God's creation, to what would promote human life and not death. Much of the drama of the Hebrew Bible revolves around Israel's struggle to remain true to her calling to be separate while being the light to the world. Israel struggled to come out from the oppressive and exploitive practices of her neighbors and live faithfully before YHWH. The covenant made with Israel stipulated that if Israel remained faithful to YHWH, YHWH's presence would remain with her. If she strayed or chased after other gods, YHWH's presence would be withdrawn. With these thoughts in mind, we have a contextual backdrop to Leviticus and the role it is to play.

Which Rules to Keep?

One does not have to read far in all of the Levitical codes of conduct to conclude that we don't practice most of them. We do not insist that someone who commits adultery be stoned, and I doubt that any Christians are going to propose that we return to such a practice. It is still practiced in some Islamic countries, but most of us are horrified by the custom. So the question is, which rules do we keep? Some? All? None? If some, who decides which ones are still applicable and which are not? And if it is some, which part? We may still believe that adultery is wrong, but we are not likely to execute any punishment other than social disapproval. Even those who adamantly reject homosexuality of any kind or expression are not likely to advocate putting a homosexual person to death, though there is one case in which a young man took it upon himself to execute Levitical judgment. In 2011, Murray Seidman, a seventy-year-old senior in Philadelphia, was stoned to death by twenty-eight-year-old John Thomas after allegedly making sexual advances toward the younger man. Thomas's defense was that he did it because the Bible says to kill homosexuals (Badash 2011).

Some attempts to resolve the problem of reading Leviticus are a bit tortured. Most of us simply ignore the Holiness Code in Leviticus—except when we don't, which is the case with the two passages some believe speak to homosexuality.

132

On a more humorous level, here are some excerpts from a letter sent to Dr. Laura Schlessinger after she declared on her radio show that homosexuality is an abomination:

> Dear Dr. Laura,
>
> Thank you for doing so much to educate people regarding God's Law. I have learned a great deal from your show and I try to share that knowledge with as many people as I can. When someone tries to defend the homosexual lifestyle, for example, I simply remind him or her that Leviticus 18:22 clearly states it to be an abomination. End of debate. I do need some advice from you however, regarding some of the specific laws and how to follow them.
>
> (a) When I burn a bull on the altar as a sacrifice, I know it creates a pleasing odor for the Lord (Lev 1:9). The problem is my neighbors. They claim the odor is not pleasing to them. Should I smite them?
>
> (b) I would like to sell my daughter into slavery, as sanctioned in Exodus 21:7. In this day and age, what do you think would be a fair price for her?
>
> (c) I know that I am allowed no contact with a woman while she is in her period of menstrual uncleanliness (Lev 15:19-24). The problem is, how do I tell? I have tried asking, but most women take offence.
>
> (d) Lev. 25:44 states that I may indeed possess slaves, both male and female, provided they are purchased from neighboring nations. A friend of mine claims that this applies to Mexicans, but not Canadians. Can you clarify? Why can't I own Canadians?
>
> (e) I have a neighbor who insists on working on Sunday (the Sabbath). In the book of Exodus verse 35:2 it clearly states he should be put to death. Am I morally obligated to kill him myself? . . .
>
> I know you have studied these things extensively, so I am confident you can help.
>
> Thank you again for reminding us that God's word is eternal and unchanging, and we should do what the bible says.
>
> Your devoted disciple and adoring fan. (Mikkelson 2012)

In a silly and entertaining way, this satirical letter does make an important point. Whatever we think of Leviticus, finding its application to our modern, Christian lives is not as easy as simply quoting a verse. This is a point upon which almost all of us agree.

How Do We Approach Leviticus?

I don't think it is simply a question of interpretation about which rules Christians are obligated to follow. Rather, I believe we must come at Leviticus as a whole and understand its role in the life of Israel in the period after the return from exile in Babylon—though the text is written as if it came down from Moses.

Leviticus lays out a Holiness Code for Israel to live by. It reflects the ancient Near Eastern cultures of which Israel was a part, and yet there is a clear distinction. Israel was to live as a light to the nations, demonstrating what justice looks like in a people. However, the code also reflects many of the cultural practices of the day, and a central part of that was the role of males in maintaining the community. Gender roles were important, but many of the practices of Israel's neighbors bent those roles to the detriment of the people, resulting in horrible injustices and harm. These practices may start with their worship, but they flowed out and contaminated their daily life. The Levitical authors insist, like most of the rest of the biblical authors, that uncleanness grew out of idolatry—the turning from God, which resulted in doing "detestable things" (Lev 18:26).

The code is not absolute and should not be construed as such, though we would certainly find within it proscriptions that we would still consider morally correct. But they must be read contextually, and the motivations behind behaviors, as well as their ends, must be what we consider as we read these texts. Most of us certainly do not subscribe to a male-dominant worldview. But we can understand the moral impropriety of male same-sex behavior that demeans one partner, adultery that destroys a marriage, bestiality that abuses God's creatures, incest that ruins families, and child sacrifice that is murder of the innocent. In each of these, the motivating factor is self-gratification at the expense of another, and in the process the family system is grievously harmed. In the language of idolatry, it is seeking to gain the focus of one's desires from something other than God. This is the central problem and will continue to be so as we proceed, as it was when we looked at the Sodom story.

The Holiness Code

Most scholars have concluded that Leviticus is a compilation of texts and traditions that didn't take its current form until after the Babylonian exile (i.e., after 536 BCE), though it includes traditions that are much older. Following the exile, Israel had "learned its lesson" about idolatry and was keen to frame the terms of its relationship with YHWH in specific stipulations that would avoid another tragedy. The book of Leviticus is comprised of two primary sections, perhaps compiled by two different schools. The first section is referred to as the Priestly Code, which deals with instructions for offerings, priests, their ordination, and the problem of uncleanness. Uncleanness was of great concern because it meant separation from YHWH. The second section is referred to as the Holiness Code. It is the portion in which the two verses we must consider are found (18:22 and 20:13). This section addresses similar themes to the first but broadens the scope to address matters beyond the work of priests. Martti Nissinen describes the Holiness Code as like a "catechism that teaches Israelites, especially adult males, God's will and, accordingly, the rules for just behavior" ([1998] 2004, 37). It includes theological and moral rules that form the basis of Israel sustaining her covenant relationship with YHWH in the land. In simple terms, "Behave this way and things are good with God. Behave in the ways specified in the code as wrong and things will be bad." Holiness is about remaining ritually clean so that God can be present with Israel. A failure to remain pure will have the necessary result of Israel again losing her place in the land. Ritual purity is about proper worship and a right relationship with God as the people of God.

Concomitant with this necessity of ritual purity is separation from the other peoples of the land. Behind the code was the motivation never again to be influenced by the surrounding peoples and their gods. *In other words, much of the Holiness Code was about avoiding idolatry.* This insistence on social, religious, and political separation from all other peoples was to grow into a monumental problem for Israel by Jesus's time. Jesus took the Pharisees to task many times because they were obsessed with determining who was in and who was out. The Holiness Code was a large part of how that delineation was defined for them. I think Jesus was trying to say to the Pharisees that Israel's vocation was to be called out (made holy) to be a light to the nations, the people through whom the peoples of the world would find God. Instead the Pharisees seem to be using the traditions to create a closed community that excludes instead of includes. In their zeal to live faithfully, the Pharisees are not fulfilling their calling. Isaiah makes this call clear: "I am the LORD, I have called you in righteousness,[11] I have taken you by the hand and kept you; I have given you as a covenant to the people, *a light to the nations*" (Isa 42:6 NRSV, emphasis added).

Abomination

Now let us turn to our Leviticus texts:

You shall not lie with a male as with a woman; it is an abomination. You shall not have sexual relations with any animal and defile yourself with it, nor shall any woman give herself to an animal to have sexual relations with it: it is perversion. Do not defile yourselves in any of these ways, for by all these practices the nations I am casting out before you have defiled themselves. (18:22-24 NRSV)

If a man lies with a male as with a woman, both of them have committed an abomination; they shall be put to death; their blood is upon them. (20:13)

An initial reading of these two texts would certainly suggest that same-sex relations between men in any way are a perversion—as are relations with animals! Whatever the practice means, it is called an abomination. Let's start with what *abomination* means.

What our English translations often translate as "abomination" is actually several Hebrew words. Our concern however is one Hebrew word—*to'eba*. This word is used consistently with regard to idolatry and various forms of practices that are found to be particularly loathsome to YHWH: "It is often used in connection with different, usually not fully defined customs of a mostly cultic nature affiliated with worship of foreign gods" (Nissinen [1998] 2004, 39).

If abomination is mostly associated with idolatry, then is it possible that the two prohibitions of our focus refer initially to an idolatrous practice including bestiality? If they do, the result is ritual uncleanness and the punishment for that is separation from the covenant community and in the case of the second version via the death penalty, the ultimate separation. This becomes our question then: Is the prohibition against male-on-male sexual behavior a ban against some form of pagan practice? I believe so.

Protecting the Clan

These prohibitions were intended to shape the life of Israel—to protect its ethnic identity. These codes were mostly directed at men. Nissinen argues that these codes were about gender and the control of social life. Gender roles were enormously important in the ancient world—including in the Greco-Roman world as we will see in the next chapter. Men were expected to maintain their honor, and how they behaved sexually was part of that. It had nothing to do with what today we would call "sexual orientation." It had to do with the role a male was expected to play in that culture. A feminized man is a disgrace to his manly honor ([1998] 2004, 43). Sociologists speak of cultural "taboos"—behaviors that are proscribed because they would in some way harm the community. The Holiness Code plays this role.

As we have seen, these codes were mostly directed at men and how they were to behave sexually—no male-on-male sex that demeaned one partner, no adultery, no incest, no bestiality, no child sacrifice. For a man to practice any of these things would destroy his honor and standing in the community because they were not consistent with the role a man was to play in the community. Specifically then, the prohibitions of same-sex behavior must be understood within this cultural framework. A man was always to be the dominant one. To play the role of the passive one, as a woman, was to damage his honor, and this would then threaten the life of the community. Threatening the community's future was what the code was intended to protect so that Israel could fulfill her vocation to be a light to the Gentiles, as Isaiah would say.

These were the things Israel's neighbors did, and they were an abomination to YHWH. Israel was not to do them if she was to remain faithful to the covenant and not be sent off again into exile. Chapter 18 of Leviticus ends with this summary.

> Do not make yourselves unclean in any of these ways because that is how the nations that I am throwing out before you became unclean. That is also how the land became unclean, and I held it liable for punishment, and the land vomited out its inhabitants. But all of you must keep my rules and my regulations. You must not do any of these detestable things, neither citizen nor immigrant who lives with you (because the people who had the land before you did all of these detestable things and the land became unclean), so that the land does not vomit you out because you have made it unclean, just as it vomited out the nations that were before you. (18:24-28)

It's about Idolatry

Cultic life and daily life flowed in and out of each other. The practices of Israel's neighbors were not to be the practices of Israel. Why? Because the practices of Israel's neighbors were rooted in idolatry. We can see that is the concern of the Holiness Code. Consider the introductory statements of each Leviticus text. The issue of idolatry is clearly in view. First is the introduction to Leviticus 18.

> Speak to the Israelites and say to them: I am the LORD your God. You must not do things like they are done in the land of Egypt, where you used to live. And you must not do things like they are done in the land of Canaan, where

He is no longer going to do that.

I am bringing you. You must not follow the practices of those places. No, my regulations and my rules are the ones you must keep by following them: I am the LORD your God. You must keep my rules and my regulations; by doing them one will live; I am the LORD. (18:2-5)

How is this about idolatry? One could argue it is always about idolatry, then and now. This was the challenge for Israel because she was forever being seduced by the cultic and social/moral practices of her neighbors. In this case it is the Egyptians and the Canaanites. Again we must remember there is no line between religious practice and regular life for any ancient people. So when YHWH says, "You shall observe my statutes," God is making a religious statement—at least that is how we would describe the intent. This becomes clearer if we look at the second passage that introduces the section in which the Leviticus 20:13 text is found:

The LORD said to Moses, Say to the whole community of the Israelites: You must be holy, because I, the LORD your God, am holy. Each of you must respect your mother and father, and you must keep my sabbaths; I am the LORD your God. Do not turn to idols or make gods of cast metal for yourselves; I am the LORD your God. (Lev 19:1-4)

Here the issue of idolatrous practice is clearly stated: "Do not turn to idols." Why? Because Israel was to be holy, set apart for YHWH. Certain practices simply were not acceptable, and here those practices are the idolatrous practices of Israel's neighbors. Again, cultic and daily practices flowed in and out of each other. Practices that turned Israel from YHWH were to be avoided.

Vinestock of Pagan Nations: Sodom and Gomorrah

What we have yet to address is why these practices were considered idolatry and therefore abhorrent to YHWH. This text from Deuteronomy focuses on Israel's failure to live according to the Torah and specifically Leviticus:

Jacob ate until he was stuffed;

Jeshurun got fat, then rebellious.

It was you who got fat, thick, stubborn!

Jeshurun gave up

on the God who made him,

thought the rock of his salvation was worthless.

They made God jealous with strange gods,
    aggravated him with detestable things.
They sacrificed to demons, not to God,
    to deities of which they had no knowledge—
        new gods only recently on the scene,
        ones about which your ancestors had never heard.
You deserted the rock that sired you;
    you forgot the God who gave birth to you!
The LORD saw this and rejected
    out of aggravation his sons and his daughters.
He said: I will hide my face from them—
    I will see what becomes of them—
        because they are a confused generation;
        they are children lacking loyalty.
They provoked me with "no-gods,"
    aggravated me with their pieces of junk.
So I am going to provoke them
    with "No-People,"
    aggravate them with a nation of fools. (32:15-21)

Jacob and *Jeshurun* are both alternative ways of referring to Israel. Jeshurun is interesting in that it is derived from the root *upright*, *just*, or *straight*. There is obviously a bit of irony here, for Israel is anything but that in the mind of the narrator. Rather, Israel is portrayed as bloated and gorged and as having abandoned her creator God. Worse, Israel has scoffed at God. How? By pursuing other gods. Israel's neighbors made God jealous with their worship of "strange gods" and "with abhorrent things," and Israel found the practices of her neighbors more attractive than her own. YHWH in turn is jealous for those gods he calls "no gods." YHWH will let Israel see what these "no gods" can do for them. Their faithlessness to the covenant will see them as "no people." The result of these behaviors is separation from their covenant God.

In short, idolatry explains the exile.

But the description continues and at 32:32 associates the nation of Israel with Sodom and Gomorrah. This passage has special importance because it comes from Moses's "Farewell Address."

Their roots run straight from Sodom—
from the fields of Gomorrah!
Their grapes are pure poison;
their grape clusters, nothing but bitter;
    their wine is snake poison,
venom from a cruel cobra.
Don't I have this stored up,
sealed in my vaults?
Revenge is my domain,
so is punishment-in-kind,
at the exact moment their step slips up,
because the day of their destruction is just around the corner;
their final destiny is speeding on its way!
But the LORD will acquit his people,
will have compassion
    on those who serve him,
    once he sees that their strength is all gone,
    that both prisoners and free people are wiped out.
 The Lord will ask, "Where are their gods—
the rocks they trusted in—
    who ate up the fat of their sacrifices,
    who drank their sacred wine?
They should stand up and help you!
They should protect you now! (Deut 32:32-38)

Their vine (i.e., the other nations Jacob finds attractive) is of the same stock as that of Sodom and Gomorrah, and this of course points all the way back to the line of Cain. This means that at the core of these religious and social practices were corruption, abuse, and exploitation of some by others. Grave injustice was practiced in the name of the gods worshipped. The narrator zeros in on how Israel's neighbors as well as Sodom and Gomorrah lived out their idolatry in verse 37. It began in their worship practice: their idolatrous practices. They ate the fat of their sacrifices and drank the wine dedicated to another god.

This was an abomination to God. It was an outrage. God had been their rock of salvation, but they abandoned YHWH for other gods. The entry in the *Dictionary of New Testament Theology* on "idols" provided the following description.

> Idols are "bdelygmata," abominations, behind which stand "daimonia," demonic powers with which one cannot come into contact without moving God to wrath....In 2 Chr 24:18 the worship of idols is equated with that of the Asherim, i.e. of the powers behind the idols.
>
> Israel often succumbed to the temptation to open the doors to these powers, especially when the rise of the Assyrian and Babylonian empires gave the impression that their gods were more powerful than the God of Israel (Isa 36:19f). Jer 44:15-19 and Ezek. 8 give graphic and terrible pictures of how widely heathen idol worship has spread in Israel in their day. The prophetic message to Israel was that the misfortune which had overtaken the people was God's punishment for falling away from Yahweh and compromising with the heathen cultus. (Isa 10:11; Jer 9:13-16; Ezek 8:17f.) (Brown 1986, 284–85)

What Was the Abomination?

If the two texts in Leviticus that reference same-sex behavior between men are about the kind of horrid, idolatrous moral practices that exploited one person for the gratification of another, then it is unlikely that they are about the kind of committed same-sex relationships that are the center of our modern discussion. Rather, they are about sexual practices that were inimical to the kind of lives they were to live together in community. In our time we would call this nonconsensual sex or sexual assault or, more to the point, rape.

One final point may provide even more clarity. It was a practice among many ancient cultures to use gang rape as a way to humiliate male prisoners; it therefore seems reasonable that this was occurring here as well: "Gang rape of a man has always been an extreme means to disgrace one's enemies and put them in their place" (Nissinen [1998] 2004, 8). Male-to-male sex was a one-way affair. The dominate partner would force himself on the other, taking what the gay community today would call the "top" position. This position required the recipient—the passive or "bottom" partner—to be penetrated. If we remember that for ancient cultures, gender roles mattered supremely, then the act of prisoner rape robbed the victim of his masculinity; from the standpoint of the community, the victim was permanently feminized (Nissinen [1998] 2004).

This was wrong from YHWH's perspective. This was not how humans were to treat others. It was not welcoming the stranger; it was exploiting and abusing the stranger who also was made in God's image. The stranger would have been the alien slave, the poor, and the powerless. This is what an abomination to God is; and that is as true today as it was in Israel's time.

A Summary of the Old Testament Texts

What can we glean vis-à-vis these Old Testament texts? It is questionable whether the Sodom story really contributes much to the conversation about homosexuality. If the central focus is on a massive failure of hospitality and the desire of the people of Sodom to show the visitors, including Lot, who was "boss," then at best it is a powerful story about what humanity looks like when it ceases to worship God. All manner of brutish, dehumanizing, immoral, and unjust behavior follows.

Relative to Leviticus, we find a code that was to shape the people of Israel, so that they did not follow again the idolatrous and often evil ways of their neighbors. Rather, it provided a framework within which their unique identity was protected and extended by outlining what was faithfulness and what was idolatry. The effect on post-exilic Jews was a defined sexual ethic that banned all sorts of things including cross-dressing (Deut 22:5), castration (Lev 21:20, 22:24; Deut 23:1),[12] and male-on-male (dominant-passive) sexual intercourse. Gender roles were important, and these were seen—rooted in ancient taboos—as a threat to masculinity and therefore to the future of the ethnic clan. Further, Israel, like many other ancient Near Eastern people, understood sexual life as a male-dominant and female-passive relationship. Anything that threatened this was a threat to society. Finally where these behaviors occurred, they were usually attended with exploitation, dehumanization, and injustice.

What does this have to do with the modern conversation about homosexuality? It says nothing about sexual orientation. It also does not say anything about an absolutized sexuality. If it did, we would still insist on maintaining male dominance for the sake of the community. It does say a great deal about how one is to live out his or her sexuality regardless of context. Dominance that exploits and behaviors that are cruel, brutal, inhumane, and rapacious are still an abomination because they are contrary to the way God intends humans to relate to each other. As such they are a few of the many faces of idolatry.

Notes

1. I am not making an epistemological statement here. I am only making a descriptive commentary on what in fact occurs.

2. Some who have written on this issue include the creation stories of Genesis 1–3, the Curse of Ham story in the Noah narratives of Genesis 9, and the rape of the Levite's concubine in Judges 19. I have dealt somewhat with the creation stories earlier. I do not believe the Curse of Ham story adds anything to this discussion, because we are not told in the story what the sin of Ham was toward Noah. Some (such as Gagnon) have written on this and built part of their argument against same-sex behaviors based upon the presumption that what Ham did that was shameful was to have homosexual sex with Noah (Gagnon 2001). I believe if we are going to use these ancient texts, especially those that most consider to be "prehistory," it should be clear what is included in the story and not make an argument from silence and speculation—which is odd vis-à-vis Gagnon because later he will object to the interpretations of those on the other side, such as Bernadette Brooten, for doing just this (2001). The rape of the Levite's concubine follows closely the Sodom story and therefore adds nothing new. A crazed rapacious crowd seeks to assault the strangers. There are also some who try to write into the David and Jonathan story, a story of same-sex love. This again, in my mind, is only labored speculation so I will leave it alone. There has been quite enough speculation on these ancient texts.

3. This is not the case in the academic world. There are many books that attempt to provide context, but these books are generally not accessible to the average reader. They can be overwhelming, and if the reader has not been exposed to the academic disciplines of theology and biblical exegesis, they can leave the one (a) confused about any of it and (b) intimidated, assuming a position is true because so much has been thrown at them—a theological "shock and awe" approach.

4. For an example, see Robert Gagnon's *The Bible and Homosexual Practice: Texts and Hermeneutics* (2001).

5. Pronouns for Israel are difficult because both a male and a female pronoun would be proper depending upon the context. When YHWH demanded that Pharaoh let Israel go, YHWH referred to Israel as God's son: "Then say to Pharaoh, 'This is what the Lord says: Israel is my oldest son'" (Exod 4:22). However, Israel is often metaphorically referred to as YHWH's "spouse" who through idolatry has played the adulteress. So to simplify this, I simply use the feminine pronoun, especially since much of this conversation is about metaphorical adultery, that is, idolatry.

6. The CEB translates the Hebrew word as "moral," while the NRSV translates it as "righteousness." Both get at the idea of doing what is right.

7. I do not mean to suggest any kind of works before grace. As a Presbyterian, I am solidly Reformed. Rather, I am trying to emphasize a fundamental biblical theme that associates faith with proper response to God in contrast to idolatry, which is in fact replacing God with a god of our own making.

8. It is not my intent to provide an exposition of this text, which can be quite controversial itself depending upon how it is read. Rather, my intent is simply to point out how important welcoming the stranger was to Jesus's message about the coming kingdom of God.

9. Contrast Gagnon, who insists that the real offense here is homosexual sex. The reading of the text simply does not make sense if the central issue is the type of sex, for in reality, the mob was most likely going to rape and kill everyone (Gagnon 2001).

10. Of course, Gagnon will go on to tie it all back to homosexuality by insisting that the sexual immorality was real instead of letting the metaphor carry through. But for a moment, there was an agreement of what the core issue was.

11. See the section on Romans in the next chapter for my discussion on the biblical concept of the "righteousness of God."

12. Some sought castration intentionally in order to be more feminized.

Chapter 7

The New Testament and
Same-Sex Behavior

Remember from a Christian perspective, the story set forth in the Hebrew Bible (Christians call it the Old Testament) is extended and brought to
its climax in the story told in the New Testament. The New Testament tells
how Jesus of Nazareth was the one that the "law and the prophets" looked
forward to. This means that there is continuity between them, and therefore
we ought to expect that the themes that are laid out in the OT will find their
expression in the NT, indeed will find their fullest expression. Loving the
stranger, justice, peace, and a world set right—these expectations are what we
find in the NT story. But the NT also warns against idolatry and all the havoc
it creates for humanity. The center of the story, however, is how the problems
defined in the OT—largely idolatry and the behaviors and consequences that
grow out of it—find their singular solution in Jesus the Messiah who comes
at last as the king who defeats sin and death (Wright 1997; 2012).

First, to understand the texts in the New Testament often associated
with same-sex behaviors, we must understand the sexual practices in Greco-
Roman society while also maintaining some level of modesty in the writing.
Second, since much of the debate has to do with certain words found in the
New Testament, we do some lexical work on them before looking at them
in their various contexts. With this work completed, we will then do an extended exegesis of the texts in which these words are found. A brief analysis
will be given for Mark 10, in which Jesus references marriage. Finally, my
summary at the end of this chapter will outline what I believe the Bible does
and does not teach about homosexuality.

145

As noted in the introduction to the OT chapter, a fair amount of detail is provided on the NT texts. As before, the reader may choose to scan the material or simply proceed to the conclusions at the end of this chapter.

Greek and Roman Sexual Practices

Before we look at the specific texts in the New Testament that are assumed to address homosexuality, it is important to provide a brief description of Roman and Greek sexual practices. I believe this excursus will help create context as we read these texts. There is a great deal of similarity (at least for my purposes) between the sexual practices of ancient Greek culture—often referred to as the Classical period—and of the subsequent Greco-Roman culture. Women were viewed similarly, and the sexual practices of men were analogous but with some specific differences. As explained below, sexual practices in these cultures did not divide along the axis that we divide matters in our modern world. Whereas we are inclined to separate people into homosexual, bisexual, or heterosexual, they separated people into "dominate/penetrative" or "passive/receptive," as is evident among the Semitic peoples of the ancient Near East. This distinction in ancient social-sexual practices affects how we read the New Testament texts, which ostensibly address these practices. We must keep in mind as we proceed that the words *homosexuality* and *heterosexuality* were not coined until the nineteenth century. These are our categories but were unknown to the biblical authors. It is our modern world that thinks in a continuum between gay and straight.

Women in Greek and Roman Society

Women were the property of Greco-Roman men (as they were in ancient Israel). Young women belonged to their fathers until they were married off in arranged marriages between the ages of twelve and eighteen—mostly on the younger side. They then came under the authority of their husbands. Some women who were not married were prostitutes or "hetaera," which in our culture would be higher-class female escorts. Married women in Greek and Roman society were expected to live virtuous lives. They were to have sex only with their husbands. Greek women often had to compete for sex with prostitutes, hetaera, and slaves who were available to their husbands in their homes. The primary role of the wife was to propagate legitimate children for her husband. In Greek and Roman culture, the woman managed the household (called the *oikos* in Greek and the *domus* in Latin). Managing the household included overseeing its daily operations, slaves, and child rearing. In the

Greek *oikos*, women were commonly kept separate from the men. They had their own quarters and consequently were seldom seen by nonfamily members. Many did not venture out from the residence. If a Greek woman did go outside the *oikos*, she had to have a male companion. In the Roman home, a woman could have more independence, but she was still mostly relegated to the household. Although she could not participate in public life, she could and did nonetheless play "political games" to advance her family's status in the class-stratified Roman social world.[1]

Female Sexuality in Greek and Roman Culture

Female sexuality was tied to social order in both the Greek and Roman cultures. Women were considered morally weak and thus kept in the controlled environment, where it was possible to monitor their sexuality. Virginity was important, and female sexuality was to be expressed only in marriage. Free women who were sexually active outside marriage lost their protection under the law as well as their social status and respect. There are not many references to sex between women in the Roman Republic, but that changed with the empire. A few documents describe lesbian sexuality usually in the form of poems and love spells.[2] In part due to the "conservative" nature of Roman culture and the influence of Stoicism, women were expected to keep their sexual desires and expressions moderated.

Greek law strictly forbid adultery by a woman and granted the husband or the family the right to seek revenge against the man while the woman was "put away." Roman law allowed the husband to put an adulterous wife to death, while it was expected that men would have sexual activities with women other than a wife. Later as the Imperial period evolved, the lax sexual standards meant that both men and women were having affairs (Bromiley 1985, 606).

Men and Sexual Standards

The sexual standards for men were different. (It would appear some things are slow to change.) In Greek society, homoerotic relationships between an adult man and a boy were known as pederasty. We must admit that this practice is offensive to our present moral sensibilities. Even though our twenty-first-century moral and legal definitions prevail, we must look at pederasty and similar practices to understand the New Testament references considered to be about same-sex behavior.

147

Pederasty already had a long history by the first century of the Common Era when Paul would have been writing. It predates Plato (428–347 BCE) and can be traced to sources even earlier. There were diverse views on the practice in the Greek city-states, some affirming and others not. In Athens and Sparta, the practice was accepted and even endorsed as normative, though for different reasons in each city. In Sparta, the practice was more closely associated with their military training and practice. In Athens, it was practiced among the aristocracy as a process of socialization of the good citizen. Pederasty was seen as a way of supporting and passing on the basic values of the community. Nissinen writes, "Pederastic relationships were at times an essential part in raising young men to be full-fledged members of society" ([1998] 2004, 58). The arts, philosophy, music, and physical exercise were all part of the young boy's upbringing for the elite of society. The Greeks justified pederasty because their gods practiced it. The story of Zeus and Ganymede is one example. Zeus in the form of an eagle swoops down and catches young Ganymede and carries him off to Mount Olympus to be his lover.

Our modern and Western perspectives about pederasty are informed by our segmentation of people into either heterosexual or homosexual groups. Thus we consciously, or more likely unconsciously, assume that such practices were choices to *be* homosexual, that is, to have a gay identity. Such an assumption is an anachronism. Sexual orientation is a modern construct in the sense of choosing to be one or the other. In reality, most men (*erastēs*) who had a boy (*pais* or *paidika*) were also married and had families. Further, the *paidika* would grow up, get married, have a family, and often become an *erastēs*. One could only become a *paidika* with the agreement of the boy's father, which occurred in his teens, at about the same age that girls were given in marriage.

Sex and Roles in Ancient Greece

In general, Greek and Roman sexuality did not break along male and female lines as it does in our culture. Sex was erotic, and it was far more about the role one played in the act of sex than the physical gender of the person with whom one had sex. As in the ancient Near East, it was about gender roles.

The role structure between the *erastēs* and the *paidika* is informative of much of the way sexual behavior was understood in the ancient world and, specifically, Greece. A boy, also called an *erōmenos*, (a beloved) was to play the passive (submissive) role. The *erastēs* was to play the active (dominant) role. Again this was not just a sexual arrangement; it was the basic structure of the relationship. Though it may be strange or appalling to us, practically this was a mentor-student relationship with "benefits." This becomes even more significant in Roman culture, in which dominance is the most important role for a male to play, which will be discussed in more detail below (Williams [1999] 2010).

The role played in the sexual act, regardless of the relationship, was significant. Whether having same-sex or other-sex, a male adult "citizen" would lose status if he played the passive role. Women, slaves, or young male youths (who were not yet citizens) had no status, so playing the passive role did not matter—and they probably in most cases had no choice in the matter anyway. The passive role was labeled *muliebria pati*, "to submit to what is done to women" and *aselgainein*, "to defile oneself." The active role in Greek was *hubrizein*, "to exert force upon another" (Bowersock, Brown, and Grabar 1999, 496).

Sex and Roles in Ancient Rome

The active/passive roles in sex were also part of Roman culture, but the Romans carried it further. For the Roman male, dominance was considered a virtue. Strong masculinity was supremely important. This association was supported by the patriarchal social structure and the patron-client system.[3] Conquest was valued, and being the active partner in a sexual encounter was a sign of one's masculinity. Freeborn Roman men could have sex with either men or women, as long as the man played the active, not passive, role in the sex act. A married freeborn Roman was expected to avoid having sex with another freeborn person but was free to have sex with male slaves, prostitutes, or women in the house who served as secondary wives. Unmarried men were free to desire women of any social status or male slaves and prostitutes. Roman men, like their Greek forerunners, had a preference for boys between the ages 12 and 20 (Williams [1999] 2010). But in all of this, it was essential for the Roman freeborn male (citizen) to play the dominant role in any sex act. Williams, in his book *Roman Homosexuality*, described the Roman male's role in colorful terms:

> First and foremost, a self-respecting Roman man must always give the appearance of playing the insertive role in penetrative acts, and not the receptive role: to use popular terminology often unfortunately replicated in the language of scholarship, he must be the "active," not the "passive," partner. This can justly be called the prime directive of masculine sexual behavior for Romans, and it has an obvious relationship to hierarchical social structures. For according to this scheme, penetration is subjugation (in the sense that the act is held simultaneously to be a figure for, and to effect, subjugation), and *masculinity is domination*. ([1999] 2010, 18, emphasis added)

149

To play the receiving role (submissive or passive) was considered weak and effeminate. The dominant role took pleasure. The submissive role gave pleasure. To give pleasure was considered servile and a threat to a man's status as a full Roman citizen.

As Rome transitioned from the republic to the empire, a more licentious culture began to emerge. More freeborn men began to play the passive role in sex, most likely as an expression of the expanding patron-client social structure that had Caesar as the ultimate paterfamilias.[4] But this role shift was also because the growing licentiousness led to ever more expansive ways to act sexually. It was in part for this reason that the first emperor, Augustus, not known for his sexual restraint, nonetheless attempted to return to more conservative Roman values and morals.

Augustus's goal in restoring public monuments and reviving religion was not simply to renew faith and pride in the Roman Empire. Rather, he hoped that these steps would restore moral standards in Rome—that is, the old ways of clear-cut rules for dominance and receptivity. Augustus also enacted social reforms as a way to improve morality. He felt particularly strong about encouraging families to have children and discouraging adultery. As such, he politically and financially rewarded families with three or more children, especially sons. This incentive stemmed from his belief that there were too few legitimate children born from "proper marriages" (Fife 2012).

We should not assume that his goals for moral revival would look like a Christian hope for moral goodness. For Augustus, it was about consolidating power and stabilizing what he saw as an increasingly unstable empire. Men were still free to act however they wanted sexually within the prescribed Roman norms, and women or men with whom Roman men had sex were still expected to play the passive role. Men however were expected to show restraint, which meant not playing the passive role. They were to restore the proper order of proving their masculinity by reclaiming the dominant role in sexual behaviors.

The other side of the Roman ideal of the dominant male is the weak or effeminate male. To be the passive one in sex meant that the person was the less powerful. Calling someone effeminate was a common way to discredit another politician and to gain political advantage. Many years past, in our own culture, the same sort of denigrating name calling was practiced.

Prostitution in Greek and Roman Culture

In ancient Greece, pederasty was not the only practice in which men had sex with young teens. Male prostitution was a thriving business. Pederasty required a large commitment of time and wealth. Those who didn't have the time or the wealth could satisfy their desires with male prostitutes. Even though prostitution of females and males was legal and even enjoyed some protections as well as taxation, it was still looked upon as socially shameful. As a result, prostitutes were either slaves or noncitizens (Dover [1978] 1989).

Ancient Greek men believed that the availability of prostitution was necessary to fulfill their needs for pleasure. There were, as stated above, different options available, from prostitutes on the streets, called peripatetic prostitutes, to the more sophisticated and educated hetaera.

Greek prostitutes were bought, stolen, or captured people who were enslaved and then put into prostitution. Many of them were captured in war and forced into prostitution as slaves. This would include both males and females. A famous ancient example of this is Phaedo of Elis. He was a Greek philosopher made famous because he was with Socrates when he died and because Plato named his dialogue "On the Soul" after him. Diogenes Laertius in his *Lives of Eminent Philosophers* tells the following story of Phaedo, explaining who he was, where he came from, and what he went on to do:

> Phaedo was a native of Elis, of noble family, who on the fall of that city was taken captive and forcibly consigned to a house of ill-fame. But he would close the door and so contrive to join Socrates' circle, and in the end Socrates induced Alcibiades or Crito with their friends to ransom him; from that time onwards he studied philosophy as became a free man. (Laertius 1972)

The Sexual Axis of Greek and Roman Practice

A great deal can be read about sexuality in ancient Greece and Rome, but after a while it becomes fairly redundant—and for my twenty-first-century sensibilities, at times disgusting. The striking impression from the literature is how different Greece and Rome were from the world in which we live. What mattered most in the male-dominated patriarchal system was the "penetrative role." The dominant/passive construct was so pervasive that men assumed female-to-female sexual practices still had to have one play the penetrative role because they could not imagine sexual behavior in any other way. This dominant/passive framework for Greek and Roman sexual practice is the axis upon which ancient sexual practices moved. Current sexual discussions tend to occur in simplistic terms on a heterosexual/homosexual continuum.[5] The following graphic expresses these different continua.

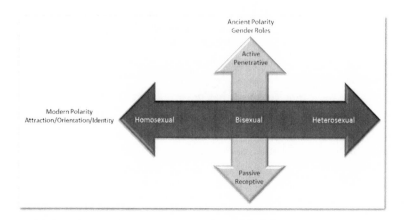

An Alternative Ethic

Lest we think all the Greeks and Romans were a lascivious lot, there were counter philosophical and religious movements that called for a more modest sexuality and the self-control of one's desires. Most of us have heard of the Epicureans and the Stoics. Both had views on sexual behavior that would moderate sexual behavior or forgo its practice entirely. For Epicureans, sexual intercourse was a natural but unnecessary desire. The Stoics believed "sexual love is a desire which does not afflict virtuous men" (Kreitner 2012).

Some scholars see in the Christian community in Corinth the influence of a religious philosophic group called the Therapeutae, a Jewish sect believed to have originated in Egypt. By the first century CE, they had spread throughout most of the known world.[6] They were ascetics who emphasized virginity and celibacy even in marriage. They lived chastely with utter simplicity; they "first of all laid down temperance as a sort of foundation for the soul to rest upon, proceed to build up other virtues on this foundation" (Philo 1993). They also eschewed material possessions: "These men abandon their property without being influenced by any predominant attraction, and flee without even turning their heads back again" (para. 18).

It's possible that some Therapeutae, at least in Corinth, had converted to Christianity and were part of the Corinthian church. A number of their teachings and practices appear in the correspondence that reached Paul. Part of 1 Corinthians addresses these. It is in the midst of such a section that one of the so-called vice lists that we are to review in 1 Corinthians 6 is found. The ascetic orientation toward otherworldly spiritual life and especially the denigration of sexuality (as this-worldly) only increases with the centuries. By the fourth century and Saint Augustine, the ascetic ideas of the Therapeutae (influenced by Platonic dualism that separated the spiritual—good and the physical—evil) had shaped at least the Western church's idea of the devoted life as well as its idea of sexuality. Ideas about sexuality were not positive and, in some Christian contexts, still aren't.

Some New Testament and Other Greek Words

Much of the discussion of the New Testament texts revolves around the meaning and usages of four different Greek words. For the purposes of this overview, I first provide an analysis of each word and its usage within its first-century context. But to do this properly, one must also consider the historical development of a word's usage. Oftentimes when we look up a word in a dictionary, we are looking for a synonym that we do know and use. Then we draw a straight conceptual line from what we know to what we don't know. Words seldom work that way.

This becomes even more of a challenge when the word is in a different language or even an ancient language like Koine Greek, which is the Greek of the New Testament. It is a beginner's error to think an interpreter can come across a Greek word, look it up in a Greek-to-English lexicon in which a translation is given, and assume "we get it." A few moments in a technical lexicon makes this obvious. Rather, the task of the interpreter is to focus on the (in our case, Greek) word in its original language and study its usage in its native context. This is what I attempt to do. But I have only provided my conclusions with necessary supporting information. That said, when we consider these words within the Greco-Roman culture of the first century, a fuller image emerges from the biblical text. Frankly, in some cases, a far more disgusting image emerges than what our English translations would lead us to believe.

Other Greek words that are associated with homoeroticism were also in common usage in the first century CE. Though they are not found in our New Testament, because they were part of the common language of the day and connoted certain types of person, I mention them here. First, one kind of man was called a *kinaidos* (*cenaedus* in Latin). It was a derogatory term referring to a man who was effeminate and only sought erotic contact with men (Nissinen [1998] 2004, 68). The second term was *androgynous*. This term also referred to an effeminate man. It is a compound word meaning "man-woman." A third word, *tribas*, was a description of a woman who preferred sexual eroticism with other women. In the descriptive categories of our modern world, these labels for individuals would likely be closer to a male

153

or female with a homosexual orientation, though any sense of orientation is our category.

Pornos/Porneia

You probably recognize this word because our word *pornography* is derived from its root. *Pornos* comes from the verb *pernemi*, which means "to sell or to be sold" (Liddell, Scott, and Jones 2014). In Classical Greek, the masculine form represented a man who prostitutes himself for hire—a harlot for hire or a catamite.[7] It also can mean "idolator" (Liddell, Scott, and Jones 2014). It came to be used universally, meaning a man who indulges in unlawful intercourse (Bauer and Danker 2001, 855). The feminine form, *porneia*, meant illicit sexual practices including prostitution but also metaphorically as idolatry (see discussion on the Septuagint below) (Liddell, Scott, and Jones 2014). The verb and its related words are often translated into English as *fornicate* or *fornication*, words that most people know have something to do with illicit sex. It is believed that our English word *fornication* originated in Latin—not Greek—with the word *fornix* meaning "done under the archway" or "vault" where prostitutes would congregate to practice their trade (*American Heritage Dictionary of the English Language*). The word *pornos* can also mean "idolater" (Liddell, Scott, and Jones 2014, 1450).

The Septuagint (LXX), the Greek translation of the Hebrew Bible, translates the Hebrew *znh*, which means "to be unfaithful," as the feminine form, *porneia*. To play the harlot is to be unfaithful. As a metaphor, it is used to describe Israel, who is unfaithful to YHWH in chasing after other gods, that is, idolatry. The northern kingdom's (Israel's) idolatry and its association with unfaithful practices are clear in this passage from Hosea. The setting is the period between 780 and 725 BCE and before people in the northern kingdom were driven into exile (ca. 734–32 BCE). The reason for the pending exile is apparent:

My people take advice from a piece of wood,
    and their divining rod gives them predictions.
        A spirit of prostitution [porneia] has led them astray;
        they have left God to follow other gods.
They offer sacrifices on mountaintops,
    and make entirely burned offerings on hills;
    they offer sacrifices under various green trees,
        because their shade is pleasant.

> Therefore, your daughters act like* prostitutes [from *porneia*],
>> and your daughters-in-law commit adultery.
> I will not punish your daughters because they act like prostitutes,
>> nor your daughters-in-law because they commit adultery;
> for the men themselves visit prostitutes [*porneia*],
>> *and offer sacrifices with consecrated workers* at temples;
> so now the people without sense must come to ruin. (Hos 4:12-14,
> emphasis added)
>
> * *Like* is an analogy.

The prophet is not saying the daughters are literally prostituting themselves nor that the daughters-in-law are committing adultery. Nor is he saying the men literally visit prostitutes. Rather, he is saying they are being unfaithful to YHWH. They are committing idolatry against their God by visiting the temples of foreign gods and offering sacrifices with the religious workers of the offending temple.[8]

The southern kingdom (Judah) was not much better. While the word *porneia* is not used, this text states that Judah practiced the same "detestable things" as Israel and other nations. These same idolatrous behaviors ultimately resulted in Judah's exile as well in 586 BCE:

> Judah did evil in the LORD's eyes. The sins they committed made the LORD angrier than anything their ancestors had done. They also built shrines, standing stones, and sacred poles on top of every high hill and under every green tree. Moreover, the *consecrated workers* in the land did detestable things, just like those nations that the LORD had removed among the Israelites. (1 Kgs 14:22-24, emphasis added)

The period after the Babylonian exile (ca. 538 BCE) is often referred to as Second Temple Judaism, which extended until the fall of Jerusalem in 70 CE. Documents from this period follow this same conceptual association but also broaden the idea of *porneia* to include all forms of illicit sexual practice. One specific document called *The Testament of the Twelve Patriarchs* provides multiple warnings against *porneia*. The *Theological Dictionary of the New Testament* explains "the first of seven evil spirits is *porneia*, to which women are more subject than men and which leads to idolatry" (Bromiley 1985, 919).

In the New Testament there is also an association of sexual immorality and idolatry. The Jerusalem Council in considering whether the Gentiles must keep the practices of Torah say no, but ask that they abstain from certain things: "Therefore, I conclude that we shouldn't create problems for Gentiles who turn to God. Instead, we should write a letter, telling them to avoid the pollution associated with idols, sexual immorality, eating meat from strangled animals, and consuming blood" (Acts 15:19-20).

The first and last items—idols and blood sacrifices—are clearly related to Greco-Roman religious/social practices. Given that *porneia* is illicit sexual behavior—and that it is sandwiched between two obvious idolatrous practices—it is likely that it too is a reference to idolatrous religious practices. But is the sexual immorality literal or again figurative of unfaithfulness to God? It is not clear, and perhaps it is both. Religious/social/political life in the Roman world was what we might call today a "mash-up."[9] As I have said previously, although we separate these, they were not separated in the ancient world. To not participate would effectively marginalize one (Bauckham 1993; Wright 2013b). Remember that the central issue between YHWH and Israel and between YHWH and all nations is idolatry. So the Jerusalem Council admonished the new Gentile Christians to avoid such practices. We will see this when we look at Romans 1. I address how the word *porneia* is used in 1 Corinthians 6:9 and 1 Timothy 1:10 below.

Arsenokoitēs

This is the word translated variously as "sodomites," "homosexual offenders," "homosexuals," or "practicing homosexuals."[10] *Arsenokoitēs* is found only in two places in the New Testament and does not appear to have been used before these instances. It is a compound of two Greek words. The first is the word for "man": *arsen*. The second, *koiteis*, is Greek for "bed" (and from which we derive our English word *coitus*). In an awkward sense, it means "man bed" or "man bedder," or, in other words, a man who goes to bed with men.[11] The Bauer and Danker lexicon (BDAG) illuminates the uncertain definition, taking issue with the English translations "homosexuals" or "sodomites" (Bauer and Danker 2001, 135).

The precise meaning of this word is difficult to obtain. It is used too rarely, so the best we can hope for is an approximation of its meaning within a field of possibilities. Some scholars believe the Apostle Paul coined *arsenokoitēs* since it is only found in 1 Corinthians 6 and was picked up by the author of 1 Timothy 1 (if not written by Paul). Paul, who was knowledgeable of the Septuagint (LXX), may have formed the word by putting together two words from Leviticus 18:22: *meta **arsenos** ouv koimēthēsē **koitēn** gunaikos bdelugma gar estin*. The words in bold are *arsen* and *koitē*, which, compounded, become *arsenokoitēs*. If this is true, then Paul would have in mind the proscription against having a male playing the female role, which Leviticus prohibited. If it is not the case that Paul coined the word from Leviticus, the meaning remains the same: "Don't bed a male as you bed a female." Robin Scroggs thinks that Paul likely has in mind a Hebrew phrase known among the Hellenistic Jewish rabbis of his day as a description of male homosexuality. The phrase *mischkav zakur* would be translated as "lying with a male" (Scroggs 1983, 108–10).[12] Nissinen believes it should be translated as "one who lies with males." This is where BDAG's definition lands as well (Bauer and Danker 2001, 135). Now this certainly sounds like male-to-male sex. Our brief review of sexual practices in the Greco-Roman world informs us that there was a great deal of diversity in how penetrative sex was performed.[13] The man was not to play the passive role—regardless of the specific form—because it was an affront to his masculinity. Although it is the case that it is difficult to pin down just what this word precisely meant, we can say it most likely referred to a practice that would have been part of the Roman culture, and it would have been tied to gender role confusion (strong/weak, penetrative/passive, insertive/receptive, i.e., male/female) (Williams [1999] 2010). Additionally, it would be fair to hypothesize that the Roman concern for "too much desire" played a part in its field of meaning. Given that it is found twice in so-called vice lists, that is something seriously to consider. The meaning in the New Testament ultimately has to be defined by its use in a specific context. That will be considered when we look at 1 Corinthians 6 and 1 Timothy 1.

Malakos

Malakos occurs in 1 Corinthians 6:9 and is paired with *arsenokoitēs*. The word group from which *malakos* is derived means "softness" or "weakness." It could range from being physically sickly to moral weakness (in the Greek and Roman sense of moral weakness, which meant lacking in self-control). *Malakos* could also mean "soft" or "effeminate" (Liddell, Scott, and Jones 2014). Moral weakness meant effeminacy and the "traditional signs of effeminacy— lack of self-control and yielding to pleasures" (Nissinen [1998] 2004, 118). Understandably then, it was also used as a label for effeminate men. It was the opposite of the ideal, dominating male of Greco-Roman culture, who had control of his desires. *A Greek-English Lexicon of the New Testament* defines the word as "effeminate, esp. of catamites" (Bauer and Danker 2001, 613). The Latin spelling is *catamitus*, a young intimate partner of a Roman man. It may be similar to the Greek practice of pederasty but with less emphasis on the formation of character and future citizenship and frankly more emphasis on the satisfaction of desire for the dominant partner.[14] The greater emphasis on sex was associated with the Greek story of Zeus and Ganymede, the beautiful Trojan youth that was abducted by Zeus and made his official cupbearer. (Nissinen [1998] 2004). Ganymede in Latin is Catamitus (Williams [1999] 2010, 59–70).[15] In summary then, *malakos* is a description of an effeminate man, which may only be a description of his behavior apart from sex. But within the field of sexual behavior, its meaning could include (1) a companion of a dominant man, (2) the practice of pederasty, or (3) prostitution. Whatever the case, when it is about sexual behavior, it is the male who plays the passive role.

Andrapodistēs

In the New Testament, the word only occurs in 1 Timothy 1. *Andrapodistēs* is another compound word. The first word is again *aner*, or "man," and the second is from *podos*, which in its many forms means "foot." It is often associated with another word, *tetrapoda*, which means "four footed," as in animals (Moulton and Milligan 1995, 40). So man footed and animal footed. The meaning is not immediately obvious of course.

Andrapodistēs is translated "man stealer" or "slave trader." These are, in effect, the same thing. First there is the theft and then the sale. There is a form of the word that refers to the person stolen as a slave; the word is *andropodon*. This word is to be distinguished from the more typical word for slave, which is *doulos* (slave or servant) and which we find often in the New Testament in phrases such as "servants/slaves of Christ." *Andropodon* connoted a much more horrific form of slavery. It could refer to captured men, women, and children who were then sold into slavery (Liddell, Scott, and Jones 2014).

We know of course that slavery was legal in ancient Rome and Greece. Yet the *andrapodistēs* was considered to be a low-life scoundrel and would be included in vice lists of those persons who were morally degenerate—along with murderers. But why, if slavery was legal, were they disparaged? Somebody had to do it. *Andrapodistēs* is the word used to connote those who captured men, women, and children and sold them into slavery. Sometimes these unsavory characters would simply steal people and sell them into prostitution, which today we would call "human trafficking." Their crime was stealing "free citizens." Greco-Roman sexual practices provided a ready market for either girls or boys. When the normal acquisition process of obtaining slaves through war captives would not meet market demand, they would kidnap free citizens. This practice is likely what the author of 1 Timothy had in mind. So when we read translations of the word as "kidnapper," we must read it with all of the horrific reality of the practices associated with it (Harrell 1999).

Now we turn to the texts in which these words are found.

1 Corinthians 6:9-10—Against a Culture of Death

The first text to examine is 1 Corinthians 6:9-10. Embedded in the middle of a discussion about fellow Christians dragging each other into court to resolve differences is a list of "vices." A list like this is placed in a text for a reason, and if one is to properly interpret it, it is necessary to discover why Paul placed it here.[16]

The letter was written by the Apostle Paul most likely when he was in Ephesus in 54–55 CE (1 Cor 16:8). Paul had founded the church in Corinth after leaving Athens but had moved on to Asia Minor. The letter was written in response to a report delivered to him regarding some behaviors in the Corinthian Church: "My brothers and sisters, Chloe's people gave me some information about you, that you're fighting with each other" (1 Cor 1:11).

Some Background on Corinth

Corinth was a crossroads between the east and Rome. It was located on a small isthmus of land between the Greek mainland and the Peloponnesian peninsula. Ships from throughout Eastern Europe, the Middle East, and Asia Minor made port in Corinth, and small boats were dragged the 3.5 miles across the isthmus from the Aegean Sea, through the Gulf of Corinth, and out into the Ionian Sea. From there, they could travel on to Rome. Because of its location, Corinth was a magnet for every philosophy and religion of the world. (Some have compared it to New York City in our time.) The people of Corinth included Greeks, Roman freedmen from Italy, and sizable Jewish communities, as well as many others. Corinth was also the home to the Temple of Aphrodite, Greek goddess of love, beauty, and fertility. Athens and Corinth celebrated the festival of Aphrodite called the *Aphrodisia*. The city was known as a center of sexual license and luxury. The cosmopolitan atmosphere of Corinth meant that it offered a smorgasbord of lifestyle choices, religious practices, and philosophies.

Setting 1 Corinthians 6:9-10 in Context

This brief background is important for understanding the multiple issues Paul addresses in his letters to the Corinthians, and especially 1 Corinthians. Starting a church in Corinth would be akin to starting one in modern-day New York City. Paul, as was his practice, began in the Jewish synagogue, but when they objected to his teaching that Jesus was the expected Jewish Messiah, he left and moved next door to the house of Titius Justis, a Gentile God worshipper, and continued his preaching ministry (Acts 18:4-8).

159

Building a church from scratch in Corinth was bound to be a challenge. Not long after Paul left, factions began to form in the Corinthian house churches. Some, influenced by what many scholars consider to be incipient gnosticism, were overly impressed with their special knowledge and wisdom. There was an ascetic party that considered themselves spiritually superior and above things of this earthly existence, like even having sex as married couples. These are the people some scholars believe may have been the Therapeutae mentioned earlier. Conversely, although we do not know the extent, it seems that some in the congregations were practicing immorality with impunity. The most blatant example was an instance of incest. There actually was a man in the church living with his father's wife.

Paul is horrified by this. How could anyone think this was OK? Even the pagans of Corinth, a city not known for its prudish sexual morality, would be shocked by what was occurring. But this is just the beginning of his disgust. It is also reported that people in the church are dragging each other into court: "When someone in your assembly has a legal case against another member, do they dare to take it to court to be judged by people who aren't just, instead of by God's people?" (1 Cor 6:1). This is the subject matter immediately prior to the so-called vice list that begins in verse 9. Paul asks some pointed questions:

> I'm saying this because you should be ashamed of yourselves! Isn't there one person among you who is wise enough to pass judgment between believers? But instead does a brother or sister have a lawsuit against another brother or sister, and do they do this in front of unbelievers? The fact that you have lawsuits against each other means that you've already lost your case. Why not be wronged instead? Why not be cheated? But instead you are doing wrong and cheating—and you're doing it to your own brothers and sisters. (1 Cor 6:5-8)

This simply should not happen in the new covenant community. Paul's alarm is that instead of convening a group within the church to adjudicate a dispute between two members of the church, they went to a court outside the community. It was very common for different religious cults and even the Jews to have internal processes and procedures for dealing with conflicts between people within their communities. This is what Paul has in mind. If they are the new covenant community, if they are the people who are finally to fulfill the original calling of humans to be God's vice regents of creation, then certainly they ought to be able to resolve this matter.

But whatever the issue was, far from being able to convene to establish justice, they were perpetrating injustice—on each other: "But you yourselves wrong and defraud—and believers at that" (1 Cor 6:8 NRSV). Paul is concerned that the Corinthians simply—as we would say today—"don't get it." This is shameful behavior, especially given who they were supposed to be. To make his point, Paul establishes a baseline principle: "Don't you know that people who are unjust won't inherit God's kingdom?" (1 Cor 6:9a).

The word translated "unjust" is *adikos*, the same word as in 6:1, in which Paul asks why they are taking grievances before the "people who aren't just" instead of the saints. For Paul, it is the unbelieving community, those without faith, who have not embraced Jesus as Lord and whose "justice" reflects the oppressive patronage system that shaped Roman culture. What Paul calls "unjust" (in some translations, "wrongdoers") are people living lives contrary to the promise and hope of the gospel and the people to whom the Corinthians were to preach and demonstrate the gospel, certainly not the people to whom they should turn to settle their disputes. The list (vice list) that follows describes what the unbelieving world looks like or perhaps more precisely, how unbelievers live and behave. I am providing two translations of 1 Corinthians 6:9-10 for comparison, the NRSV and the CEB:

> Do you not know that *wrongdoers* will not inherit the kingdom of God? Do not be deceived! Fornicators, idolaters, adulterers, *male prostitutes, sodomites*, thieves, the greedy, drunkards, revilers, robbers—none of these will inherit the kingdom of God. (NRSV, emphasis added)

> Don't you know that *people who are unjust* won't inherit God's kingdom? Don't be deceived. Those who are sexually immoral, those who worship false gods, adulterers, *both participants in same-sex intercourse*, thieves, the greedy, drunks, abusive people, and swindlers won't inherit God's kingdom.[17] (emphasis added)

In Paul's mind none of these behaviors correspond to the gospel he had shared with them—namely, why Jesus came and what he has done and is doing for them.

The unjust (the wrongdoers) are persons still lost in idolatry. Remember, idolatry is not just about worship. It is a life orientation defined by who or where a person places his or her trust, namely, the immorality that attends idolatry. (For more on idolatry, see the section on Romans 1 below.) The same point was made earlier about Sodom. Abraham was called righteous precisely because he trusted God. Sodom was unrighteous, meaning it was going after other gods and all of the behaviors that followed such idolatry such as all forms of immorality. This immorality was the expression of an oppressive and exploitive society that used and abused the stranger and the weak. This was the cry that went up to YHWH's ears and called for judgment. In the same way here in Corinth, what Paul is writing about in general terms is a culture of idolatry that translates into multiple forms of human degradation and depravity. Some of these behaviors would have actually been part of cultic rituals. Some would have just reflected the culture's values—though the line between these is thin. But all were antithetical to what righteousness should look like. God was calling his people out of that to just and holy lives—lives humans were intended to live.

Paul then says in verse 11:

> That is what some of you used to be! But you were washed clean, you were made holy to God, and you were made right with God in the name of the Lord Jesus Christ and in the Spirit of our God. (1 Cor 6:11)

Vice lists were a common literary motif used by writers in this period as a way of describing moral flaws in society. Paul employs a known vice list to make a specific point. The Corinthians used to be these kinds of people, living these kinds of vices. But having heard the gospel of Jesus the Christ, they no longer had to be. Now their lives were to reflect the character of their Lord. This was not the kind of life Jesus had called them to. His death was the defeat of evil; his resurrection, his vindication as the true Lord of heaven and earth. To strengthen and help them resist temptation, Jesus gave them the gift of the Spirit to convict and empower them to be God's new creation. But here they were behaving worse than the unbelieving community. And it appears that some were even proud of it. It was an expression of their new "freedom" in Christ. But they had been set apart (sanctified) for God, vindicated before God (justified) in the name of Jesus, and they had the Spirit of God with them now. Paul closes this section with these powerful words: "Or don't you [all] know that your body is a temple of the Holy Spirit who is in you? Don't you [all] know that you have the Holy Spirit from God, and you don't belong to yourselves? You [all] have been bought and paid for, so honor God with your body"[18] (1 Cor 6:19-20).

Paul wanted the Corinthians to know that they were now on the road to what humans were intended to be. John Wesley, founder of the Methodist movement, would have said that they were "on the road to perfection." The presence of God was with them. They together as a community were the place where heaven and earth meet. That possibility had been costly. Therefore, they were no longer their own. Rather now they were intended to reflect God's glory in their life—to be a living temple of God, not walking in the ways of their former lives.

The Vice List

By placing the vice list in context, we see that Paul's concern is about the holiness of the Corinthian Christian community. The gospel called people out of a culture of death into a culture of life made possible by the love of God, most fully expressed in Jesus. The logic is simple. Live a new life because you *can* live a new life.

Look at the list again in 1 Corinthians 6:9b-10

> Don't be deceived. Those who are sexually immoral, those who worship false gods, adulterers, *both participants in same-sex intercourse,** thieves, the greedy, drunks, abusive people, and swindlers won't inherit God's kingdom. (emphasis added)
>
> *The CEB translates the two Greek words *malakos* and *arsenokoitēs* as "both participants in same-sex intercourse."

In the following table each of the vice words are provided along with a list of optional translations and what I believe is the preferred translation. These options reflect the alternative ways a word was used historically.

Word	Translation/Usage Options	Preferred Translation
pornoi	A male prostitute Illicit sex practices (fornicator) Any sexual immorality Metaphor for idolatry	Illicit sex practices (fornicator)
eidōlolatrai	An idolater	An idolater
moichoi	An adulterer Figurative for unfaithfulness to God	An adulterer
malakoi	A male prostitute who plays the passive role	A male prostitute who plays the passive role
	A male slave who plays the passive role	A male slave who plays the passive role
	A boy in a pederastic relationship	A boy in a pederastic relationship

163

arsenokoitēs	A man bedder	The adult/active side of pederasty
	The adult/active side of pederasty	A man who takes the active role having sex with a male prostitute
	A man who takes the active role having sex with a male prostitute	
kleptai	A person who steals from another	A person who steals from another
pleonektai	A person who is greedy for gain	A person who is greedy for gain
	A covetous person	A covetous person
ouvmethusoi	A drunkard	A drunkard
ouloidoroi	An abusive person (verbally)	An abusive person (verbally)
ouxarpages	One who takes by force	One who takes by force
	A rapacious person	A rapacious person
	A swindler	A swindler

From this brief analysis we can say with certainty that these are pretty nasty people doing pretty nasty things. Each term, and the terms in the aggregate, presents the antithesis of God and what God wants for or expects from humanity. If we compare this list to several items on the earlier list of practices considered abominations in the Old Testament, we will see a definite correlation. Paul was a rabbinic Jew, and he knew the Hebrew scriptures. He knew what was an abomination to God. Remember, an abomination is something deeply outrageous. In rabbinic Judaism, it meant that the Lord must separate from them and that they would lose their place in the land as God's covenant people. Idolatry, illicit sex, male (and female) prostitution, exploitation of the weak, cheaters, thieves, and those who oppress the poor and needy—the consequences of these would be on Paul's mind. All of these things are antithetical to God and the people God is calling into being. They are forms of injustice—things not as they ought to be—the very things from which God is redeeming his creation.

Three specific examples from the Old Testament will make the point. The first text is from the prophet Jeremiah. Notice the themes of injustice and idolatry or justice and faithfulness to YHWH that are clear in each:

If you truly reform your ways and your actions; if you treat each other justly; if you stop taking advantage of the immigrant, orphan, or widow; if you don't shed the blood of the innocent in this place, or go after other gods to your own ruin, only then will I dwell with you in this place, in the land that I gave long ago to your ancestors for all time. And yet you trust in lies that will only hurt you. Will you steal and murder, commit adultery and perjury, sacrifice to Baal and go after other gods that you don't know, and then come and stand before me in this temple that bears my name, and say, "We are safe," only to keep on doing all these detestable things? (Jer 7:5-10)

Jeremiah's concern was for justice in the land of Israel. God will dwell with God's people wherever they deal justly with one another. But if they begin to chase after other gods and morally devolve into stealing, murder, adultery, making false statements, and making offerings to Baal, still assuming all is good, they are mistaken. They need to know that such things are an abomination to the Lord, and God will separate from them, leaving them to their own devices. They will create a culture of death instead of life. From the prophet's perspective, indeed from the perspective of the Old Testament, such courses ultimately result in the destruction of the community and its culture.

The association of all of these behaviors with idolatry is clear. A second text adds to the understanding and again is reflected in the vice list:

Judah did evil in the LORD's eyes. The sins they committed made the LORD angrier than anything their ancestors had done. They also built shrines, standing stones, and sacred poles* on top of every high hill and under every green tree. Moreover, the consecrated workers** in the land did detestable things, just like those nations that the LORD had removed among the Israelites. (1 Kgs 14:22-24)
* In Hebrew, *asherim* are perhaps objects devoted to the goddess Asherah (CEB).
** Traditionally, these are cultic prostitutes (CEB).

Once again it is the unfaithfulness to YHWH by chasing after other gods and the behaviors that typically attend the shift in worship/cultic practice that are an abomination.

The third text is from the prophet Ezekiel. This is an extended text that is informative because it sets the benefit to faithfulness to YHWH against unfaithfulness. Faithfulness propagates justice in the land, and unfaithfulness, injustice:

People are declared innocent when they act justly and responsibly. They don't eat on the hills or give their attention to the idols of the house of Israel. They don't defile the wives of their neighbors or approach menstruating women. They don't cheat anyone, but fulfill their obligations. They don't rob others, but give food to the hungry and clothes to the naked. They don't impose interest or take profit. They refrain from evil and settle cases between people fairly. They follow my regulations, keep my case laws, and act faithfully. Such people are innocent, and they will live, proclaims the Lord God. But suppose one of them has a violent child who sheds blood or does any one of these things, even though his parents didn't do any of them. He eats on the mountains, defiles his neighbor's wife, oppresses the poor and needy, robs others and doesn't fulfill his obligations, pays attention to the idols and does detestable things, and takes interest and profit. Should he live? He should not. He engaged in all these detestable practices. He will surely die, and his blood will be on him. (Ezek 18:5-13)

Two different lives, and two different lives lived. One promotes a culture of life; the other, death. From the Old Testament perspective, it is not possible to separate faith in YHWH and life in the land lived as it should be. Conversely, neither can one separate living in the land unjustly—life as it ought not to be—from idolatry. Each goes hand in hand with the other. We have seen this time and again in our study.

Now we will get back to Paul and 1 Corinthians and the vice list. This is not just a list, but it is also behaviors that are indicative of a culture that does not know God. But it is not an irreligious culture. No culture is, even those that deny God in our day. But specifically in the Corinthian context, Paul saw a culture chasing after all kinds of gods, sometimes in cultic practices, sometimes not. What he sees is a culture that is giving itself to all sorts of things that ultimately result in death not life. All would be idolatry. In our modern analysis, we would look at these as manifestations of systemic evil.

The kind of people represented in a vice list lived humanly debasing lives; they not only degraded themselves but also degraded everyone who came in contact with them. It is these types of people practicing these types of behaviors that create a culture of death. This is why these shall not inherit the kingdom of God. Their choices move them in the opposite direction. But we must also remember that it is these very people Paul expected the Corinthians to reach *and* that such were they when he found them: "And this is what some of you used to be" (1 Cor 6:11 NRSV).

Malakos and *Arsenokoitēs*

The focus now turns to the two words that are traditionally associated with homosexuality. Based upon the lexical study of the words above and the context in which they are found in 1 Corinthians 6, I believe these refer to truly loathsome practices.

Paul pairs *malakos* with *arsenokoitēs* in this vice list. It seems clear that the two reflect the two roles played in any sexual act in Roman culture, as discussed above; and in this sense, the Common English Bible translation gets it right in the note on the text where it says, "submissive and dominant male sexual partners." *Malakos* means "soft" or "effeminate." The effeminate in Roman culture was not necessarily a person with a homosexual orientation as we would describe it today. Remember, sexual orientation is a modern construct. Rather, a *malakos* would have been the person who played the receptive or passive role in intercourse. A *malakos* could be a male or a female though in this context it is likely a male. The *arsenokoitēs* is a man who takes the dominant/active or penetrative role in intercourse. Many biblical translations are not far from this. However, understanding requires more specificity as to what Paul was talking about. I believe there are three possible readings and one unlikely one. The focus in each one is what is meant by *malakos*. Once this word is understood, the meaning of *arsenokoitēs* becomes pretty clear.

Three Possible Readings and One Unlikely

Practice of Pederasty: Pederasty is the practice wherein an older man would have his "call boy" with whom he maintained a relationship. This would not be the kind of idealized pederasty of Classical Greece, but rather a more sexually focused relationship as a sexual outlet for an older man (Scroggs 1983, 62–65).

Boy Slaves: We have seen earlier that it was an accepted practice to require slaves to have sex with their masters. This sex could be with a male or female. But it had two important characteristics. First, the slave was forced to have sex with his or her master—though again in this case, the master was male. Second, the slave was to play the passive/receptive role in all sexual behaviors. There was no choice here.

Male Prostitute: We have also seen that there were male prostitutes that would sell their services to a whoremonger—a man who frequents prostitutes for sex. These prostitutes could have chosen to be a prostitute, or they could have been boys captured and sold as slaves to whoremasters. In the latter case, the boy had no choice.[19]

Unlikely Reading: Based upon this analysis, it seems pretty unlikely that Paul had in mind general same-sex relations. I do not mean that he thought some same-sex relations were valid. Rather, I am saying that when he talks about the despicable, he has specific practices in mind. I am suspect of the idea that Paul thought about what we know today as committed same-sex relationships and lumped them all in together. What Paul objects to and considers despicable, we do as well. In our day such practices would be called human trafficking, child abuse, molestation, and pedophilia. We, too, will not stand for such behaviors. Our culture today would be on the side of Paul, with some modifications based upon our greater biological and psychological knowledge.

Summary

Paul is concerned that the Corinthian Christians understand how they have been called out of the world of idolatry and loose living in which they had been living. This means that they should not be hauling one another into court. And even more, they should not defraud or treat one another unjustly. This was how they were; it is not how they should be.

1 Timothy 1:10—A Horrid Practice

A Brief Introduction to 1 Timothy

This letter to Timothy is one of three traditionally called the Pastoral Epistles. This is because they are written to either Timothy or Titus with the intent of providing them wisdom for dealing with some problems in the churches they were serving. Topics range from living as faithful Christians to church leadership and the way to guide teachers who were off the mark theologically. In fact, 1 Timothy admonishes Timothy to deal with people teaching a doctrine different than the one he had received:

> When I left for Macedonia, I asked you to stay behind in Ephesus so that you could instruct certain individuals not to spread wrong teaching. They shouldn't pay attention to myths and endless genealogies. Their teaching only causes useless guessing games instead of faithfulness to God's way of doing things. The goal of instruction is love from a pure heart, a good conscience, and a sincere faith. (1:3-5)

The author[20] explains that the aim of instruction (by teachers of the faith) is loving—lives flowing out of hearts that have been captured by authentic faith. But there were some teachers within the church that Timothy was sent to serve who were teaching something else. At least part of what they were teaching had to do with Torah. In effect, the author is saying that they don't know what they are talking about. So he sets the record straight, explaining what and who Torah is for:[21]

> Because they missed this goal, some people have been distracted by talk that doesn't mean anything. They want to be teachers of Law without understanding either what they are saying or what they are talking about with such confidence. Now we know that the Law is good if used appropriately. We understand this: the Law isn't established for a righteous person but for people who live without laws and without obeying any authority. They are the ungodly and the sinners. They are people who are not spiritual, and nothing is sacred to them. They kill their fathers and mothers, and murder others. *They are people who are sexually unfaithful, and people who have intercourse with the same sex. They are kidnappers,* liars, individuals who give false testimonies in court, and those who do anything else that is opposed to sound teaching. Sound teaching agrees with the glorious gospel of the blessed God that has been trusted to me. (1 Tim 1:6-11, emphasis added)

The Vice List

First Timothy 1:9-10 again has a vice list. As mentioned previously, vice lists were a common literary motif, and the author, as in 1 Corinthians, has used one to associate what is contrary to God. It is clear from the text that it is for these kinds of people that law is meant, not for the "righteous." In the context of this letter, the "righteous" would mean the faithful Christians. It is not clear exactly what doctrine the false teachers were expounding. Some suggest they were trying to teach the Jewish Torah but did not really understand it. Others suggest it is a reference to an incipient gnosticism (the meaningless talk). It may have been some mixture of both. The author does make it clear that their understanding of the purpose of law was not correct.

Many commentators see in this list direct allusions to the Ten Commandments (Mounce 2000, 30; Oden 1989, 39). The CEB is a dynamic translation so it is difficult to point to a Greek word and know the English equivalent. To make this possible structure easier to see, the NRSV has been provided so that the corresponding Greek and English words can be laid out in the table below. Verses 9-10 have been segmented and labeled in the table somewhat to reflect such allusions. Notice that items in rows A through C each have to do with a relationship to God. Rows D through F have to do with relationships with others. This follows somewhat the structure of the commandments as is illustrated:

Some people have deviated from these and turned to meaningless talk, desiring to be teachers of the law, without understanding either what they are saying or the things about which they make assertions. Now we know that the law is good, if one uses it legitimately. This means understanding that the law is laid down not for the innocent but for the lawless and disobedient, for the godless and sinful, for the unholy and profane, for those who kill their father or mother, for murderers, *fornicators, sodomites, slave traders,* liars, perjurers, and whatever else is contrary to the sound teaching that conforms to the glorious gospel of the blessed God, which he entrusted to me. (1 Tim 1:6-11 NRSV, emphasis added)

Just how precise the author was trying to be in his list is open to interpretation. But that he had the commandments in mind is compelling because of the statement that the false teachers do not have a proper understanding of Torah and the commandments represent a summation of Torah. This is not the place for an extended discussion of the proper understanding of Torah. But the author's point is that Torah is not for the innocent but for people who practice these behaviors, presumably because it points out the behaviors as being unjust.

Row	Greek Text	Behaviors (NRSV Translation)	Offense Committed
A	*anomois de kai anypotaktois*	lawless and disobedient,	Against God
B	*asebesin kai hamartōlois*	the godless and sinful,	Against God
C	*anosiois kai bebēlois*	the unholy and profane,	Against God
D1	*patralōais kai mētralōais*	those who kill their father or mother,	Dishonor of mother and father
D2	*androphonois*	murderers,	Murder
E1	*pornois arsenokoitais*	fornicators, sodomites	Adultery
E2	*Andrapodistais*	slave traders (kidnappers),	Stealing
F	*pseustais epiorkois*	liars, perjurers,	Bearing false witness

G	*kai ei ti heteron tē hygiainousēa didaskalia antikeitai*	and whatever else is contrary to the sound teaching	Against anything else contrary to faith

Close examination reveals that they are not just a string of fourteen words (and a phrase to catch anything else he had not covered). Some are paired intentionally by the addition of the Greek word *kai* (English, "and"). Others appear to be thematically related, such as liars and perjurers. This leaves the three words in rows E1 and E2 (shaded in gray). There are two possible interpretations. The first is that the two words of E1 are related and must be seen as a unit. E2 then stands alone as a specific example of stealing. However, as explained above, slave traders were known not only to trade slaves but also to capture people and make them slaves or to steal slaves from one owner and sell them to a different owner. So, a second interpretive possibility is that E1 and E2 form a single piece together, the three representing a social practice that the author finds to be a violation of two commandments: committing adultery and stealing. This latter interpretation, I believe, makes the best reading of the text.

The Three Words

We are now ready to apply the results of the prior word studies. The three words are *pornois*, *arsenokoitais*, and *andrapodistais*. The following table, like before, provides possible translation options for each of the three words in 1 Timothy and then what I believe to be the preferred interpretation of each.

Word	Translation/Usage Options	Preferred Translation
pornois	A male prostitute A catamite Any sexual immorality Metaphor for idolatry	A male prostitute or catamite

arsenokoitais	A man bedder The adult side of pederasty A man who takes the active role while having sex with a male prostitute	A man who takes the active role while having sex with a male slave or prostitute
andrapodistais	A slave dealer or kidnapper A man who steals humans and sells them into slavery, often prostitution	A man who steals humans and sells them into slavery, often prostitution

Putting it all together then, *pornos* probably meant a male prostitute or at least a male who performed the passive role in same-sex behavior, often under compulsion. The *arsenokoitēs* was a man who used a male prostitute (catamite) as a passive partner or a man who used his slave boys under compulsion. This is suggested due to the proximity of the word *andrapodistēs* to the other two words. Therefore, it is likely that it reflects the practice of using boy slaves as sex objects. These boy slaves could have been captured and sold into prostitution by the *andrapodistēs* (the slave trader), or they could be the personal slaves of the *aresenokoitēs* who perhaps obtained the slave boy via the *andrapodistēs*. Either way it is an ugly practice. Today we would call it human trafficking, the sex trade, and pedophilia. Recall that Greek and Roman sexual practices expected the man to play the dominant or active role. But the practice is obviously more horrific than the role played. Most of these men (*aresenokoitēs*) would be considered heterosexuals (or at least bisexual) by our modern definition. The three words together list the typical Greco-Roman practice of a dominant male expressing his sexual desire with another male; in all probability it was a young male slave or a prostitute who was probably a slave or possibly a freedman who had been stolen and sold into slavery. The author of 1 Timothy had in mind practices that today would get a person locked up for life. These were terribly abusive acts of self-indulged men.

Romans 1:18-32—Idolatry and Its Outcomes

Although many who are opposed to same-sex marriage and LGBT ordination may agree that the Sodom story and the abomination of Leviticus are not really germane to the current discussion, they give heavy significance to Paul in his letter to the Romans. This text, above all others, they believe, makes it clear that Paul was opposed to same-sex behavior of any kind.

What Is Paul Talking About?

Is Paul talking about the modern same-sex couple who lives in a long-term committed relationship and behave, in all other ways, like a loving, committed married opposite-gender couple? Is this Paul's concern? Does he have in mind the middle-aged lesbian couple who has quietly lived their lives together for 25 years? Is he thinking about the seventy-year-old man who sits beside the bed of his aging male partner of 40 years who is dying of cancer? Are these the people Paul has in mind? The disparity between these two instances and Paul's description in Romans 1 is enormous. So what does Paul mean when he speaks of exchanging one kind of sexual behavior for another? We must answer these questions in our study of this primary New Testament text that clearly is talking about some form of same-sex behaviors.

Paul is clear about his main concern. As he looks out at Greco-Roman culture and its sexual practices (along with many other practices and behaviors), he sees a world drowning in destructive idolatry and, again, the degrading practices that attend idolatry. We must be clear about what is meant by idolatry, however.

The Righteousness of God Reprised

Any exposition of Romans 1:18 and following must begin with Romans 1:16-17. This is because it is the initial statement of Paul's entire argument that extends to the end of chapter 11. Chapter 12 then develops the practical implications of the theology that has preceded it.[22] Here Paul is telling the story of God's faithfulness to God's covenant promise to heal, restore, and complete creation. Paul calls this the gospel—the good news story—and it is for everyone who has faith, who trusts in the one true God and nothing else. We can only assume that Paul is aware that this "good news" was different than the "good news" about the salvation offered through Caesar.[23] Rather, this gospel gives the "righteousness of God" full expression: "I'm not ashamed of the gospel: it is God's own power for salvation to all who have faith in God, to the Jew first and also to the Greek. *God's righteousness* is being revealed in the gospel, from faithfulness for faith, as it is written, *The righteous person will live by faith*" (Rom 1:16-17, emphasis added).[24]

N. T. Wright has dramatically opened up this key phrase "the righteousness of God" for many of us who have struggled to understand the argument of Romans by reanchoring this phrase in the covenant history of Israel. Wright summarizes his exposition of Romans as follows:

> Romans is the letter in which he (Paul) plants this goal of the mission and unity of the church in the firmest possible theological soil, i.e., the exposition of the righteousness of God—which I take to mean essentially the covenant faithfulness, the covenant justice, of the God who made promises to Abraham, promises of a worldwide family characterized by faith, in and through whom the evil of the world would be undone. (1993, 234)

We discussed this in the earlier chapter on creation theology. As a Christian and someone from a Reformed theological background, I was taught that this phrase referred to something I was given as a believer—namely, God's righteousness. This of course would be consistent with an interpretation that Romans 1–8 is about how I am saved, justified, sanctified, glorified, and so on. Now all of that is certainly addressed in Romans 1–8, but that is not the primary thrust. The primary thrust, as Wright has insisted, is about God's covenant faithfulness. It is God's own righteousness that has been revealed. God faithfully keeps the covenant promise to creation, and God is calling out a new Israel, a new covenant community comprised of all kinds of people— Jew and Gentile. (Galatians takes this further.[25]) That covenant faithfulness is captured better in the phrase "God's righteousness" as translated in the CEB. So it's not about me or something I get for having faith; it is about God and who God is and how God has fulfilled that covenant promise. This emphasis comes to a focal point at Romans 3:21-23: "But now God's righteousness has been revealed apart from the Law, which is confirmed by the Law and the Prophets. God's righteousness comes *through the faithfulness of Jesus Christ* for all who have faith in him. There's no distinction. All have sinned and fall short of God's glory" (emphasis added). The covenant faithfulness of God has been fully expressed through the faithfulness of Jesus to be faithful to his calling, even to the point of death.[26]

If we go back to the beginning and look again at Romans 1:16-17, Paul's overarching concern is with how God has acted to fulfill God's covenant promise. The story of Jesus is how God has acted, and it is about this that Paul is not ashamed.

With this auspicious beginning, Paul launches into his argument. Romans can be a complicated book, so before we zoom in on the relevant text in chapter 1, we need an overview through 3:24. Romans was written to inform the Roman church—which Paul had not started and had never visited—that he intended to stop there on his way to Spain (15:21). *But in addition and perhaps more to the point, he is writing to the Roman church that is comprised of Jews and Gentiles, who are not getting along.* Paul intends to show how all of the threads of humanity end up in one large family of God that is both Jew and Greek (i.e., Jew plus everybody else). Evidently some Jewish Christians were acting a bit superior to their Gentile converts. Conversely, as demonstrated later in chapters 9 through 11, some Gentiles did not fully appreciate the role the Jews had played in working out God's new creation project.[27] So amazingly, Paul writes the most mind-blowing letter in history to emphasize God's covenant promise to heal creation.

The first part of the argument from 1:18 to 3:24 levels the playing field. Is there a place for the Jews to feel superior to the Gentiles? At first it would appear so, for Paul, in 1:18-32, brings forth unflattering images of what Jews thought about Gentiles. Every good Hellenistic Jew[28] would have recognized his language and the centrality of the Gentile problem of idolatry, as we will see momentarily. The language Paul uses in 1:18-32 is reminiscent of language in the Wisdom of Solomon, which he would most certainly have in his literary repertoire along with the Hebrew scriptures.[29] The echoes of Wisdom 14 are obvious to anyone who has read 1:18-32. It would have certainly been clear to Paul's Jewish readers. But as Nissinen says, it's a "rhetorical trap" for his imaginary Jewish conversation partner (scholars refer to this as an interlocutor): "The description of the corruption of humankind in Romans 1 is an introduction to chapters 2 and 3, where Paul proceeds to assert that the Jews are really no better off than the gentiles if they imagine they can be saved because of the Law and circumcision" ([1998] 2004, 111). "So what are we saying? Are we better off? Not at all. We have already stated the charge: both Jews and Greeks are all under the power of sin. As it is written, *There is no righteous person, not even one.*" (Rom 3:9-10).

With this larger backdrop in mind, we zoom in on chapter 1.

Without Excuse

In Romans 1:18, Paul begins to lay out the problem. In other words, why is it that God has had to act in such a manner to begin with (i.e., to reveal God's righteousness)? He begins with the worst Gentile behavior and specifically idolatry. It is a fairly typical Jewish critique of Gentile culture. Humans have turned from a living relationship with their creator and replaced that relationship with the worship of gods they have made out of things that are merely part of the creation:

God's wrath is being revealed from heaven against all the ungodly behavior and the injustice of human beings who silence the truth with injustice. This is because what is known about God should be plain to them because God made it plain to them. Ever since the creation of the world, God's invisible qualities—God's eternal power and divine nature—have been clearly seen, because they are understood through the things God has made. (Rom 1:18-20a)

In response to this faithlessness, God's wrath has been revealed as well. Wrath sounds scary, but it is not for the reasons people often assume. Too often God is portrayed as a large, powerful, usually male being enraged by unfaithful humanity and ready to strike down people for their sinfulness. But this is not what the "wrath of God" means. The wrath of God is a way of saying, "You want to worship something or someone other than me; then have it your way." And further, to put it in a phrase that seems to be popular today, "How is that working out for you?" More seriously, God lets us have our own way, and God lets us suppress the truth about God, even though everywhere we look, we see God's creation. This is consistent with the over-view of creation and the kind of universe God created with its freedom. Here we see that very thing worked out from Paul's theological perspective; that is, he expresses how human choice to reject God had worked out among the Gentiles. So Paul continues:

So humans are without excuse. Although they knew God, they didn't honor God as God or thank him. Instead, their reasoning became pointless, and their foolish hearts were darkened. While they were claiming to be wise, they made fools of themselves. *They exchanged the glory of the immortal God for images that look like mortal humans: birds, animals, and reptiles.* (Rom 1:20b-23, emphasis added)

Humans cannot claim that God is not made known. The evidence for a creator is all around. The Gentiles simply choose to reject what is obvious and go their own way, doing their own thing. It is pitiable if nothing else! Let's again step back and generalize from the text to include our modern society. The creator of the universe creates humans in the divine image to be vice regents or stewards over the rest of God's creation. Yet instead of embracing that, we turn our backs, and our thinking becomes foolish. How so? Look at what we exchanged for a relationship with God! We even turned animals into little gods; and though they are precious to God's creation, they are not God. In fact, they are not on the same level as humans, who alone were created in the image of God. Yet that is what we did/do. If that is not foolish, I don't know what is! Idolatry among many other things is foolish.

Paul is setting the trap. Look at what these foolish Gentiles have done. They make little images, set up little alters in their houses, and worship what they made with their own hands. Keeping with the typical Jewish critique of Gentile idolatry, the Wisdom of Solomon, which is a book of the Apocrypha, tells a story to show how pathetic it is:

> Imagine this. A woodcutter with some skill cuts down a pliable shrub. He carefully strips the outside covering of the plant and then, because he has some skill, shapes it into a tool for daily use. Afterward he picks up the left-over bark that he had stripped away and uses it to cook a meal for himself. He eats his fill and then picks up one of the leftover pieces of wood, one that wasn't good for anything, a crooked hard piece with broken ends where the branches had been. Having nothing else to do, he takes this piece of wood and starts carving. By a process of trial and error, he's finally able to give it a human shape, or he fashions it into something that vaguely resembles some miserable creature. He covers it with red paint, giving it a rosy hue where the creature's flesh is supposed to be. He covers over every flaw in the wood. Finally, he makes a perfect little shrine for it and fastens the shrine securely to the wall with a nail so that it doesn't fall down. He knows full well that it can't do anything for itself. After all, it's only an image, and it requires help. (13:11-16)

We saw the emphasis on idolatry earlier in the Old Testament texts, and it is at the forefront here as well. For the Jews, all evil has its origin in idolatry. The Wisdom of Solomon makes this precise point:

> The very notion of idols was the beginning of immoral sexual activity. The invention of idols ruined human life. (14:12)

> The worship of nameless idols is the origin of all evil—its cause as well as its result. (14:27)

N. T. Wright, commenting on the Wisdom of Solomon, says that the author "did not believe that the created order was itself evil, but that human beings, by committing idolatry, distorted their own humanity into sinful behavior and courted corruption and ultimately death" (2003, 727).

Degrading Passions and Idolatry

Where do things go from here? Once a person starts down the road to foolishness (i.e., idolatry) and away from the God who alone can show us where life is to be found, things go badly. When Paul says, "so God abandoned them to their hearts' desires," he is saying again, God let us—humanity—have what we wanted and what our hearts would produce if left to our own devices (Rom 1:24). C. S. Lewis says in *The Great Divorce*: "There are only two kinds of people in the end: those who say to God, 'Thy will be done,' and those to whom God says, in the end, '*Thy* will be done'" (2009, 75). Exchange the truth for a lie, exchange the glory for the worship of anything else, and one will quickly devolve into all manner of debauchery and promiscuity. This is consistent with the analysis of Genesis 19:1-11, Leviticus 18:22-24 and 20:3, and 1 Corinthians 6. All point to what happens to human society when we turn our back on God. We humans have to worship something, even if we make it up. Even one of Bob Dylan's songs from the 1970s, when for a brief moment he embraced the Christian faith, says:

> You're gonna have to serve somebody.
> Well, it may be the devil or it may be the Lord, but you're gonna serve somebody. (Dylan 1979)

Paul continues in Romans:

> So God abandoned them to their hearts' desires, which led to the moral corruption of degrading their own bodies with each other. They traded God's truth for a lie, and they worshipped and served the creation instead of the creator, who is blessed forever. Amen. That's why God abandoned them to degrading lust. Their females traded natural sexual relations for unnatural sexual relations. Also, in the same way, the males traded natural sexual relations with females, and burned with lust for each other. Males performed shameful actions with males, and they were paid back with the penalty they deserved for their mistake in their own bodies. (1:24-27)

This is the text where interpreters see Paul declaring that same-sex behavior is a degrading passion. In fact, it very much looks like he is saying just that; and in fact, within Paul's frame of reference as a first-century Christian Jew, he is. But remember that the larger theme is about idolatry and idol worship, so we must consider again what idolatry means and then apply it to this text.

Recall that idolatry is choosing to worship something other than the creator God. But what does that mean? To worship something is to ascribe value to it and then *desire* that thing, to give yourself to it. Again, Dylan's song: "You're gonna have to serve somebody." Wright comments, "Humans are worshipping creatures, and even when they don't consciously or even unconsciously worship any kind of god, they are all involved in the adoring pursuit of something greater than themselves" (2013b, 36). To worship anything, we must draw the conclusion that if I give myself to this god, this god will do something for me. There is a transaction at work. We give ourselves to those things (gods) that we believe will provide us the "life" we long for and the prestige we so desire. If you believe a necklace with a jeweled reptile will protect you, you will also be inclined to give yourself to that reptile and do what you have been told it expects of you. If you believe that always being seen with so-and-so will bring you the prestige you so long for, you will do what you have to in order to be seen with them—perhaps at any cost. If you believe that sexual orgasm easily and often is the road to making you feel powerful and virile, you will look for it wherever, whenever, and however you can. In every one of these scenarios, it is behavior based upon the believed promise that promotes choices. In every case, from the simple idol worship of a reptile to the insatiable pursuit of sex, a person gives a piece of herself or himself away in exchange for the promise made by the object of pursuit—the idol. When Paul says they "burned with lust for each other" (Rom 1:27), he is providing an apt description of persons who have given themselves fully with the expectation that there is a payoff for doing so.

Given the sexual morality of ancient Rome and especially in Corinth where Paul probably was when he wrote Romans, it is not difficult to see how his description of human idolatry would look. Corinth was a notoriously corrupt and promiscuous city. If there was a place where human sexual passions had run amok, it was Corinth. Paul's description is not an abstract expression of how we humans turn creation into gods to which we give ourselves. In such settings as Corinth, sexual desires were unleashed—men with women, men with men, women with women. One can barely imagine how perverse, exploitive, and abusive such practices were. Idolatry destroys humanity. Desires run amok. This is what I believe Paul means when he says, "they were paid back with the penalty they deserved for their mistake in their own bodies" (Rom 1:27; Nissinen [1998] 2004, 108–9).

From a theological standpoint, I do not believe Paul's concern is that "you are deserving of judgment because of all of your horrible, bad behavior" (my paraphrase). Rather, I think Paul's concern is for how destructive idolatry is to human beings who were created to bear God's image. So, far from expressing that image in their relationships with one another and even themselves, they were using one another for their own consumptive purposes. If idolatry is the transaction that says to the object of worship, "You be to me all that I need for life. In exchange I will give myself to you and your demands even if they are exploitive, abusive, tyrannical, rapacious, overbearing, dominating, and deceitful." These actions are simply the way people give themselves in order to receive what the god promises. Paul saw human life being sucked out of people at every level of society. When he uses the phrase, "received in their own persons the due penalty of their error," he is not happy that they got their just deserts. He is appalled and weeps, for this was not why God created us. God gave them over to what they desired, but false gods cannot deliver; and in the end, all they got was death. This is the tragedy of the human story—or, more precisely, human sin.

Dehumanized Humanity

The result is dehumanized humanity. Far from reflecting the glory of the living God, humans begin to shrink and shrivel, and given enough time, they cease to be human. N. T. Wright says:

> When people continually and consistently refuse to worship this God, they progressively reflect this image less and less. Instead, they reflect the images of what they are worshipping. Since all else other than the true creator God is heading for death, this means that they buy into a system of death. Thus, failure to worship the God revealed in Jesus leads, by one's own choice, to an eventual erasing of that which makes us truly human. I think this is the way a doctrine of hell might be restated today. (2014)

In *The Great Divorce*, C. S. Lewis observes this specific dynamic. Humans who are continually given the opportunity to enter heaven reject it and in the process become less and less human, more and more separated from others into the gray world of their own imaginings. In his book *Mere Christianity*, he follows this same theme: "The most dangerous thing you can do is to take any one impulse of your own nature and set it up as the thing you ought to follow at all costs. There's not one of them which won't make us into devils if we set it up as an absolute guide" ([1952] 2009, 11).

When we read in Paul's letter the language about giving up natural intercourse for unnatural, don't read it as heterosexual versus homosexual sex. It should be read as life versus death.

About That "Natural" Word

What about the language that would appear to specifically address some kind of same-sex behavior? Is that what Paul means or isn't it? I think it would be hard to argue that he has something other than same-sex behavior in mind. We must remember he was a good Jew. And it is clear that he is well versed in Second Temple literature such as the Wisdom of Solomon. For post-exilic Jews, same-sex eroticism was repugnant. It was not considered natural for a woman to play the role of a man—that is, the active or penetrative partner. Such behavior masculinized the active partner. It was not natural for a man to play the female role and allow himself to be penetrated. Such behavior feminized the passive partner. Paul meant this more in the sense of the normal order of things and that to depart from this was to turn social order upside down (Nissinen [1998] 2004, 106–8). Men are the active partner; women are the passive partner. Exchanging these roles disrupts life. It is "unnatural."[30]

Those who want to absolutize the idea of *natural* miss the central point, not just of what Paul is saying, but of what God has said and Jesus clearly said. Humans were created to love God and love one another. Idolatry turns one away from love, and healthy desire morphs into lust. Lust is not love, and it is lust that Paul is pointing to. But let us not forget how Paul completes Romans 1:

> Since they didn't think it was worthwhile to acknowledge God, God abandoned them to a defective mind to do inappropriate things. So they were filled with all injustice, wicked behavior, greed, and evil behavior. They are full of jealousy, murder, fighting, deception, and malice. They are gossips, they slander people, and they hate God. They are rude and proud, and they brag. They invent ways to be evil, and they are disobedient to their parents. They are without understanding, disloyal, without affection, and without mercy. Though they know God's decision that those who persist in such practices deserve death, they not only keep doing these things but also approve others who practice them. (vv. 28-32)

In summary, whatever Paul means in Romans 1, it is not to be compared to all same-sex relationships. If there is a comparison to make, it is with behaviors that originate in desires not directed toward the love of God and the other. That is what the rest of chapter 1 points to.

- We do not know much of anything about same-sex relationships in Paul's era that approximate modern same-sex partners in a long-term committed relationship based upon love.

- We do know many of the sexual practices of Greeks and Romans. We know those practices would be more comparable to the kinds of promiscuous lifestyles we see practiced today by both same-sex and opposite-sex persons.

- The most we can say then, relative to Paul and current same-sex committed relationships, is that Paul is silent on the issue, though as a Hellenistic Jew whose understanding of social structures was fairly consistent with the rest of the Jewish people, he would have found same-sex behavior an affront to the natural order—meaning male as dominant, female as passive.

- We can (and must) conclude that his concern is what happens to human beings, created in the image of God and who are meant to live that way. When they turn from God and make gods out of anything else, they debase their own humanity as well as that of others. That was Paul's concern, and that ought to be ours.

Jude 5-7—A Strange Text

Some who oppose same-sex marriage and homosexuality in general refer to Jude 7. This short letter is a truly odd one. The issue is common enough: concern that Christians are allowing pagan influences to infiltrate their community. To counter that, the author wants to remind them of a couple of stories and what happened in them. The first is easy enough for us to understand, for it is the story of Israel: "I want to remind you of something you already know very well. The Lord, who once saved a people out of Egypt, later destroyed those who didn't maintain their faith" (Jude 5).

But starting with verse 6, things turn fantastically strange:

> I remind you too of the angels who didn't keep their position of authority but deserted their own home. The Lord has kept them in eternal chains in the underworld until the judgment of the great day. In the same way, Sodom and Gomorrah and neighboring towns practiced immoral sexual relations and pursued other sexual urges. By undergoing the punishment of eternal fire, they serve as a warning. (vv. 6-7)

Two additional reminders are given, but only the first is of concern to us. It is a reference to an equally odd text (odd to us, anyway) in Genesis 6:

> When the number of people started to increase throughout the fertile land, daughters were born to them. The divine beings saw how beautiful these human women were, so they married the ones they chose. In those days, giants lived on the earth and also afterward, when divine beings and human daughters had sexual relations and gave birth to children. These were the ancient heroes, famous men. (vv. 1-2, 4)

182

Our only concern with these texts is the intermarriage between human women and divine beings. What follows this story is the great flood. The author of Jude in the tradition of other Second Temple writings concluded that at least part of the reason for the flood was the intermixing of divine and human beings, thus blurring the line between the heavenly and earthly. Consequently, these divine beings await their final judgment. (Second Peter 2:4-6 also relates to this story.) Next the author references Sodom and Gomorrah. Second Temple Judaism's interpretation of that event was not about potential homosexual behavior but about crossing the line between divine beings (Lot's guests) and humans. The rape would have been against divine beings (Nissinen [1998] 2004, 90–93)

The author of Jude is trying to warn his Christian friends about the danger of following "in the footsteps of Cain" (Jude 11). The text has nothing to do with homosexuality—or perhaps more precisely homoeroticism. Furthermore, we have already seen that the "sin of Sodom" was not homosexuality. The sin of Sodom was idolatry that manifested itself in wanton disregard for basic moral decency and social justice even for the Middle Eastern nations of the time.

Mark 10:2-12—Jesus and Marriage

This text, perhaps more than any other, has caused me to pause over the years. Here we are, dealing with the reported words of Jesus. You don't get any closer to the mind of God than this: "Jesus said to them, 'He wrote this commandment for you because of your unyielding hearts. At the beginning of creation, *God made them male and female. Because of this, a man should leave his father and mother and be joined together with his wife, and the two will be one flesh.* So they are no longer two but one flesh" (Mark 10:5-8).

If we were to isolate all of scripture to this text, it would be difficult to avoid the conclusion that Jesus does not support same-sex marriage. But before rushing to judgment we must, as I have said previously, take these words in their context. What is the issue? It is clear from verse 5 that Jesus is responding to something, and his answer is intended to address whatever was inquired of him. So who was he responding to, and what was the issue? Let's look first at the larger context. Here is a full reading of the text.

> Some Pharisees came and, trying to test him, they asked, "Does the Law allow a man to divorce his wife?" Jesus answered, "What did Moses command you?" They said, "Moses allowed a man to write a divorce certificate and to divorce his wife." Jesus said to them, "He wrote this commandment

for you because of your unyielding hearts. At the beginning of creation, *God made them male and female. Because of this, a man should leave his father and mother and be joined together with his wife, and the two will be one flesh.* So they are no longer two but one flesh. Therefore, humans must not pull apart what God has put together." Inside the house, the disciples asked him again about this. He said to them, "Whoever divorces his wife and marries another commits adultery against her; and if a wife divorces her husband and marries another, she commits adultery." (Mark 10:2-12)

The inquirers are the Pharisees, and the issue is divorce. We know that the Pharisees sometimes asked Jesus questions in order to trap him. They wanted to see if he would say something that they could use against him. It is no different here. They wanted to know if he would support their reading of Torah. As they read it, Moses allowed men easily to dismiss their wives. In their culture, that meant a woman was cast out of her home and hopefully back to her original family. But to be sent back was a disgrace on the family and possibly a hardship. This does not even begin to describe what it meant for the woman. So, far from supporting this callous practice, Jesus points out that the only reason Moses allowed the practice of divorce was because of their stubborn hearts. The certificate of dismissal was meant to protect the dispossessed wife. The husband could not merely kick her out. When breaking a covenant, he did have obligations. But this was not how God intended human relationships to unfold. A marriage partnership—a covenant—was intended to be permanent. By appealing to Genesis 2, Jesus makes this point.

Does this insight about divorce preclude same-sex marriage? It really doesn't. Same-sex marriage was unheard of in first-century Judaism. It was barely heard of in Rome. Jesus was talking about how relationships between men and women should be committed and permanent in that culture, in which women had few rights.

Jesus's response to the Pharisees is germane to any type of marriage, however. It speaks to a culture that sees relationships as transient. When we consider the affirmation of same-sex marriage, the expectation of a lasting commitment must be part of that discussion. This is difficult for many couples, whether gay or straight. Yet it is ironic that in most church traditions today, divorce is common, and people who have been through a divorce are not precluded from full participation in the life of the church, including ordained leadership and remarriage.

184

Summary of the Biblical Texts

What can we say then about these texts that are the traditional sources of the whole range of beliefs about homosexuality?

- The "sin of Sodom" pertains to a society whose idolatry had devolved into a culture of degradation and injustice and whose victims cried out for justice.

- The offense of the Sodomites was a radical failure of hospitality that, consistent with the evil that had engulfed the culture, included a crowd intent on violent gang rape. It was not an issue of heterosexual versus homosexual behavior. Their determination to do violence to the stranger —and in the perception of Jude, a divine stranger—was the offense.

- The ancient Near Eastern cultures, the Classic Greek culture, and the Greco-Roman culture all subscribed to a natural order in which the male was to play the insertive or active role and the female the receptive or passive role. Sex was conditioned by gender roles, which is what Paul means in Romans by "according to nature." To act "against nature" was to have men playing the role of a woman, which meant the passive, receptive role.

- The idea of *nature* in biblical times does not have the same meaning as *nature* over the past thousand years, when philosophers or scientists describe the "laws of nature," which reflect alleged rules that cause the universe to unfold as it does. To read the modern scientific use of the term back into Paul's use of the concept of nature is to misinterpret Paul.

- The abominations to which the Leviticus passages refer are practices that exploit and abuse the other. Within the cultural context of post-exilic Israel, they referred to practices that threatened the clan by compromising the "natural" order of male dominance. These were the practices of Israel's neighbors that Israel was to avoid.

- Prostitution practices exploited and abused the stranger: the immigrant slave, the poor, and the powerless, who were also made in the image of God; therefore these acts were an abomination.

- Paul rejected the practice of whoremongers (*arsenikoitēs*) who (a) used and abused their own boy slaves or those boys sold into prostitution for

185

sexual gratification, (b) used male prostitutes (*malakos*) who may have offered sexual services for a fee, or (c) practiced pederasty. He may have meant all of them. In all cases, the *arsenikoitēs* used sex for self-serving pleasure at the expense of the *malakos*.

- The issue in Romans is human idolatry, the rejection of the creator God whose presence is obvious all around them and the choice to worship other things; and with that worship comes practices that are comparable to what today most people would consider promiscuous lifestyles.

- Theologically, these kinds of behaviors are consistent with idolatry—turning sexual pleasure into a god and giving oneself to it and taking what one can to satisfy selfish desires.

To the extent this analysis is faithful to the biblical stories, one can conclude that the Bible is silent on the forms of committed same-sex relationships that are the center of the modern discussion. At the same time, the Bible is exceedingly clear about the dehumanizing effects of turning sexual pleasures and their pursuits into gods, regardless of the kinds of sexual expression—gay or straight.

Notes

1. For more reading on the life and roles of Roman women, see *Roman Women* by Eve D'Ambra (2006) or *Women in the World of the Earliest Christians: Illuminating Ancient Ways of Life* by Lynn H. Cohick (2009).

2. Most of the literature we have from the ancient world was written by upper-class men. This means their perspectives and values were reflected in what they wrote. There was a female writer named Sappho (ca. 630 BC) who lived on the Island of Lesbos. It is from this island and Sappho that we get our word *lesbian*. (Nissinen 1998 [2004], 74–76).

3. The relationship was hierarchical, but obligations were mutual. The *patronus* was the protector, sponsor, and benefactor of the client; the technical term for this protection was *patrocinium* (Quinn 1982, 117).

4. In a patron-client social structure, there is always someone to whom you owe allegiance as well as someone who owes it to you. Within such a structure, a man may have someone with whom he plays the active role. But likewise, there may be someone to whom he is subservient, and thus he plays the passive role.

5. We have already explored the current viewpoint that human sexuality falls along a continuum between heterosexuality and homosexuality, with most humans falling somewhere between. But the point is that it was binary in the ancient world.

6. They were a Jewish ascetic sect. In some ways they were like the Essenes, yet they were different in that they were also influenced by Hellenism and therefore Platonism. For more information, visit the website for the Jewish Encyclopedia, http://www.jewish encyclopedia.com/articles/14366-therapeutae.

7. A catamite was a boy or man who was the receiving partner in sex. It comes from the Latin word *catamitus*.

8. This text and many others like it have been traditionally understood as referring to sacred prostitution. Recent scholarship has cast a pretty dark shadow over the whole constructed world of sacred prostitution. It is not in the purview of this book to go into this, for it does not support my argument. See *The Myth of Sacred Prostitution in Antiquity* by Stephanie Lynn Budin (2008).

9. A mash-up is a product that brings together several different content pieces and puts them together—or mashes them together.

10. All of these words we read through our twenty-first-century lenses, importing what we know into how we understand them.

11. Gagnon subscribes to the reading of the compound word *man bedder*, meaning a man who goes to bed with males: "It is a neologism, occurring for the first time in extant literature here in 1 Cor 6:9 and later in 1 Tim 1:10" (2001).

12. Scroggs goes on to limit the meaning to Greek pederasty, but subsequent scholars have mostly set this view aside.

13. Penetrative practices included vaginal (in women), intercrural, anal, and oral.

14. The Greek words usually associated with formal pederasty were *erastes* for the dominant partner and *eromenos* for the passive.

15. See also Nissinen [1998] 2004.

16. It has become customary within scholarly circles to look at these vice lists used by New Testament authors as relatively standard lists that would have been commonplace in the first century. Paul, for example, pulls from these lists multiple times and in different configurations to meet his purposes. These lists would have been known to his readers. See Harrell 1999.

17. The CEB conflates the two Greek words *malakos* and *arsenokoitēs* into the phrase "both participants in same-sex intercourse."

18. The Greek is the plural second person pronoun. It is important in this text to understand that Paul is speaking to them collectively. Thus I have inserted the word *all* in brackets to emphasize this point.

19. There are some who would suggest that a fourth alternative would be male sacred prostitutes. But as mentioned before, current scholarship has brought the entire sacred prostitute theory into question. Further research would be required for this to be added to the list here.

20. The letters say they are from Paul, but many scholars do not think Paul the apostle is in fact the author. But for the purposes of this discussion, it really does not

matter. The Pastoral Letters are part of the "received text" and as such are part of our rule of faith.

21. There is a secondary discussion that is beyond the scope of this study that considers the question: Who really was under Torah? In reading Paul in Romans, it is clear that the Jews alone were under Torah. Gentiles were still accountable to God for their idolatry but not because of a failure to live according to Torah, which was part of the covenant God made with Israel.

22. I do not mean to suggest there were not Christian life implications prior to chapter 12. Rather, my point is that it is at Romans 12:1 that Paul himself gives a large *therefore* that points forward. Given all that has proceeded, these are some real implications for life together in the Roman church that is comprised of Jews and Gentiles alike.

23. The most divine Caesar...we should consider equal to the Beginning of all things...; for when everything was falling [into disorder] and tending toward dissolution, he restored it once more and gave to the whole world a new aura; Caesar...the common good Fortune of all...the beginning of life and vitality....All the cities unanimously adopt the birthday of the divine Caesar as the new beginning of the year....Whereas Providence, which has regulated our whole existence...has brought our life to the climax of perfection in giving to us [the emperor] Augustus, whom it [Providence] filled with strength for the welfare of men, and who being sent to us and our descendants as Savior, has put an end to war and has set all things in order; and [whereas,] having become [god] manifest (*phaneis*), Caesar has fulfilled all the hopes of earlier times... in surpassing all the benefactors who preceded him..., and whereas, finally, the birthday of the god [Augustus] has been for the whole world the beginning of good news (*euangelion*) concerning him [therefore let a new era begin from his birth]. (Dittenberger 1905 in Horsley 2003, 27–28)

24. In the CEB, the phrase *dikaiosunē theou* is translated "God's righteousness."

25. Gal 3:28-29: "There is no longer Jew or Greek, there is no longer slave or free, there is no longer male and female; for all of you are one in Christ Jesus. And if you belong to Christ, then you are Abraham's offspring, heirs according to the promise" (NRSV).

26. See Phil 2:8.

27. This phrase comes from the tagline of a new church in Irvine, California, that my wife Debbie and I often participate in. It is called Canvas Church: Inviting everyone to join in God's project of new creation (see CanvasOC.org).

28. Hellenistic Jews were those who did not live in Palestine and who were more likely to be influenced by Greek and Roman culture.

29. Paul may have used the Septuagint (LXX), which was a Greek translation of the Hebrew scriptures. The Wisdom of Solomon would have been part of that collection.

30. This is consistently Gagnon's view, but as I have said, I believe this reflects his own presuppositions. There are good arguments regarding "what is natural" referring to what are the normal—for them—practices. We see this in the situation in 1 Corinthians when Paul states that it is not natural for a man to have long hair.

Chapter 8
Constructing a Theology of Inclusion

A Fixed Point in an Evolving World

I was having coffee one day with a friend and pastor colleague, the Reverend Kirk Winslow. I don't even remember the content of our discussion other than it was theology. Kirk and I are inclined to talk theology when together. He was referring to something Miroslav Volf told him when he was a graduate student at Fuller Seminary. Volf said, "You are going to have to put one anchor pole in the ground, and everything else must be understood in light of that." I continue to think about that comment because of its simplicity. For all of the profound and challenging and exciting ideas that make up the biblical story in all of its diversity and complexity (and sometimes contradictions), is there one single and simple idea that makes sense out of it all? Is there a single anchoring idea that gives meaning and definition and by which everything else must be evaluated or judged? With the question put that way, I think most of us who have been Christians for a while would answer, "Yes, it is love."

I would agree. But having made this claim, do we really let it play that defining role or do we fudge on it? Do other ideas sometimes take precedence over love? Does love consistently guide and shape our behavior as individuals and as the church? This chapter addresses these issues, but it will also provide a framework for a theology of inclusion. Obviously the primary focus of this book is inclusion for LGBT people, so we will look back to strides we have made to be inclusive of the "other" as well as look forward toward groups who remain in the "other" category. My approach will use the stories and teachings of Jesus because they are real, accessible, and concrete.

189

Love as the Anchor

We begin with the idea of love as the anchor. What does that mean? How can love be that one single anchoring pole? What makes love more than a romantic affection or idealistic moral value? Put simply, love is defined as that which God extends to all of creation. God loves creation, "all creatures great and small." This love is reflected in the message of God's coming kingdom and enacted in the death of Jesus on the cross. It was vindicated in Jesus's resurrection from the dead. And Jesus now extends it as Lord of heaven and earth, where he has been enthroned at the right side of the Almighty. This is the image in Daniel 7.

> As I continued to watch this night vision of mine, I suddenly saw one like a human being* coming with the heavenly clouds. He came to the ancient one and was presented before him. Rule, glory, and kingship were given to him; all peoples, nations, and languages will serve him. His rule is an everlasting one—it will never pass away!—his kingship is indestructible. (vv. 13-14)
> *Like a son of man.

Everything is redefined around this one central idea/action. This is the one pole. I anchor everything in my life to the notion that God exists and that God loves creation. Further, God loves the tremendous diversity that has unfolded within creation. That same love "weeps" over the brokenness that we humans have created, but that sorrow has not diminished God's love for us. In fact, on the cross, God has demonstrated the extent to which God will go to rescue us from our own self-destruction and the world from demonic evil. In John's Gospel this is summed up in that often-repeated verse, John 3:16: "God so loved the world that he gave his only Son, so that everyone who believes in him won't perish but will have eternal life."

This one statement captures God's love for us. Unfortunately, John 3:16 is used so often and out of context that it produces a negative reaction in people. It is inevitable that someone will print *John 3:16* on a poster and make sure it gets in front of a camera at sporting events. It is not a little amusing that most people under thirty have no idea what John 3:16 means! But consider what it says. God loved creation so much that God sent Jesus to be for the world what it could not be for itself, so that we humans might have life in the age to come.[1]

Paul's letter to the Romans has always been a home and comfort for me because it so brilliantly outlines how God loves creation. One text from Romans 5 adds to our conceptualization of God's love for us, and it also ties back to Romans 1, where we started our conversation about Romans in the previous chapter. In Romans 1, Paul begins his argument by stating that humans have exchanged the glory of God for gods of their own creation and let their desires run amok. We saw this when looking at Romans 1 in the prior chapter. God honored human choice and left us to our own devices. Paul called that the wrath of God. But while God let us pursue our own desires, because of God's great love for us, God covenanted to bring healing and reconciliation even when we were in that state of rejection. These verses summarize that:

> But God shows his love for us, because while we were still sinners Christ died for us. So, now that we have been made righteous by his blood, we can be even more certain that we will be saved from God's wrath through him. If we were reconciled to God through the death of his Son while we were still enemies, now that we have been reconciled, how much more certain is it that we will be saved by his life? (Rom 5:8-10)

God's love is God acting on our behalf even when we did not know or acknowledge our need of rescue. This is not just an idea; this is what God has done. Love is an action. Ephesians 2:4-5 captures this extremely well: "However, God is rich in mercy. He brought us to life with Christ while we were dead as a result of those things that we did wrong [i.e., idolatry]. He did this because of the great love that he has for us. You are saved [rescued] by God's grace!"

This is the center of my theology, and I believe it reflects the core and primary motive of the entire biblical story. It is all about the love of God. In fact, I believe this is the central anchor point that must inform all others.

Rob Bell's controversial book, *Love Wins: A Book about Heaven, Hell, and the Fate of Every Person Who Ever Lived*, makes a similar point. Gather together all of the various threads of the biblical story, and they tie into a single message: God loves creation. God has acted to redeem creation. I believe all of the other ideas that we associate with God are subordinate to this one single idea.

Several church leaders condemned Bell. Mark Galli immediately wrote a book titled *God Wins: Heaven, Hell and Why the Good News Is Better Than Love Wins*. While I was speaking in our church about *Love Wins*, one person brought Galli's book and, holding it up, insisted that justice was just as important as love. I agreed that justice is important. Justice is about God setting the world right. But that is not the view of justice this particular person held. For him justice was about punishing the evildoer. Many conservative Christians need the evildoer to be punished. God maintains integrity this way. If

God lets anyone off, then God is not fair or just. So justice has to be equal to love. If it isn't, then love is reduced to sentimentality in their minds.

This dualistic thinking is not the biblical view of love or justice. If justice is about setting right what is wrong, bringing creation back (or forward) to what it should be, then it is not about punishing the evildoer, it is about fixing what is not right. And what is the motive behind this? The scriptures teach us that it is the covenant love and faithfulness of God. (See discussion in chapter 2 about *hesed*.) Because God loves creation, God makes a covenant with it to bring it fully into its potential, a potential that is diminished by human sin and rebellion but restored by grace—substantially in this life and fully in the life to come. Justice only has meaning within the matrix of love. God's acts of love always win out.[2] That truly is "good news" for all of us.

All of the rest of the biblical story is the working out of the love of God for creation. It is the one fixed point in an ever-changing world. Faith, hope, and love, but the greatest is love.[3] Justice, mercy, and grace, as well, have their origin in the love of God. It is the anchor. Thus when we approach the question of homosexuality theologically, the love of God for creation must be the place we begin. All other pieces of the conversation must revolve around and be evaluated by this central message, a message that was enacted by God in the incarnation of Jesus, ultimately expressed in his death, and vindicated in his resurrection.

How Do We Respond to Such Love?

How does one respond to such love? The obvious answer is to receive and reciprocate that love. To address this question I turn to the Gospel of Luke:

> A legal expert stood up to test Jesus. "Teacher," he said, "what must I do to gain eternal life?" Jesus replied, "What is written in the Law? How do you interpret it?" He responded, "*You must love the Lord your God with all your heart, with all your being, with all your strength, and with all your mind, and love your neighbor as yourself.*" Jesus said to him, "You have answered correctly. Do this and you will live." But the legal expert wanted to *prove that he was right,** so he said to Jesus, "And who is my neighbor?"[4] (10:25-28)
> *Many translations use the phrase "justify himself."

A legal expert was trained in Torah instruction and thus a specialist in its proper and traditional teaching.[5] He wants to test Jesus to see if he will depart from the traditional readings and perhaps find cause for taking action against him. Jesus, however, turns it around and asks the expert a question.

The Summary of Torah

So what was the expert's question? "What must I do to inherit eternal life?" This is quite a question. Let's first look at what the words *eternal life* mean and then what question he is *not* asking. How we translate these two words and then what we generally assume they mean creates a major disconnect in properly understanding the question. Within the Judaism of Jesus's time, it was believed that the current evil age would finally come to an end when God returned as king to set the world right. When that happened, this world with its sickness, evil, oppression, poverty, and heartache—death itself—would give way to true life as God intended it and last forever. The promise of the covenant was that God's people alone would enjoy the blessings and benefits of the new age, the everlasting age to come. This is what the Torah expert is asking about: What must I do to make sure I inherit the blessings of the new age?

Now let's consider what it does *not* mean. It does not mean, "How do I get saved so I can go to heaven?" meaning stepping out of this space-time universe and into some kind of timeless eternal reality. The real question is: What must I do to participate in the coming kingdom of God and all that comes with that?

Jesus answers by turning it around and asking the Torah expert a different question. "What is written in the law (Torah)? What do you read there?" Jesus is not referring to some abstract law that sets the rules by which people get in or not. He is referring specifically to the Torah, and he is challenging this expert in Torah to summarize the teaching of Torah. The lawyer says "to love God" and "love your neighbor as yourself." These two commandments come from two different places in the Old Testament. The first comes from Deuteronomy 6, which is also called the "Shema": "Israel, listen! Our God is the LORD! Only the LORD! Love the LORD your God with all your heart, all your being, and all your strength" (vv. 4-5). The second comes from Leviticus 19:18: "You must not take revenge nor hold a grudge against any of your people; instead, you must love your neighbor as yourself; I am the LORD."

Let's look at the first of these two more closely before we consider how they answer the question. What does it mean to love God with your whole heart, whole being, and all your strength? The simple answer is to give one's self totally to God. But how many of us can say we do that? Perhaps a better way of coming at this is through the idea of trust—trust God with your whole self. To love is to trust, and to trust is to believe there is a good reason to trust; that in not trusting, something will be lacking. Love and trust go together, but they are not abstract ideas in Deuteronomy. Israel's God was the

God who delivered them from slavery, who made a covenant with her ancestor Abraham. Israel's God was YHWH, who promised to heal and restore and set right all that is wrong through the Israelite people. So if you are going to trust in someone, trust in YHWH, love YHWH, because YHWH had promised to love Israel and made a covenant that stipulated that promise.

If we look at the somewhat parallel story in Mark 12, we have an additional element. In Mark, the question is asked, and it is Jesus who answers, and the Scribe says, "Well said, Teacher. You have truthfully said that God is one and there is no other besides him. And to love God with all of the heart, a full understanding, and all of one's strength, and to love one's neighbor as oneself is much more important than all kinds of entirely burned offerings and sacrifices" (vv. 32b-33).

Jesus agrees; that is the right answer. In these two commands, one finds the entire teaching of the Torah brought to a single point. So Jesus says, "Do this, and you will live." He means if you live this way, you will inherit the blessings of the age to come. Do this, and you will be assured of your inheritance as a child of God. It's as simple as that. To love God and neighbor is more important than all of the temple practices. These practices that defined Israel as Israel are relativized—that is, they only have meaning to the extent they are expressions of loving God and neighbor, not in place of.

Who Is My Neighbor?

But wait, is that correct? Can we merely love God and our neighbor and be assured of a place in the kingdom of God? We of course answer, "No! Because we can't!" Correct? That would mean one could "earn" one's salvation, and we all know that is not correct—or so we are told, at least within the Reformed tradition of which I am a part. And our objections seem—pun intended—justified because of what comes next:

> But the legal expert wanted to prove *that he was right*, so he said to Jesus, "And who is my neighbor?" Jesus replied, "A man went down from Jerusalem to Jericho. He encountered thieves, who stripped him naked, beat him up, and left him near death. Now it just so happened that a priest was also going down the same road. When he saw the injured man, he crossed over to the other side of the road and went on his way. Likewise, a Levite came by that spot, saw the injured man, and crossed over to the other side of the road and went on his way. A Samaritan, who was on a journey, came to where the man was. But when he saw him, he was moved with compassion. The Samaritan went to him and bandaged his wounds, tending them with oil and wine. Then he placed the wounded man on his own donkey, took

him to an inn, and took care of him. The next day, he took two full days' worth of wages and gave them to the innkeeper. He said, 'Take care of him, and when I return, I will pay you back for any additional costs.' What do you think? Which one of these three was a neighbor to the man who encountered thieves?" Then the legal expert said, "The one who demonstrated mercy toward him." Jesus told him, "Go and do likewise." (Luke 10:29-37, emphasis added)

Luke tells us that the expert wanted to "prove that he was right" or, as many translations say, "justify" himself, so he asked Jesus another question, "Who is my neighbor?" But what is meant by this? When some Protestants—at least Reformed ones—hear the word *justify* they think *sola fide* or "justification by faith alone without works." That would seem to be the opposite of someone wanting to justify himself or herself. And so we add to this story the idea that if we were perfect and without sin, we could love God and our neighbors as we ought to, then we could justify ourselves; but of course we are not perfect so we cannot. But if we read it like this, we have departed from the meaning and flow of the text, and we have certainly misunderstood both the prior question, "How do I inherit the blessings of the life to come?" and this new one "Who is my neighbor?"

We would better understand this comment about justifying oneself if we read it like this: "But wanting to vindicate or prove himself as a true Jew..." In other words, what is it that makes one a true child of the covenant? Where is the line? Who is in and who is out? I want to make sure I am in. It all revolves around where the line is between the neighbor and nonneighbor. The neighbor question is intended as a boundary marker, which defines who I am obligated to love according to Torah. And behind this is the entire religious/ political system and structures of status, privilege, and power of which he was a part and player—and had much to lose (Wright 1997, 304–5).

To answer his question, Jesus tells him a story. A Jew heads down the road from Jerusalem to Jericho, perhaps on his way home from participation in some temple festival or practice. It is a dangerous road as everyone knows, and he is attacked, robbed, beaten, and left for dead. Fortunately, a priest was coming down the road behind him, who, perhaps having completed his temple obligation, was also heading home, but he passes him by. Likewise a Levite, who most likely was also a priest and perhaps had also just completed temple obligations, passes him by. But a Samaritan comes along and stops and gives him aid. This is a curious example for Jesus to use because in Luke 9, Jesus's request to pass through the land of the Samaritans had been rejected.

There was a visceral hatred between the Samaritans and the Jews.[6] And yet here is a Samaritan moved by pity and showing compassion on this poor Jew.

How are we to think about this parable? First, this is not primarily a moral tale about how we ought to show compassion to those in need—though it certainly teaches this. Second, it points out that the real question of the expert was not, "Who is my neighbor?" Instead he wants to know, "Who is not my neighbor?" He needed to know so he would know to whom he was obligated to care about according to Torah. Third, outsiders were living faithful to the Torah and thus coming into the kingdom, living the life of the kingdom in their actions, while those who presumed to be the children of the covenant by birth were not. Fourth, this meant the boundaries that defined Israel were being radically redrawn by Jesus, while he remained faithful to the true, core teaching of Torah. In the redrawing, some who assumed they were in may not be, and many assumed to be out were indeed in. Finally, this would suggest that covenant community membership was not based upon status or ancestry but upon love that enacts love.

Who Was the Neighbor?

Jesus answers the expert by asking him a question: "Which of these three was a neighbor to the poor Jew?" The expert answers: the one who showed mercy to the person in need. Loving the neighbor is about action, not ancestry. So Jesus tells him, "Go and do likewise and you too will inherit the blessings of the new age as a child of God" (my paraphrase). We don't know what the lawyer did. We don't know if he chose to embrace what Jesus was teaching or rejected it. But we do have a much clearer understanding of Torah and how to be a child of the new age. N. T. Wright in response to the question, "What must I do to find life in the age to come?," says,

> follow Jesus in finding a new and radicalized version of Torah-observance. Loving Israel's covenant god meant loving him as creator of all, and discovering as neighbors those who were beyond the borders of the chosen people. Those who followed Jesus in this way would be "justified"; that is they would be vindicated when the covenant god acted climatically within history. "Go and do likewise." (1997, 307)

Now back to our original question. What must we do to inherit eternal life? Is the way we gain it different than what Jesus has told this expert? No, if we understand what he says here. For the question being asked is not how we get into heaven. Our inheritance and destination, as our expert correctly understood, is a place in the age to come. But assuming this, is it by grace or works? The singular voice of the entire biblical witness is that participation in the life of God and God's new creation is and always has been by God's all loving grace expressed in the covenant with creation to heal, restore, and set it right. And this great hope and gift is and always has been ours by faith, that is, by trust in God.

This brings us back to the summary teaching of Torah to love God and our neighbor. To love God is, at minimum, to trust God, to cast ourselves on God's grace and the divine promise that indeed all things will be made new, that creation will one day be as it ought to be, including our very selves. As God's children, as members of the new covenant people, we share our unbounded love of others who are all part of God's creation. We do not draw lines around status or ethnicity or nationalism or sex or gender or orientation. This is how we reciprocate God's love for us: we love. We do not try to create artificial boundaries that include some as neighbors and others as not. In fact, for Israel, her own history reminded her of the need to love not just other Israelites but also the "stranger." In Deuteronomy 10, Moses reflects on the journey after the smashing of the first set of tablets upon which were cut the Ten Commandments. Moses asks, "What does the LORD your God ask of you?" (v. 12b). He answers: to love the Lord, to keep God's commandments, and not to forget where they came from. Their lowly estate in slavery should remind them of how to treat one another because that is how the Lord is, and that is who they were: "He enacts justice for orphans and widows, and he loves immigrants, giving them food and clothing. That means you must also love immigrants *because you were immigrants in Egypt*" (Deut 10:18-19, emphasis added).

The election of Israel ("But the LORD adored your ancestors, loving them and choosing the descendants that followed them—you!—from all other people." [Deut 10:15]) was so that through Israel the entire world would be rescued. She had been called out of the world in order to be a gift back to the world. She had been a stranger but was so no longer, and now she was to embrace the stranger. Who is the stranger? The stranger is the person who at least at the moment of encounter is outside the covenant community. But the vocation of Israel was to embrace the stranger and introduce him or her into the covenant community where the stranger encounters the true God.

So how does one respond to the wonder of God's love? We should give ourselves to God to live as God has called us to live, which strangely means to be like God; we should love as God loves, and love whom God loves: your neighbor, which includes the stranger.

Two Jesus Stories of Inclusion

While reading the Gospels, one is immediately impressed with how Jesus consistently embraced the social outcast and the stranger. This is how the kingdom comes. I am not saying that the LGBT person is a stranger. But from a social standpoint, especially in large quarters of the religious community, LGBT people are treated as social outcasts. The challenge to us within the religious community is concrete if we actually look at how Jesus dealt with this problem vis-à-vis the Pharisees. Therefore, to extend the principle that to love God is to love the neighbor (who includes the outcast), we look at two stories in which Jesus addressed the issue of inclusion.

Saving All the Wrong People

The first story comes from that moment in Luke when Jesus shows up in the synagogue in his home community of Nazareth. In Luke's telling of the Jesus story, Jesus begins his public career in his hometown, where he announces his manifesto:

> Jesus went to Nazareth, where he had been raised. On the Sabbath he went to the synagogue as he normally did and stood up to read. The synagogue assistant gave him the scroll from the prophet Isaiah. He unrolled the scroll and found the place where it was written: *The Spirit of the Lord is upon me, because the Lord has anointed me. He has sent me to preach good news to the poor, to proclaim release to the prisoners and recovery of sight to the blind, to liberate the oppressed, and to proclaim the year of the Lord's favor.* He rolled up the scroll, gave it back to the synagogue assistant, and sat down. Every eye in the synagogue was fixed on him. He began to explain to them, "Today, this scripture has been fulfilled just as you heard it." (4:16-21)

Jesus announced that he had come, as Isaiah had prophesied, to set free the captives.[7] Then, having read from Isaiah, he says, "Today, this scripture has been fulfilled just as you heard it." What follows is a somewhat confusing story of how this message was received, following several exchanges between Jesus and the people of his village. First they respond with amazement: "Everyone was raving about Jesus, so impressed were they by the gracious words flowing from his lips. They said, "This is Joseph's son, isn't it?" (Luke 4:22). But suddenly they were enraged and sought to kill Jesus. Why? What sent them into murderous rage? We could easily imagine them tearing their clothes and freaking out with the initial words Jesus said about what's happening, now, here, today. But initially they were impressed "by the gracious words." What initially impressed and then enraged them? Some read it as an evaluation of his speaking ability; as in he speaks really well! But is that what Luke cared about? Most likely not. The Greek syntax or word order has "words of grace," where *grace* translates as *charis*. I believe an alternative reading proposed by N. T. Wright makes better sense of the overall passage and how they go from being impressed to being in a killing rage. Wright suggests that a better reading would be, "They were amazed at his teaching about grace—God's grace." This is what the Isaiah passage is talking about: the grace of God that promised the restoration of all people. So what about the comment about Joseph's son? Think of it as Jesus being a "favorite son." If you have been doing good things out there, what are you going to do for us? You speak about grace, so what grace will you show us, your own people?

Jesus, from the perspective of Luke, knows what is really behind their comments. They expect him to show them special treatment, and so he responds to the unspoken presumption with two statements. First, he says that they will tell him cure himself—that is, to do here at home what he has done elsewhere; surely he is going to take better care of them. They see Jesus as theirs, and that should provide them some advantage. If he did so much in Capernaum, he should do even more in Nazareth! But Jesus stands their expectation on its head with a proverb about a prophet never being accepted in his hometown. Now I can imagine the crowd barely having recovered from his first comment before being thrown again by the second. He is saying that his people won't accept him. Why? Before one can even begin to answer, he throws out two examples of just how Israel had done the same thing twice before, first to the prophet Elijah and then to Elisha.

The reference to Elijah refers to the time there was a famine in the land because of Israel's sin. Elijah is sent to help a non-Israelite widow and her son. The reference to Elisha refers to the time that Elisha healed not only a non-Israelite but also a general of the Syrian army, an enemy of Israel who was also a leper. What is going on here? What is true about both of these stories? In both cases a prophet of God extends grace to an outsider, to a person whose social status was outside the covenant boundary. The first was a Sidonian widow. She was not an Israelite; and while Israel suffered, she received grace from the prophet of God. The second was Naaman, a Syrian general. Again, he was not an Israelite and was the general of the enemy army; and what's worse, he was a leper! Neither of these people should have been the recipients of God's grace according to the common understanding of the day. In fact, this illustrates once again the problem. Israel, the chosen people, was called to be the light to the world but instead sought to keep the light for themselves.

And here is Jesus saying, I am like Elijah and Elisha. I am proclaiming and effecting release to all the poor, especially those outside the bounds.

That was it! That is what drove them into a rage! As N. T. Wright says, based upon what Jesus was saying, God was about to rescue the wrong people! Jesus was not going to be the favorite son, giving special favors to Nazareth. He was going to set everyone free! Good news to the poor did not just mean Israel under Rome and the Herods. Good news to the poor included the widow, the unclean, the Gentile, and any of low status. He was not coming to destroy Israel's enemies; he was coming to extend God's grace to everyone and heal them. God's kingdom was an inclusive kingdom. It was to be a dominion in which love and grace and mercy were extended to all, regardless of social status or ethnicity (Wright 1997, 264–74).

Jesus and a Crippled Woman

The second story is found in Luke 13:10–17:10, which is an extended narrative whose primary focus is on what qualifies a person for, and therefore who will participate in, the kingdom of God (Green 2010, 516–615). In a real sense, it is a direct confrontation with the exclusivity that had become normative for Second Temple Judaism. This exclusivism is historically understandable if we remember that the problem for Israel was always sliding off into unfaithful idolatry. To counteract this, there was a strong emphasis on the separateness of the children of Israel. Some groups such as the Essenes physically separated themselves by moving off into desert enclaves to avoid contact with the unfaithful even in Israel. Others, such as the Pharisees, did so by strict purity and Sabbath regulations based upon Torah. The result was to create clear boundary markers between different Jewish groups and ethnic Israelites and their Gentile neighbors (Wright 1997, 301–7) Of special note in this passage is the group of people referred to as "sinners." This was a derogatory term with somewhat fuzzy boundaries for some Jews, who from the perspective of the religious—the Pharisees—were second-class citizens because they did not live in strict accordance with Torah. Within this group would have been those who clearly acted contrary to Torah, such as thieves, prostitutes, tax collectors, and those afflicted with some kind of mental or physical malady, but it also included poor Jews who simply did not have the time or resources to follow all of the religious regulations.

The Pharisees wanted to purify Israel, believing that doing so would quicken the return of the Messiah as king. To accomplish this, they drew firm boundaries between those who were considered part of the covenant people of God and those who were not. But this was contrary to Israel's calling. Israel's election as the people of God was so that she could be the light to the world.[8] You don't light a lamp and hide it under a table. You set it on the table where it can spread its light around the room—even to the four corners of the world. Within Second Temple Judaism, the Messiah was expected to return as a king and redeem the true Israel. And that is why it was important to know who was "in" and who was "out." The Pharisees had a scheme worked out, and Jesus hit that scheme head on:

> Jesus was teaching in one of the synagogues on the Sabbath. A woman was there who had been disabled by a spirit for eighteen years. She was bent over and couldn't stand up straight. When he saw her, Jesus called her to him and said, "Woman, you are set free from your sickness." He placed his hands on her and she straightened up at once and praised God. The synagogue leader, incensed that Jesus had healed on the Sabbath, responded, "There are six days during which work is permitted. Come and be healed on those days, not on the Sabbath day." The Lord replied, "Hypocrites! Don't each of you on the Sabbath untie your ox or donkey from its stall and lead it out to get a drink? Then isn't it necessary that this woman, a daughter of Abraham, bound by Satan for eighteen long years, be set free from her bondage on the Sabbath day?" When he said these things, all his opponents were put to shame, but all those in the crowd rejoiced at all the extraordinary things he was doing. Jesus asked, "What is God's kingdom like? To what can I compare it? It's like a mustard seed that someone took and planted in a garden. It grew and developed into a tree and the birds in the sky nested in its branches." Again he said, "To what can I compare God's kingdom? It's like yeast, which a woman took and hid in a bushel of wheat flour until the yeast had worked its way through the whole." (Luke 13:10-21)

What Jesus Saw

The scene is a Jewish religious gathering. In that time the men and women were separated for prayers and Torah reading, with priority given to the men. Imagine Jesus sitting in the center of the gathering space with the leader next to him. It is no doubt a terribly awkward situation, for Jesus was well known by now and the leader would have been of the Pharisees. The leader was influential in the community and had high social standing. Yet here is Jesus, this upstart, self-proclaimed teacher/prophet ready to teach in his synagogue. Jesus looks out at the crowd and sees a woman crippled and bent over in the women's section, most likely at the back of the room—perhaps even outside the door—certainly not immediately visible. She was most likely a social outcast living on the margins of the community—invisible in their midst, suffering from some unknown disease. Yet this is the person Jesus sees and to whom he calls out. But even more, if we keep in mind the way the synagogue would have been laid out, Jesus is not near her, and yet Luke's next comment is that he laid hands on her. Given her condition, Jesus had to have gone to her, a totally scandalous act itself. Reaching her, he touches her (another taboo) and sets her free of her ailment. She stands up and praises God.

This is the first time Jesus teaches in a synagogue in Luke's telling, since that opening declaration of his manifesto described in Luke 4. And what was the center piece of that manifesto? "The Spirit of the Lord is upon me, because he has anointed me to bring good news to the poor. He has sent me to proclaim release to the captives and recovery of sight to the blind, to let the oppressed go free, to proclaim the year of the Lord's favor" (vv. 18-19 NRSV).

Here he is, doing exactly what he had declared, setting free a captive. He is doing exactly what the Messiah was supposed to be doing. What Jesus saw was a "daughter of Abraham," who was suffering physically but who was also suffering as one outside the covenant community. Her maladies would likely have left her unable to fulfill the practices of Torah as defined by the Pharisees. She was unclean, and yet this is the person Jesus sees and touches.

What the Synagogue Leader Saw

What did the synagogue leader see? Did he see the one expected to come and set captive Israel free? Did he see the woman who had been hanging around the fringes of their gatherings each week for eighteen years, suffering? No! What he saw was a teacher disregarding one of the rules about the Sabbath! He worked! He broke one of the Sabbath practices that marked him off as a true child of the covenant.

Perhaps an analogy will help us better understand. I have heard on more than one occasion the complaint about how some kids and adults dress when they come to worship. One person actually said, "They can dress like that all week if they want; why can't they dress like they should on Sunday when they come to church?" Such well-intentioned church people may be completely blind to what is actually going on with these inappropriately dressed people. What immediately jumps out to these parishioners is that others are not living up to the rules and expectations. In fact, in the complaining parishioner's mind, these people are really socially marginal—not really inside *our* community.

Jesus was breaking a rule that was more important in the leader's mind than the captivity of a distressed woman. Jesus wasted no time in his response. Visualize again the scene. Jesus is tending to the woman when the leader makes his statement. I can see Jesus turning on his heels and looking toward the front where all the important people in the community sat. Focusing his full gaze on them, he calls out, "Hypocrites! Don't each of you on the Sabbath untie your ox or donkey from its stall and lead it out to get a drink? Then isn't it necessary that this woman [and note what he calls her], a daughter of Abraham, bound by Satan for eighteen long years, be set free from her bondage on the Sabbath day?" (Luke 13:15-16).

Two Parables of the Kingdom

Jesus proceeds to teach using two parables to help people understand what he intends to do, namely, bring in God's kingdom. The first compares the kingdom to a mustard seed that is sown and when grown becomes a tree so big that birds nest in it. The kingdom will grow over time. This is in contrast to the coercive power and immediate confrontation many thought was needed to establish the kingdom. Not only that, but others from the outside will find a home in it and take advantage of its safety. The kingdom becomes a place of welcome and refuge, which had always been Israel's calling. The second parable compares the kingdom of God to yeast. Take just a little bit; mix it into a people, and the process will begin to transform them all. What is the kingdom transforming? A people enslaved under the domain of the Satan and all who represent evil.

So, here is this socially inconsequential woman; yet for those who can see, Jesus is planting the kingdom. Satan's kingdom has been invaded with the yeast of God's kingdom, and the result is a woman freed from captivity. Or consider the mustard seed; the kingdom has been planted so even the social outcast can find her rightful place at home.

The Trouble with Boundaries

Israel's fundamental error was drawing a boundary line around itself and assuming only ethnic Israelites were the true people of God. This was what the Pharisees were doing, and as a result they excluded any who they thought failed to live up to their religious scruples or meet their standards. They spent a great deal of time defining where the boundary line was, defining who was in and who was out. The injured man in the Samaritan story was unclean because of his injuries. The townspeople of Nazareth tried to kill Jesus because he suggested that the grace of God extended to those outside of Israel. The crippled woman was out due to her social status as a woman and because she had a physical defect.

It is a human thing to create boundaries between people based upon some quality or characteristic. But Jesus's full embrace of all social outcasts speaks loudly. His critique of the religious leaders who excluded persons speaks even more loudly. Yet we humans make groups, and groups always have either spoken or unspoken rules of membership. In the field of set theory, such behavior is about the creation of a "bounded set" (Hiebert 1994, 110–33).

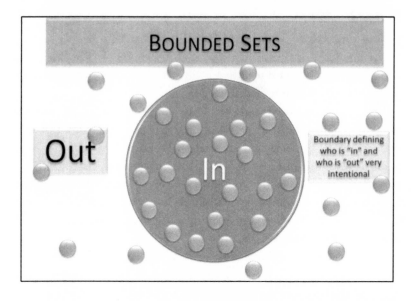

In a bounded set, a line is drawn based upon rules. These rules determine who is included and who is excluded. The graphic above clearly shows the line between in and out. Those excluded may not even know what the rules are. Those included do, mostly. The Pharisees' behavior was about establishing the rules of the bounded set of Israel and then monitoring the boundaries to make sure nobody was included that should not be. This was much of what their motivation was about in following Jesus around and questioning him at various moments. They were trying to catch him making an error so that they could exclude him: "As he left there, the legal experts and Pharisees began to resent him deeply and to ask him pointed questions about many things. They plotted against him, trying to trap him in his words"[9] (Luke 11:53-54).

Jesus however was throwing out the bounded set, saying it was and still is contrary to God's purpose of setting the world right. Rather, he is calling all to choose to follow him in what set theory would call a "centered set." If you examine a centered set, you can see it has shape and form, but it is based upon the fact that everyone included within the set is somewhere along the path toward the center, who is Jesus. In this model, the set that is defined is based upon self-selection. Those included are all traveling toward the same destination. There is no official boundary line based upon a set of rules. True disciples are those who by faith choose to orient their life around Jesus and to follow him while being faithful to what he is calling his new people to be about. Coming full circle, he is calling his people to love the neighbor.

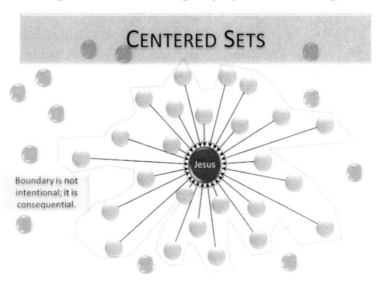

What does this have to do with the issue of full inclusion of LGBT persons? Boundary definition is innate to all groups, even to religious organizations. We can't help ourselves. There is an impulse to draw a line somewhere that defines who is included with all rights and privileges and who is not. In the church's past are many examples. Not many years ago, churches and their members bought and sold slaves based upon the belief that whites were superior to Africans and that the Bible supported this view. In 1885, the publisher Parker Pillsbury published a book by the Honorable James G. Birney titled *The American Churches, the Bulwarks of American Slavery.* His purpose was to chronicle the ways in which the churches in America participated in slavery and resisted its abolition. It is a compilation of quotes from newspapers and official denominational proceedings. The following quote is an example:

Chancellor Harper, of South Carolina—"It is the order of nature and of GOD, that the being of superior faculties and knowledge, and therefore of superior power, should control and dispose of those who are inferior. It is as much in the order of nature, that men should enslave each other, as that *other* animals should prey upon each other." (Birney 1885, 12)

This comment is valuable to this discussion for two reasons. First, it shows boundary definition used as a way to legitimate slavery. But second, it appeals to "the order of nature and of God." The second is curious because those most ardently opposed to embracing LGBT people are those who also appeal to "the order of nature" for justification.[10]

Later, after slavery was abolished, black people were still excluded from membership in white churches, in some cases deep into the twentieth century. Many white Methodist churches in the South did not allow blacks to worship with them as late as the 1960s (Nittle 2014). A truly sad example of very recent race-based boundary marking was the statement made by Bob Jones University (BJU) public spokesman at the time, Jonathan Pait, who in 1998 commented on the university's policy banning interracial dating:

God has separated people for his own purposes. He has erected barriers between the nations, not only land and sea barriers, but also ethnic, cultural, and language barriers. God has made people different from one another and intends those differences to remain. Bob Jones University is opposed to intermarriage of the races because it breaks down the barriers God has established. ("Bob Jones University Apologizes" 2009)

Fortunately, in 2008, BJU president Stephen Jones issued an apology for the university's past segregationist practices.

Women of course have known boundary marking that put them on the outside for most of human history. Indeed the chapters that detail the social structures of the ancient Near East and the Greco-Roman cultures provide plenty of examples of how women were to be kept in their place—sexually and otherwise. Bible verses are marshaled to support these boundary markers. For example, even our letters from Paul demonstrate that he, inspired though he was to provide us the best insights into how God is redeeming creation, was a man of his culture. Recent times have provided many examples of (sometimes tortured) interpretations of comments he made about the place and role of women as in this text from 1 Corinthians: "Like in all the churches of God's people, the women should be quiet during the meeting. They are not allowed to talk. Instead, they need to get under control, just as the Law says.

If they want to learn something, they should ask their husbands at home. It is disgraceful for a woman to talk during the meeting" (14:33b-35).

Fearing a compromise of biblical authority, some interpreters have worked overly hard to explain (away?) this text. Some insist to this day that this is how it is supposed to be. But most mainline Protestant denominations have long since drawn a line between Paul's central theological teaching and some of his teaching that showed him a man of his culture. Based upon these kinds of views, women were excluded from positions of leadership and were certainly not to teach men. Sadly and in contrast, our New Testament has many examples of women actively involved and providing leadership in the early decades of the church: Mary mother of Jesus, Martha and Mary of Bethany, Mary Magdalene, Tabitha, Junia, the Apostle, Phoebe, a deacon, and Priscilla; and these are just the ones mentioned. Surely there were more.[11]

It also was not long ago that divorced persons were not allowed to participate in church leadership (and still cannot in some extremely conservative churches). Those in power insisted that any of these people were welcome to attend worship (and one assumes to contribute money), but that was to be the extent of their proper participation. This, too, has changed, fortunately, in many church traditions.

Each of these examples demonstrates that there were in fact classes of "citizenship," and your class defined your status vis-à-vis membership. Those who tried to cross over into a different class—or, returning to our "set theory" model, those who tried to cross over into a different set where they were excluded—found that crossing lines was perilous. It did not take long before they discovered that there were rules and there was a line drawn and they were outside of it. Fortunately in many churches these exclusions have been removed; and African Americans, women, and divorced people are granted full membership based solely on their confession of faith in the faithfulness of Jesus. But the structures of many of these same churches that have broken down the walls of separation have kept them up relative to LGBT people.

In the ongoing LGBT debate, those promoting full inclusion often use slavery/segregation and the women's movement as models. For them it is a civil rights issue. (It is also a moral issue but often only engaged as civil rights issue.) It has also now become predictable that opponents of full inclusion of LGBT people will try to draw a distinction (boundary marking again) between slavery and the women's movement as true civil rights issues on the one hand and the LGBT issue as a moral issue (only) on the other. Though even a casual reading of material around each of these social movements shows much in common, those who oppose insist that there is a clear line between race and gender identity on the one hand and sexual orientation on the other when making their case.[12]

Let us return to our two stories of inclusion: the story of the crippled woman and the story about Jesus saving all the wrong people. These two stories reveal a theme that is fundamental to God's kingdom that Jesus was inaugurating. The returning king was returning for all people, and he condemned the "bounded set" practices of the Pharisees and other religious people who marginalized anyone. In fact, Jesus made it his habit to "hang out" with those most despised by the religious community. I suspect that today Jesus would be found hanging out with people from the LGBT community and that many religious folks would, like the Pharisees, stand outside and complain to his disciples about him associating with such iniquitous people. From the perspective of many religious communities, LGBT people are outside the bounds of God's covenant community, especially if they do not renounce, if not their orientation, then at least any same-sex behavior.

New Creation

Inclusion in the covenant community in the teaching of Jesus was simply about hearing and trusting him. Those who opened their hearts to him to follow became part of his new Israel. Paul understood this. The calling out of a new people of God was a central theme for him. Paul argues strongly more than once (but especially in Galatians) against any effort to make the Gentiles become Jews first. He understood that God was forming a new worldwide people in which all of the cultural boundaries and systems that divided people and segmented them were removed—even if he was not always consistent with this. This is stated most clearly in that classic statement from Galatians 3: "There is neither Jew nor Greek; there is neither slave nor free; nor is there male and female, for you are all one in Christ Jesus. Now if you belong to Christ, then indeed you are Abraham's descendants, heirs according to the promise" (vv. 28-29).

I remember this specific text especially well because it was on the exegesis portion of my ordination exams. I knew then that it was important to give the correct interpretation. In the mid-1980s, that interpretation needed to demonstrate why the inclusion of women in ordained leadership was supported by scripture. I must have handled it well enough because I passed my exams. But I am also sure that I really did not understand Paul. I did not understand that in this text, he is working out the theological and practical implications of the inauguration of the kingdom of God as expected in the

Hebrew scriptures. In Jesus's time, the expectation of the coming of the king was that Israel's enemies would be vanquished. But this was not really what the prophets had proclaimed. Rather, when the king returned, he would establish justice in Jerusalem. His rule would include both Jew and Gentile as one whole people of God. Paul would refer to this new people as the new or true Israel of God—a new creation. The enemies to be vanquished were sin and death and the evil that robs God's creation of life.

The End of Boundary Markers

Second Corinthians says, "So then, if anyone is in Christ, that *person is part of the new creation.* The old things have gone away, and look, new things have arrived!" (5:17, emphasis added). We often tell new believers they are a new creation. But it is a total abstraction that usually has little meaning to them. It is also not what Paul is saying. He is saying that those "in Christ" are those who by faith have been brought into the new people of God. The kingdom of God has been inaugurated. The new creation has begun even as the old creation continues. For those who have trusted Jesus to be the long expected Messiah who came to take away the sin of the world and be the firstborn of a new creation, they too have become part of this new creation. This means they have the hope that what has been started in them will be completed in the age to come.

A necessary component of this new creation is the end of those things that separate people. No longer should someone or a group be demeaned or excluded. Paul often encountered Jewish teachers who insisted that any Gentiles who became Christians first needed to become Jews, and for men that meant circumcision. Paul took a stand against this, and it was not because he sensed a proto-Pelagian works theology.[13] These leaders were not insisting that one needed circumcision in order to earn righteousness (right standing with God). Rather, for these teachers, circumcision was a sign of being "inside." For them it was about boundary markers. It was about a bounded set. The only way to really be a part of the people of God was to keep all of the practices of Torah. Paul stood adamantly against such teaching. So as he brings his letter to a close, Paul says, "Being circumcised or not being circumcised doesn't mean anything. What matters is a new creation" (Gal 6:15-16).

In God's kingdom, old boundary markers have no place. What matters is where the new creation is to be found. That is in those who (again) by faith have embraced the faithfulness of Jesus and all that it means.

One New Humanity

Perhaps nowhere is this idea of a new creation more clearly stated, even though the phrase is not used, than in Ephesians 2:

> But now, thanks to Christ Jesus, you who once were so far away have been brought near by the blood of Christ. Christ is our peace. He made both Jews and Gentiles into one group. With his body, *he broke down the barrier of hatred that divided us.* He canceled the detailed rules of the Law so that he could create one new person out of the two groups, making peace. He reconciled them both as one body to God by the cross, which ended the hostility to God. When he came, he announced the good news of peace to you who were far away from God and to those who were near. We both have access to the Father through Christ by the one Spirit. So now you are no longer strangers and aliens. Rather, you are fellow citizens with God's people, and you belong to God's household. As God's household, you are built on the foundation of the apostles and prophets with Christ Jesus himself as the cornerstone. The whole building is joined together in him, and it grows up into a temple that is dedicated to the Lord. Christ is building you [all] into a place where God lives through the Spirit. (vv. 13-22, emphasis added)

The boundary wall that separated Jew from Gentile via the Torah with its commandments has been brought down in Christ. He has abolished the wall that separated, not only God from us, but also us from one another. Jesus, the first born of a new creation, suffered, died, and rose again so that a new humanity might be born. In Christ, we have all been reconciled together as one new humanity.

This removal of the boundaries between people was huge for Paul. If we return to Galatians 3:28-29, we can see this. What Paul says here is world shattering, not just for the Jew/Gentile separation. Paul pushes this further than was even imaginable for Rome. Roman culture and its economy were built largely on a slave labor, slave trade, and proper household/patriarchal hierarchies in which women were kept in their proper place. Here is Paul saying there is neither slave nor free! And to bring down the separation between men and women, putting them on equal footing, was unheard of. This is a truly radical statement. It is as radical in that time as is the statement today that LGBT persons ought to be granted full rights and opportunities within the church.

This alone ought to cause us to pause.

Could It Be Prejudice?

The calling of Levi and the banquet at his house provide a keen insight into how subtlety we can become ossified in our views of how things ought to be and, as a result, find ourselves on the wrong side of the movement of the Spirit. Even recent church history in the United States reflects how easily this can happen.[14]

Jesus was in conflict with the religious leaders of his day because he kept hanging out with the wrong people. The calling of Levi (Matthew) to be a disciple is a good example. It reveals what is often the case for us religious folk when it comes to change: "Afterward, Jesus went out and saw a tax collector named Levi sitting at a kiosk for collecting taxes. Jesus said to him, 'Follow me.' Levi got up, left everything behind, and followed him. Then Levi threw a great banquet for Jesus in his home. A large number of tax collectors and others sat down to eat with them" (Luke 5:27-29).

Jesus calls Levi the tax collector to follow him. We can hardly appreciate how appalling this would have been for the Pharisees. Tax collectors were near the very bottom of the social-religious ladder in first-century Palestine. Not only were they extremely impious relative to keeping Torah practices, but also they were actually collaborators with the oppressor, Rome and Herod (Wright 1997; Bauckham 1993). From the standpoint of the religious leadership (self-appointed in many cases), they were on the same social status level as prostitutes, lepers, and Gentiles.

That Jesus calls this kind of person to follow him was scandalous; but he goes a step further and agrees to dine with Matthew and other tax collectors. Practicing Torah included strict dietary laws that made it impossible for a good Jew to eat with such people. To do so would put Jesus outside the boundary.

The dialogue in the story, however, is not between Jesus and the tax collectors; it's between Jesus's disciples and the Pharisees, and then Jesus chimes into their conversation: "The Pharisees and their legal experts grumbled against his disciples. They said, 'Why do you eat and drink with tax collectors and sinners?' Jesus answered, 'Healthy people don't need a doctor, but sick people do. I didn't come to call righteous people but sinners to change their hearts and lives'" (Luke 5:30-32).

Now if you think about it, this is an odd response to the Pharisee's question. They want to know why he eats with people whom he must know will make him ceremonially unclean vis-à-vis Torah regulations. The true Messiah would never do such a thing. But Jesus's response stands their world on its head. The "righteous"—that is, those who believe they are the true Israel—

211

don't need healing and thus the healer. Sinners, however, know they are out-side the covenant community. Here is Jesus inviting them in to the new cove-nant community through repentance and then celebrating that in a banquet.

What did Jesus mean by that? the Pharisees had to be wondering. They did know they were the righteous. That was not a question. In fact, the real ques-tion in their mind was whether Jesus was righteous. So they ask Jesus why his disciples don't fast like theirs and even those of John the Baptist:

> Some people said to Jesus, "The disciples of John fast often and pray fre-quently. The disciples of the Pharisees do the same, but your disciples are always eating and drinking." Jesus replied, "You can't make the wedding guests fast while the groom is with them, can you? The days will come when the groom will be taken from them, and then they will fast." (Luke 5:33-35)

At first glance this seems like Luke made an awkward transition, jam-ming together two sayings of Jesus. They ask why Jesus goes banqueting in-stead of fasting. Jesus replies oddly about celebrating rather than fasting when the bridegroom is still present. We are piling up the metaphors here—a physi-cian and now a bridegroom? But there is powerful symbolism at work. If Jesus is the one from God, then eating a banquet would indicate (as it does often in Luke) anticipation that the final messianic banquet as depicted by the prophet Isaiah that was to occur once the king had returned and set the world right. But only the righteous would be seated around that table. However, those seated around the table would be from all peoples or all nations, not just from Israel. It would include former sinners who also have been rescued:

> On this mountain, the LORD of hosts will make *for all peoples* a feast of rich food, a feast of well-aged wines, of rich food filled with marrow, of well-aged wines strained clear. And he will destroy on this mountain the shroud that is cast over *all peoples*, the sheet that is spread over *all nations*; he will swallow up death forever. Then the LORD God will wipe away the tears from all faces, and the disgrace of his people he will take away from all the earth, for the LORD has spoken. It will be said on that day, Lo, this is our God; we have waited for him, so that he might save us. This is the LORD for whom we have waited; let us be glad and rejoice in his salvation [*rescue*]. (Isa 25:6-9 NRSV, emphasis added)

Luke uses this same banquet motif consistently many times to illustrate that the people with whom Jesus eats are also consistently the wrong people or, perhaps better, the wrong kind of people. But Luke always has the final banquet symbol in mind. Who will be seated at that table? All kinds of people will be in attendance that the religious leaders did not expect. Although Jesus affirms the traditional imagery of God's rescue, he modifies it or, perhaps more precisely, restores it to its original intent. This is something new, and yet this was pointed to by the prophet. Jesus makes just this point with two brief parables about garments and wineskins:

> Then he told them a parable. "No one tears a patch from a new garment to patch an old garment. Otherwise, the new garment would be ruined, and the new patch wouldn't match the old garment. Nobody pours new wine into old wineskins. If they did, the new wine would burst the wineskins, the wine would spill, and the wineskins would be ruined. Instead, new wine must be put into new wineskins." (Luke 5:36-38)

What the two stories mean on their surface sounds more like practical wisdom than typical parables. Hearers would say, "Well of course." And perhaps if we were there, we might also ask, "So what is the point?" Jesus is saying that something new is happening. But it really ought not to be unexpected. This is what the coming of the kingdom of God would look like. When the great messianic banquet occurs, all peoples will partake—including the social outcasts who were considered beyond the pale. This new thing is like a new garment. This new thing is like new wine. You don't patch a new garment with old material, and you don't put new wine in wineskins that have already been used to let wine age. The old and the new do not mix. Thus in addition, he is saying, the new thing that is happening (the coming of God's kingdom) cannot be attached to what is—including the agenda of the Pharisees. Luke adds a final interpretive flourish: "No one who drinks a well-aged wine wants new wine, but says, 'The well-aged wine is better.'" (5:39). This rather pointed comment to the Pharisees says that if you like the old, you probably will not want to have anything to do with the new.

As with any story, we find ourselves identifying with some of the characters. I believe many of us Christians identify with Matthew. Here was a sinner whom Jesus embraced, just like we are sinners whom Jesus has embraced. While that is certainly true, I think we might also want to consider whether or not we ought to identify with the Pharisees. In what sense? In the sense that many of us still want to draw lines of exclusion to full fellowship for some persons. LGBT people for many religious people are outside the bounds, in the same social status as the tax collectors, prostitutes, and Gentiles. We are being challenged today with the findings of science that inform us that sexual orientation is fixed before birth. That is a game changer relative to how we ought to see such people. Suddenly we are confronted with the fact that this is not a choice and that perhaps we have been wrong in how we have understood homosexuality and how we have been unwilling to include LGBT persons into full fellowship and participation of God's people. And yet the resistance in some quarters of the religious community is becoming more aggressive, not more open and accepting. In this sense we are like the Pharisees. Given the option between new wine and old, we will take the old.

The Pharisees' affront at tax collectors and other sinners we would call prejudice. Their exclusion of these groups from the covenant community we would call discrimination based upon exclusionary religious convictions. To the extent we are doing the same toward any person, are we not guilty of the same? Could it be that we are either consciously or perhaps unconsciously prejudiced against LGBT people because of their otherness? Could we be saying we like the old wine—the way it was—more than the new?

The movie *Lincoln*, directed by Steven Spielberg, has parallels to the current social debate about full inclusion, including marriage of LGBT people. In one scene during the debate over passing the Emancipation Proclamation, one legislator is heard to say (this is a paraphrase), "If we do this, next women will want to vote!" If we open up to LGBT people, what will be next?!

The Church and the Stranger

When Debbie and I were in Rome on a tour of the ancient city, our guide told us a story about the early Christians, who came out in the night and would go through the garbage heaps looking for cast-off babies. There was something that drove that early community to break the social barriers to rescue all kinds of people, including unwanted babies. They believed these children were part of the creation God loves and that they should therefore love them as well—these were their neighbors too. I believe the way the church deals with LGBT persons ought to follow in the same way. From the standpoint of many churches, the LGBT person is a social outcast.

Rather, the church informed by science and guided by scripture should see the LGBT community as people whom Jesus embraces fully. For too long LGBT children growing up in our churches have felt like outcasts, listening to their youth leaders tell them that homosexuality is an abomination to God. For too long parents of gay children have had to sit silently, sometimes feeling shame because their faith condemns who their children are. If there is any community of people that ought to be the first to open their doors to the LGBT community, it ought to be the church because that is what Jesus would do.

The early Christians understood themselves to be the new Israel under the new covenant. They were to be for the world what ethnic Israel had failed to be. Israel had failed to love the stranger. Rather, she had become a bounded set that was concerned only for the future of herself. Frankly in my years working with churches of all denominations, conservative and liberal, across the United States, I have seen far too often a similar behavior. If I am honest, I have colluded in this by not speaking up for LGBT persons. My own internal conflicts over the issue, plus the fact that it did not affect me personally for so many years, rendered me complicit by inaction.

Jesus loves all people in their manifest diversity. Our calling is to do no less. When we do, we find ourselves as religious people in the same role as the young Torah expert who asked Jesus, "Who is my neighbor?" Jesus's answer then and now is to be a neighbor to anyone, regardless of gender, social status, race, ethnicity, or sexual orientation. This, to continue Jesus's answer, is how we inherit the blessings of the kingdom of God.

But this question might still trouble you. Am I saying that we ought to include everyone and it doesn't matter what anyone does? The short answer is no, I am not saying this. This would mean there is no morality; there is no right and wrong. I am certainly not saying that; far from it! In the next chapter the issue of morality will be considered. But this chapter has been about developing a theology of inclusion. The anchor is the love of God for all of creation that was most concretely displayed in the Incarnation. In response to this great love, we, who would presume to be God's people, are called to love God and to love the neighbor. There are no boundary markers that signify one people as neighbor and others as not. We are called to be neighbors to all people including LGBT people. Christians are to be especially sensitive to the social outcasts among us. It is not any harder or complex than this. Now certainly showing this kind of love is a challenge because our own human failure to love as we ought to love. But what we are called to is not hard to understand. Based upon an observation of Jesus's own actions, we are without excuse when we turn our backs on, or worse, outwardly reject LGBT persons just because they are gay.

One last observation: it is ironic that the real offence of the Sodomites was failing to show justice to the weak among them and hospitality to the stranger. I believe we are guilty of the same offense today when we condemn gay people for something that is innate and exclude them from full participation in the life of Jesus's church. It would appear that the outcast is alive and well. Perhaps we are the real Sodomites.

Notes

1. English-speaking Christians misunderstand what the Greek means when we render eternal life. For too many Christians, eternal life means going to heaven and the end of this space-time universe. But this was not the Jewish hope. Judaism of Jesus's day thought in terms of two ages: the current age and the age to come. The age to come would see the dawn of the kingdom of God during which God returns and establishes just rule on earth so that our prayer, "your will be done on earth as in heaven," would finally be realized. In referring to this text, N. T. Wright says in *Jesus and the Victory of God*, "The long night of exile, the 'present evil age,' would give way to the dawn of renewal and restoration, the new exodus, the return from exile, 'the age to come'" (1997, 48).

2. My comments are not intended to support Universalism.

3. See 1 Cor 13:13.

4. See Deut 6:5; Lev 19:18

5. Often translated as "scribes."

6. See Luke 9:51-56.

7. See Isa 61:1-2; 58:6.

8. See chapter 2, where Israel's election is discussed.

9. See also Luke 5:30; 6:7; 15:2; 19:47; 20:1-2.

10. See Gagnon (2001) He insists that the order of nature as demonstrated by the complementarity of male and female is absolute.

11. See writings and blog posting by Rachel Held Evans, author of *A Year of Biblical Womanhood* (2012).

12. See Gagnon (2001) and Webb (2001).

13. Most Protestants read the Pauline texts as a battle between Judaizers (who try to reintroduce works of the law as necessary to salvation) and Paul (who takes a strong stand against Judaizers). The stand Paul takes is against those who would insist that all Gentiles who became Christians must adopt all of the Jewish Torah practices, such as food and purity laws, circumcision, and separatism. For Paul, this was contrary to the message of his gospel, which includes all as they are. He of course assumed that where true faith was found would be people seeking to live lives that turned from evil (sin) and death and pursuing lives of love.

14. How the church justified slavery and the separation of whites and blacks in our country is well documented. The process of allowing women and divorced persons full participation in leadership is as well. For more detail I would refer the reader to Jack Rogers's book, *Jesus, the Bible, and Homosexuality* for a review of the historical process the church in the United States went through. The lessons learned there are applicable to this discussion.

Chapter 9

Is There a Moral Line?

If love is the fixed point that defines everything else, then when we approach the moral questions associated with homosexuality, love must be at the center of the discussion. However, it is not as easy as declaring this a principle and then assuming questions of morality have been solved. Moral questions arise, and one is confronted immediately with two questions. *How* do we draw the moral line? One might think that I have stated this wrong. Shouldn't the first question be: *where* do we draw the moral line? No, that question comes second; we must speak to the "how" question first.

There are multiple beginning points in the "how" discussion, but for our purposes, I am only concerned with two approaches. The first is what is called natural law. So I begin with it and then propose an alternative "how." Second, the conversation must address the human experience of "attraction." This at first would not appear to be a question of morality, but given how it is understood in some quarters vis-à-vis same-sex attraction, it is and therefore is a question to which we must attend. Having looked at these two, then I propose both *how* and *where* I believe we should draw the moral line and the implications of doing so for all expressions of sexual behavior.

Natural Law

My reason for beginning with natural law is simple; natural law, in one form or another is consistently the basis for rejecting any form of same-sex expression within the conservative community, especially among Roman Catholics. Natural law provides an ethical framework for approaching moral questions. It is a method because it provides an answer to the "how" question. If you find this section too philosophical or theological, again, please skip to the next section. But there are many, especially among conservatives—both Catholics and Protestants—who anchor much of the moral debate in natural law, so it's important to cover the ground.

So What Is Natural Law?

Natural law has a long history, and any summary will not do it complete justice. It goes back in Western civilization to the Greek philosophers Plato and Aristotle. Saint Augustine sought to integrate it into Christian thought and notably on the subject of human sexuality. Its Christian formulation was further refined as a way of thinking by Thomas Aquinas. In short, natural law is an approach to ethics and the articulation of "laws" by which humans should live that is discernible in nature using human reasoning. A similar approach in the science domain begins from the premise that there are natural laws in nature, and those laws are discoverable using reason and observation. These can then be used to make predictions. For example, if you stand on top of a building and drop a rock, it is reasonable to assume before releasing it that it will drop to the ground. Why is this reasonable? Primarily because it happens every time, and so it is reasonable to assume it will happen again. Science defines this as the law of gravity, and based upon that law, we can predict future behavior, that is, that the rock will drop.

In the domain of ethical inquiry, natural law seeks to derive those self-evident principles in nature that, if followed, will promote the "good." Like science, the means of derivation is human reason, but unlike science, there is no observational element. Laws are derived exclusively through the cognitive process of human reason. It is a form of what is called rationalism: "Rationalists claim that there are significant ways in which our concepts and knowledge are gained independently of sense experience" (Markie 2013). Natural law conversations often quote the following from the Stoic Roman political philosopher Cicero: "True law is right reason in agreement with nature; it is of universal application, unchanging and everlasting. It summons to duty by its commands and averts from wrongdoing by its prohibitions" (1877, bk. 3, chap. 22).

In other words, that which is moral is that which is derived from proper reasoning. What reasoning concludes is in agreement with the way things are supposed to be (i.e., according to nature), always and everywhere. This is the good.

It is in the definition of the good that many alternative opinions can be found. In general the idea of the good is that which promotes human flourishing (Volf 2013).[1] For both Aristotle and Aquinas, goodness meant something fulfilling its nature—what it is and its intended goal or purpose (Koritansky 2007). Nature would indicate that the human person ought to live well and reproduce. That is our purpose, our end. Natural law principles point out what a person must and must not do for the good to be achieved. These ideas are tied to Aristotle's fourth cause—the final cause, "the end, that for the sake of which a thing is done" (Falcon 2012).

Thomas Aquinas, a pivotal theologian and later saint in the Roman Catholic Church, taught that there were certain natural laws that all humans could discern (via reason) that ought to determine how they live and which served the good. Aquinas, like many Bible interpreters believed that this basic ability to discern the good was what Paul appeals to in Romans 2. Although the Gentiles were not given Torah (the Law), they nonetheless can discern what is the good because their consciences convict them:

> Gentiles don't have the Law. But when they instinctively do what the Law requires they are a Law in themselves, though they don't have the Law. They show the proof of the Law written on their hearts, and their consciences affirm it. Their conflicting thoughts will accuse them, or even make a defense for them, on the day when, according to my gospel, God will judge the hidden truth about human beings through Christ Jesus. (Rom 2:14-16)

The assumption being made by Aquinas, and certainly by many other even modern interpreters, is that Paul believed humans have some kind of innate sense of what is right and wrong and that this is written into creation and therefore in humans by their capacity for reason. Whether this is what Paul was actually saying is another matter. Here I would refer to N. T. Wright, who makes a strong argument that we often have it wrong. Wright proposes that the Gentiles Paul has in mind are not the "great unwashed" hoards of non-Jewish people. Rather, he argues that Paul has the Roman Gentile Christians in mind. If Wright's interpretation is correct—and it makes a whole lot of sense for Romans 1–4 if it is—then one cannot begin to build natural law assumptions based upon the notion that all humans have the moral law imprinted on their hearts based upon the Apostle Paul. Removing Paul does serious damage to its—religious at least—foundations (2002, 440–41; 2013b).[2] This does not mean that humans are not without excuse; indeed, that is also part of Paul's argument—that neither Jews nor Gentiles are without excuse because the marks of a creator God are evident in creation.[3] It just means one cannot argue from Paul that the moral law is innate in human reason.

Aquinas expounded that there were four kinds of law: eternal, natural, human, and divine. The eternal law is divine providence by which all of creation is governed by the divine reason. Natural law pertains only to humans who alone share in the divine capacity to reason. Aquinas says, "the natural law is nothing else than the rational creature's participation of the eternal law" (1947, Q91, A2). Applied to humans, it is the basis for morality and politics. Human law is what is referred to as "positive law," meaning laws articulated and applied by societies and their governments. Divine laws are those that humans only obtain through revelation as provided in scripture.

Positive laws that are at odds with natural law are not considered to be true laws. Thus within the worldview of natural law advocates, laws that are not discernible within nature, regardless of who espouses or implements them, are not true laws. This follows in the tradition of Augustine who said, "An unjust law is not really a law at all" (1993, Books 1 and 5). This is important because there are some natural law proponents who will reject laws supported by the people because they believe them to be against nature's laws, such as abortion and same-sex marriage, to name a couple of examples.

Aquinas has greatly influenced how natural law proponents view human sexual behavior in general, and they appeal to him as a basis for rejecting same-sex marriage. At first glance one might think Aquinas could support same-sex marriage. This may seem like an odd statement, but if we begin where he begins, it makes sense. We rational beings are to pursue the doing of the good and not evil. But how are we to know what is the good we are to pursue? He would say that we are to follow our "natural inclinations." These inclinations include, first, "preserving human life and warding off its obstacles." Second, we have inclinations toward sexual intercourse, which we share with other animals in order to reproduce. Finally, we have inclinations that are exclusively human due to our rational capability, such as our desire to know God and live in societies. But all of these are subject to human fallenness, and so simply acting on our inclinations will not produce the morally good. Grace is required.

Considering the second inclination to sexual intercourse, Aquinas saw it as a good because it supported a greater good: "For Aquinas, sexuality that was within the bounds of marriage and which helped to further what he saw as the distinctive goods of marriage, mainly love, companionship, and legitimate offspring, was permissible, and even good" (Pickett 2011). Sexual inclinations encouraged people to partner with another promoting love and companionship and reproduction. Same-sex marriage could almost fall within this definition, except perhaps for the production of offspring. Aquinas was aware that some couples were sterile, and yet sex was still considered to be a good because it supported a loving relationship. But Aquinas also became extremely explicit in what kind of sex was moral. In short (and without becoming too explicit), only sex that was, at least in theory, reproductive was moral:

> Aquinas, in a significant move, adds a requirement that for any given sex act to be moral it must be of *a generative kind*. The only way that this can be achieved is via vaginal intercourse. That is, since only the emission of semen in a vagina can result in natural reproduction, only sex acts of that type are generative, even if a given sex act does not lead to reproduction, and even if it is impossible due to infertility. (Pickett 2011, emphasis added)

There it is. This is the natural purpose or goal of sex (referring us back to Aristotle). To use sex otherwise is contrary to natural law (Koritansky 2007). If the sex act does not at least have the possibility of reproduction, it is against nature and thus morally wrong: "Natural law theorists, if they want to support their objection to homosexual sex, have to emphasize procreation. If, for example, they were to place love and mutual support for human flourishing at the center, it is clear that many same-sex couples would meet this standard. Hence their sexual acts would be morally just" (Pickett 2011).

Modern natural law proponents follow Aquinas on the whole range of sexual practices. For example, the Roman Catholic teaching on contraception is fairly well recognized. But perhaps the details are not as well known. For those seeking answers to Catholic doctrinal teaching, there are several websites that can be queried. The following quote is from the website Catholic Answers to Explain and Defend the Faith. This article is titled "Birth Control":

> Contraception is wrong because it's a deliberate violation of the design God built into the human race, often referred to as "natural law." The natural law purpose of sex is procreation. The pleasure that sexual intercourse provides is an additional blessing from God, intended to offer the possibility of new life while strengthening the bond of intimacy, respect, and love between husband and wife. The loving environment this bond creates is the perfect setting for nurturing children.
>
> But sexual pleasure within marriage becomes unnatural, and even harmful to the spouses, when it is used in a way that deliberately excludes the basic purpose of sex, which is procreation. God's gift of the sex act, along with its pleasure and intimacy, must not be abused by deliberately frustrating its *natural end*—procreation. (2004, emphasis added)

Sex is wrong when it deliberately excludes the purpose (i.e., the natural end) of sex, which is procreation. This then becomes the basis for, not only the rejection of contraception, but also any form of sexual expression that cannot lead to reproduction—including many activities I suspect many modern (and Christian) married couples do. This is at the core of the natural law argument against gay sex and same-sex marriage. Natural law says that for sexual intimacy to be "good" it must always have, as part of its aim, procreation.[4]

In more recent times there has emerged what is referred to as a "new" natural law band of proponents. Building solidly on the Aquinas tradition, they attempt to buttress his insistence that reproduction must be possible in theory (meaning vaginal penetration and male ejaculation) for sex to be moral. Even though there are variations to the arguments proposed, there are two arguments that specifically oppose homosexual sex: personal integration and marriage.

Personal integration says that humans are acting agents. The good is integration between a person's intentions and his or her "embodied self." To use one's body as only a means to pleasure is disintegrative or "self-alienating." To be integrative, the intended action must conform to our body's reproductive purpose. Thus masturbation is self-alienating as is sex just for pleasure that does not include vaginal penetration. The second argument relates to the first as a completion. It could be possible to engage in vaginal penetration but outside the bonds of marriage. So even though sexual intercourse occurs, the intention does not conform to the proper context for such intimate expression. In other words, only when the vaginal intercourse comes to completion between two married persons is it a good (George and Tollefsen 2008). "This argument requires drawing how marriage is an important good in a very particular way, since it puts procreation at the center of marriage as its 'natural fulfillment'" (Pickett 2011).

Rebuttal to Natural Law

Natural law rejects any form of sexual expression that does not end in vaginal penetration and male ejaculation. As already mentioned, this would be news to a lot of people, including a lot of Roman Catholics and conservative Protestants. I suspect, on the Protestant side, some would not be willing to go that far, but they would argue that the "natural" function of sex is to be reproductive, and then some would get a little fuzzy on some other behaviors. But it is important to understand that the root of much conservative rejection of same-sex marriage is rooted in this natural law principle.

I do not accept this principle. First, natural law sees sexual pleasure as a good if it leads to generative behaviors. Sexual pleasure that does not is not a moral good; in fact, it is immoral. How many boys and girls have been made to feel dirty over the years because they were told masturbation was immoral? How is this conclusion reached? It is rooted in Aristotelian causality and Aquinas's interpretation of him. Briefly, there must be a cause behind a result. So far so good. But some causes and their outcomes (their goals) are secondary in that they make the final cause and its outcome (goal) possible. In natural law, sexual pleasure is a secondary (or essential) cause that makes the final cause—sexual intercourse—possible, the goal of which is reproduction.

This way of thinking, apart from the LGBT issue, denigrates the gift of sexual pleasure. From an evolutionary standpoint, our sexual drive and its promise of pleasure encourage humans to couple and reproduce. But it also encourages us not to be alone and to receive one of life's joys. Are these not "goods" in themselves? Are not companionship, intimacy, and pleasure, which are part of being human, good ends in themselves if pursued within the context of love? At least a classic Protestant view of sexuality embraces and promotes this view. Further, it is rooted in a more biblical creation theology. Creation is God's good work and gift. Humans were intended to enjoy God's gifts. It is our squandering of his gifts that creates so much heartache and evil.

Second, natural law reduces human sexuality to biological necessity. Persons who have looked deeply into the eyes of a lover in those moments of deep intimacy know that sex is more than just a generative biological necessity. It may have its roots in our biology, but it promotes more than reproduction. In the language of Volf, sexual intimacy and pleasure in the right context promote human flourishing. The sterile couple still find great joy in the intimacy they share, knowing full well that there can be no reproduction.

Third, the fundamental premise of natural law, especially in some of its new expressions, goes against the Protestant principle of "sola scriptura"—scripture alone.[5] Certainly this idea has evolved over the centuries since the Reformation; but it still stands for most Protestants that the life, death, and resurrection of Jesus are the definitive revelatory events in human history. Our understanding of the right and the good is defined in these events, and all else that is right and good is a mere shadow. But one of the key proponents of the new natural law, Robert P. George (professor at Princeton, conservative law professor, and a Roman Catholic), makes it clear that he believes moral law can be discerned in nature without any outside source. A reporter writing about and quoting George says: "What makes his natural law 'new' is that it disavows dependence on divine revelation or biblical Scripture—or even history and anthropology. Instead, George rests his ethics on a foundation of 'practical reason': 'invoking no authority beyond the authority of reason itself'" (Kirkpatrick 2009).

Protestant theology becomes uncomfortable with a moral theory that creates a framework within which, if a person lived consistently, he or she could reach the good without grace or even know what the good is without revelation—specifically the revelation given to us in Jesus.

Finally, natural law quickly devolves into casuistry. Casuistry has a descriptive and a pejorative meaning. Descriptively it means case-based reasoning. That is, it means the building up of a position held by logical reasoning through cases. Its pejorative meaning comes from its reasoning processes that at times appear to be overworked rationalism. Using the image of Ockham's Razor, it means to multiply things needlessly. My personal reaction is that all things being equal, the simplest explanation is probably the best. In its worst case, for the untrained observer, it appears that there is too much hair splitting. While the sincerity of natural law proponents is not questioned, their method is, and it is the method that rationalizes that all sexual behaviors that do not (in theory) lead to procreation are wrong—whether homosexual, heterosexual, or autosexual (masturbation).

Positive Assertion of "How"

We are still working on the "how" question. How do we approach the question of a moral line? I have presented the natural law view that is employed by many conservatives who oppose same-sex marriage and behavior and why I believe it is not the proper method. Now I must lay down a positive assertion of how I believe these questions need to be approached.

Theologically, it is essential we understand the larger picture of what God is doing. But it is also important that we reflect on what God is calling us to do. This is where ethics enters. I believe the Bible presents us with a good God who wants justice in God's world. God wants things to be as they ought to be, and God is committed to that end. Part of setting those things right is for us as creatures to pursue lives that are just to the extent that we are able by God's grace and the work of the Holy Spirit.

Following my Protestant tradition—though it has evolved over time—I do believe that certain things are right and certain things are wrong. But I believe that the foundation of that knowledge is revealed to us in scripture and more directly in the life, death, and resurrection of Jesus. I believe that morality exists because there is a moral God who is creator and sustainer. Things are right because they reflect the character of God, even though a large portion of human society does not subscribe to this. I do believe we can see goodness in creation, and we sense goodness, even if darkly, when we encounter it. C. S. Lewis in *Mere Christianity* illustrates this point: "My argument against God was that the universe seemed so cruel and unjust. But how had I got this idea of just and unjust? A man does not call a line crooked unless he has some idea of a straight line. What was I comparing this universe with when I called it unjust?" ([1952] 2009, 38).

I also believe there is a teleological (purposeful) element in morality. When the Bible calls upon God's people to live a certain way, it is because God wants us to live in such a way that the outcome is life, not death; that is what I mean by human flourishing. Nowhere is this clearer than this covenant renewal passage from Deuteronomy:

> Look here! Today I've set before you life and what's good versus death and what's wrong. If you obey the *Lord* your God's commandments that I'm commanding you right now by loving the *Lord* your God, by walking in his ways, and by keeping his commandments, his regulations, and his case laws, then you will live and thrive, and the *Lord* your God will bless you in the land you are entering to possess. But if your heart turns away and you refuse to listen, and so are misled, worshipping other gods and serving them, I'm telling you right now that you will definitely die. You will not prolong your life on the fertile land that you are crossing the Jordan River to enter and possess. I call heaven and earth as my witnesses against you right now: I have set life and death, blessing and curse before you. *Now choose life—so that you and your descendants will live—by loving the Lord your God, by obeying his voice, and by clinging to him.* That's how you will survive and live long on the fertile land the *Lord* swore to give to your ancestors: to Abraham, Isaac, and Jacob. (30:15-20, emphasis added)

In the Bible, the good is life with God. It is those behaviors that promote life that determine what is right. *The means of producing life is to live a life shaped by love.* The Incarnation was God's way of showing us what is the good—namely, love that promotes human flourishing. As we saw in the prior chapter, when Jesus was asked how to summarize all of Torah, he said to love God and love the neighbor.

The ethical test for a moral life is whether it is a life that actively seeks to love God and one's neighbors with the lives we have been given. Some natural law proponents, such as Robert George, it would appear, want to separate divine law from natural law, making natural law declarations absolute and deciding what is on the list of stipulations. Sadly the natural law approach to ethics means that LGBT persons have no moral recourse that allows them to fully accept their identity.

Although Protestants have much in common with Roman Catholic believers—most important a commitment to Jesus as Lord—we differ on this theological approach to ethics. Protestant commitment to "sola scriptura" provides a different foundation from which to build the "how" of Christian ethics.

Attraction and Humanness

Like many, I have been trying to figure out what love is most of my life, in large part, because I have tried to get my hands around the meaning of the love of God for creation and what that means for me as one called to love the other. It might be easier if it were not for the fact that we also speak of love when we speak of human attraction for each other.

Attraction gets a bit mixed up as well because it is generally recognized that there are biological and psychological elements to attraction. Sexual attraction is a mix of these two. But what is attraction about? At the most basic biological level, we all know that attraction is nature's way of making sure we reproduce. But most of us also know from real life experience that it is more than that.

Attraction and Community

Attraction draws us to other people, and that serves to mitigate a basic need we have—to address a sense of loneliness. Most of us long to be part of someone else and part of a community in which we have a sense of belonging. That desire to belong creates communities. Individuals in caring and supportive communities are more likely to be psychologically healthy persons who flourish. Attraction, a most fundamental human desire, is creation's way of promoting healthy, contributing humans.

From a theological perspective, we say that God created us to live in relationship with others, first with God and then other humans. This is why Genesis 2 says: "Then the LORD God said, 'It is not good that the man should be alone; I will make him a helper as his partner'" (v. 18 NRSV).

Of course one wants to immediately insist that here is a text that is about marriage between a man and woman, but that is not what the text does first. The text first says it is not good for the man, the human, to be alone. And so God creates a being that is of his kind. Yes, in the story he creates a woman, and the story continues with the formation of the first couple who are told to "be fruitful and multiply." But it is the aloneness and the need for the other to participate with Adam in fulfilling his calling as steward of God's creation that give the text its greatest power, even when used, as I often have, in a marriage ceremony between a young man and a young woman.

In a biological sense, attraction does obviously have a sexual element. In fact, it may have a role in all kinds of attractions to other people each day. But clearly, the strongest attraction is that wonderfully mysterious thing that happens when that special someone catches the eye. All sorts of biological things begin to happen. Certainly there is sexual longing. But there can also

226

be nervous stomachs, shyness, anxiety, an unusual desire to show off; all kinds of things go on. The result of this "dance," as it is often called, is two people growing closer together and building a bond of emotional and at some point physical intimacy.

With this background, let's ask the obvious psychological question. Is same-sex attraction normal or abnormal? From a moral perspective is it wrong? And from a theological perspective is it sinful?

From a psychological perspective, attraction is attraction. There is, of course, cause for concern when attractions become unhealthy. A man obsessed with a female celebrity to the point that he begins to exhibit strange intrusive behaviors does not have a healthy attraction. Attraction that drives a person to oppress another is not healthy, and certainly attraction that leads one to rape another is way beyond not healthy. That is a sickness. But is the sickness due to one's sexual orientation? The mainstream psychological community would not judge a same-sex attraction (desire) negatively. They would make a declarative, descriptive statement: person A is attracted to person B.

Let's consider the question from a moral and theological perspective. I had a friend tell me that homosexual attraction itself was sinful. In other words, the fact that a gay person was attracted to another person of the same sex made the attraction sinful. Were that person to be attracted—to feel the same desires—toward a person of the opposite sex, it would not be sinful. But can this really be true? If attraction is what we have been discussing it to be, it is simply a human phenomenon that in good circumstances creates human community and, in specific instances, propagates the species. I do not believe same-sex attraction is any more sinful than opposite-sex attraction. Attraction brings people together. Once again C. S. Lewis points us in the right direction: "No natural feelings are high or low, holy or unholy, in themselves. They are all holy when God's hand is on the rein." But he continues, "They all go bad when they set up on their own and make themselves into false gods (2009, 100). This leads us to the issue of when attraction crosses the line.

When Attraction Becomes Wrong

Clearly attraction can become a moral issue and therefore wrong. Let us return to the previous illustration. When a person becomes so obsessed with another person that behaviors begin to be harmful for the person who is the object of attraction, that is not only psychologically unhealthy but also wrong because it is a desire to take from another for one's own satisfaction with little to any regard for the other. That is certainly not love. What is it? In most cases it is lust!

Here is another illustration my friend shared with me. He insisted that he lusted every day because every day he saw beautiful women and felt attracted to them. But is the mere fact of sensing attraction lust? If that is the case, then most of us would have to confess that we spend a large portion of every day lusting—unless we have cloistered ourselves so as to avoid human contact! When does attraction move from being simply human to lust? Of course knowing the exact line is impossible to determine, but I think it's safe to say that when we proceed to "camp" on the object of attraction and begin to imagine things that we could not morally justify, then we have crossed over. When we begin to consider the person only as an object of our satisfaction, as an object we want to use in some way, we dehumanize that person, and we cross over into lust. I suspect most of us know that line and know that we cross it.

Attraction is human. Lust is attraction or desire that has been perverted by our thoughts so that it becomes base self-satisfaction at the expense of the other. More simply, lust is natural desire run amok. In Romans 1, what Paul finds problematic is the normal desires that have crossed over into lust followed by actual behaviors. Paul calls this idolatry. It is turning a natural and good human experience into a god and throwing oneself at it expecting it to provide life.

Love, however, as I have indicated previously, seeks the good of the other, seeks life instead of death. To use another is to bring death. Paul, as we saw earlier, expresses this as the experience of the wrath of God, not because God is actively bringing down destruction on people, but rather as the consequence of choosing to pursue behaviors that do so. The Bible will refer to God as "hating" such things. God hates such behavior because they rob God's creatures (we humans) of what God really intends for us—to flourish, to live. God does not hate any of us creatures. As we have seen, quite the contrary, God loves each one of us.

Human attraction turned to lust dehumanizes both the object of lust and the person doing the lusting. Lust is not limited to one sexual orientation.

The Moral Line

We have addressed the question of how we draw the moral line. Now the question becomes: is there then a moral line we can draw and if so, where is it? The traditional and most conservative way of drawing the line is to say that homosexual attraction is sin because it is a perversion of God's design—this is the natural law position. But I don't believe this to be true. Attraction is attraction. Others somewhat less conservative may be more generous and concede that people are born as LGBT persons and may not be able to help the attractions they have, but if they pursue those attractions, at that point they become sinful.

One Way to Draw the Moral Line

The following graphic reflects how many in the conservative community would draw the moral line. There are two axes in the graphic. The vertical axis separates behaviors based upon the extent they are motivated by love of the other, seeking the welfare of the other, or by selfish desires to use the other for one's own pleasure. In theory one would hope most Christians would see loving the other as our primary calling. The horizontal axis separates behaviors based upon one's sexual orientation. We have seen previously that psychology sees sexual orientation as a continuum. But when it comes to moral choices, more conservative folks see only two options: other-sex behavior or same-sex behavior. Thus the regions considered immoral encompass the gray areas.

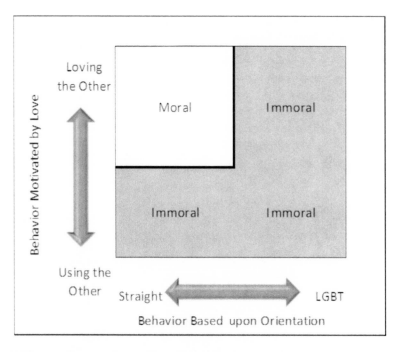

A Different Way to Draw the Moral Line

It has always troubled me that the church:

1. knows its very existence and future hope is tied to the ultimate act of love,

2. proclaims that love and vigorously insists on salvation by grace alone, and
3. still draws lines between themselves and the other.

I believe we have only gone part way toward that which we so boldly assert: to trust that loving the other, on no other grounds than that the person is the other, as God has done in Christ, is our calling. I am not saying there is no role for law. We still live with feet in both the new and the old kingdom.[6] But within the Christian church, our feet are solely planted in the kingdom of God where Christ's rule is undisputed. It is within this community that there never should be a question about inclusion of the other. So can we draw the moral line differently regarding human sexuality? Based upon love of the other as the fixed point—that is, pursuing behaviors that promote life, not death—and the comments about attraction and when it becomes sinful, perhaps we ought to draw the line only along the horizontal axis. Instead of the vertical Straight–LGBT division, what if we draw the line between love and commitment on one side and lust and exploitation on the other? Does this not reflect more accurately what we observe in the New Testament, in the life and message of Jesus?

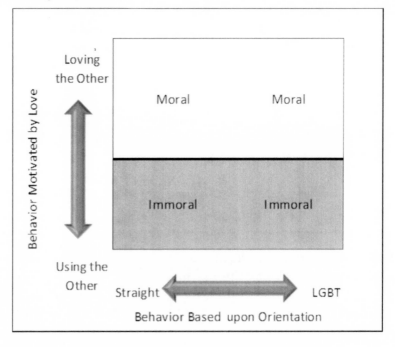

In this model, the line is drawn based upon how one human being relates to another and in my mind approximates more the core message of God's kingdom: love your neighbor as yourself. It is love that brings life, and it is abuse and exploitation that destroy it. Behaviors along the sexual-orientation axis are neutral. Clearly the two models are abstractions. Human life is never this tidy. But this is a conceptual framework for thinking morally about the natural reality of persons whose attractions may not be mostly heterosexual.

Is it possible that in cultures in which the strong emphasis on hetero-sexuality as God's design is practiced that it also can provide a cover for lust, abuse, and exploitation of women? Are we not saying this at times when we describe some actions as "boys will be boys"? How many women suffer in marriages in which the husband simply assumes it is his right to "have" his wife whenever he wants, however he wants? Would we not all agree that such brutish behavior is wrong? Why? Because the Bible teaches us that we are to love our wives. They are not possessions. Wives are gifts, and men are called to be Christ-like in loving them.

There is, I believe, a moral line. But it is not between straight and gay. In my understanding of the biblical story and specifically of the actions of Jesus, the moral line is drawn between behaviors that flow from love versus those that flow from lust or power or greed or fear. God's hope for humans is that we flourish, and it is love that leads to that flourishing. *So the question we should ask of each other, whether gay or straight, is this: what will our choices produce: life or death?* Does a particular action or lifestyle bring you closer to an expression of love as God loves, or does it come from some other place? This approach to the moral question would, in my mind, bring many behaviors practiced by both gay and straight people into question. I do not mean to express a judgmental attitude. Rather, it comes from a place of sadness. God wants life for us, and we too often choose death—then call it living. We settle for less. We desire too little.

I was in my mid-twenties the first time I read the essay called *The Weight of Glory* by C. S. Lewis. I, like so many Christians, considered the Christian life to be about fighting off evil desires in order to live faithfully. But Lewis introduced me to an idea that has captured my imagination for my entire adult life, and to my wondrous surprise, is biblical as well. He says: "It would seem that Our Lord finds our desires not too strong, but too weak. We are half-hearted creatures, fooling about with drink and sex and ambition when infinite joy is offered us, like an ignorant child who wants to go on making mud pies in a slum because he cannot imagine what is meant by the offer of a holiday at the sea. We are far too easily pleased" (2001, 26).

231

This is another way of talking about idolatry. We humans settle for too little and then convince ourselves that we are living. So many of the moral choices we make are mud pies. There may be choices being made around us that reflect the heart of God, but we cannot see them. There may be people who have made commitments out of a deep love for the other that is bringing life for them both and to those who will let them touch them. But we may not even see it. In fact, we may call it evil.

It reminds me of another C. S. Lewis piece from his last book in the Chronicles of Narnia series, *The Last Battle.* The dwarves, who have been tricked and exploited by everyone, including a false Aslan (the Christ figure), decide that "the Dwarves are for the Dwarves." As the story nears the climax, all of the true Narnians and a few others have passed through (or were thrown through) a shed door and into the true Narnia, Aslan's country. It looks much like the old Narnia, only bigger and more real and more beautiful. The Dwarves were some who were thrown through the shed door, but they are having a much different experience. While the others can see the wonders of the new Narnia, the Dwarves only see darkness and smell a dirty stable. Lucy tries to help them realize where they really are, but they will have none of it. We pick up the dialogue at this point. (If you do not know the story, I advise you to pick up the books and read them. Your life will be richer for having done so.)

> "Oh the poor things! This is dreadful," said Lucy. Then she had an idea. She stooped and picked some wild violets. "Listen, Dwarf," she said. "Even if your eyes are wrong, perhaps your nose is all right: can you smell that?" She leaned across and held the fresh, damp flowers to Diggle's ugly nose. But she had to jump back quickly in order to avoid a blow from his hard little fist.
>
> "None of that!" he shouted. "How dare you! What do to you mean by shoving a lot of filthy stable-litter in my face? There is a thistle in it too. (1976, 180–82)

The Dwarves are convinced that they have it right, that by their deciding only to depend upon themselves, there is no chance they will be fooled again or taken in the wrong direction. A distressed Lucy goes to Aslan for help. Aslan comes up to the Dwarves and tries to communicate with them. But again, they will have none of it:

> "Well, at any rate there's no Humbug here. We haven't let anyone take us in. The Dwarfs are for the Dwarfs."

Lucy is heartbroken, but Aslan tries to comfort her:

"You see," said Aslan. "They will not let us help them. They have chosen cunning instead of belief. Their prison is only in their own minds, yet they are in that prison; and so afraid of being taken in that they cannot be taken out. But come, children. I have other work to do." (Lewis 1976, 180–82)

I realize there is some danger in my using these examples from Lewis. It would be easy to assign roles in this debate to the various characters. That is not my intent. My only intent is to use story to remind us that God may be at work among us in ways we would not have expected. Are we willing to see?

Social and Religious Conservatives and Social Policy

Having established where I believe the moral line ought to be drawn will help us look at several moral claims that are made by social and religious conservatives about homosexuality and LGBT people. There are five problems that are repeatedly raised. These include (1) the promiscuity problem, (2) the poor parenting model problem, (3) the same-sex relationships don't last problem, (4) the domestic violence problem, and (5) the slippery slope problem, which is a bit of a catchall category. The goal in each is to make the case against same-sex marriage because same-sex practices bring with them these social problems and thus become an issue of social policy. Appeals are made to social and psychological research to support conclusions that same-sex partnerships are unstable and unhealthy and therefore inimical to our traditional views of marriage and family. Therefore members of the LGBT community ought not be granted legal protection or granted legal status. Frankly the materials written by most social and religious conservatives appear to be a thinly veiled cover for their à priori assumption that the Bible teaches that same-sex relationships are evil and must be stopped.

The Promiscuity Problem

Some religious conservatives claim that homosexuals are more sexually promiscuous than heterosexuals. In the pamphlet *The Slippery Slope of Same-Sex Marriage*, the Family Research Council (FRC) writes: "Data from the 2000 U.S. Census and other sources indicates that only a small percentage of homosexual households choose to raise children. One reason for this is that the raising of children is inimical to the typical homosexual lifestyle, which as we have seen typically involves a revolving bedroom door" (Dailey 2004). The FRC references the 2000 Decennial Census, which indicates the small percentage of homosexual households with children, which was no doubt the case, at least as far as it was possible to derive this information from census data. But what I find curious is the juxtaposition of a statement of findings from the census with the second statement. It says that one reason for the low percentage of same-sex households choosing to raise children is that it would cramp the lifestyle of promiscuous homosexuals. First of all, the Census Bureau statistics do not report choices regarding raising children. They report the number of households raising children by type of household. Further, the second statement is not supported. Where does the rationale that LGBT people think children cramp their lifestyle come from? It certainly does not come from the Census Bureau's report.

This idea of the promiscuity of gays and lesbians has reached mythic proportions, largely because such ideas are repeated over and over. For example, in a FRC "research" paper on homosexuality, author Timothy Dailey makes this statement, "Research indicates that the average male homosexual has hundreds of sex partners in his lifetime" (2014).[7] Is this really true? Where is the data to support it? Most researchers concede that the data on homosexuals and their behaviors are often inadequate because the percentage of the population that is LGBT is relatively small, as we demonstrated in chapter 4. This problem is compounded by the challenges of recruiting LGBT persons to participate in surveys—a problem recognized by all parties (LeVay 1997). So to make such blanket and, frankly, over-the-top statements not only is bad research but also contributes to negative stereotypes of gay people. Furthermore, much of the research that has been done has focused on males. To generalize to all LGBT people from this is additionally unwarranted and hurtful.

Is there research that can address the question about promiscuity? After all, many of us can remember the late '70s and early '80s when promiscuity among young adults had mushroomed. But for those of us who remember those days, one's orientation was really not the issue. There is some data that does not line up with the claims of the FRC or other groups who repeat this claim.[8] The following graph presents data from the General Social Survey (GSS), collected by researchers at the University of Chicago since 1972 to the present (2014). The graph displays men only who were divorced, separated, or never married. Along the vertical axis is the number of sexual partners in the past five years. The black bars represent men who had male sex partners, and the gray bars represent men who had female sex partners. The horizontal axis represents what percentage of each group by the number of sexual partners (N=number of partners).

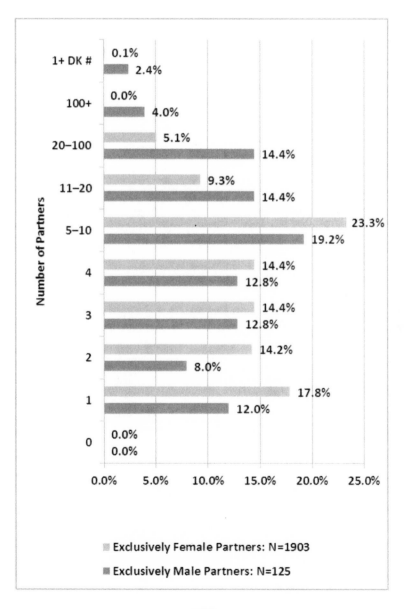

Number of partners in last five years expressed in % of Total (N)		
No. of Sex Partners	Exclusively Male Partners: N=125	Exclusively Female Partners: N=1903
0	0.0%	0.0%
1	12.0%	17.8%
2	8.0%	14.2%
3	12.8%	14.4%
4	12.8%	14.4%
5–10	19.2%	23.3%
11–20	14.4%	9.3%
20–100	14.4%	5.1%
100+	4.0%	0.0%
1+ DK #	2.4%	0.1%

The graph and table show that the number of sexual partners for gay men tracks closely with the number of sexual partners of straight men. It is only in the extreme that gay men begin to demonstrate a promiscuous pattern. In those reporting twenty or more partners in five years, it only represents 18 percent of all gay men. But even 5 percent of the heterosexual men reported as many, making the difference between them only thirteen points. These data suggest that on average both straight and gay men have about five partners in five years. Odd as this conversation is to discuss, it does belie the exaggerated statement of the FRC that "the average male homosexual has hundreds of sex partners in his lifetime." Such statements do not serve an honest dialogue about the merits or otherwise of same-sex marriage or the propriety of same-sex committed relationships. And it certainly does not bring any honest clarity to the question of the quality of same-sex couple parents as models for children.

I do not take lightly the level of promiscuity that is demonstrated by some gay men. But neither should we take lightly that of straight men. It is a true moral problem for our society, and the church does have something to say on the subject. Promiscuity does not secure for its perpetrators what they think it acquires. Like so many human pursuits, it is just another form of idolatry that promises life but leaves in its path a wasteland of death. That is truly sad. God wants more for us.

The Poor Parenting Model Problem

Social and religious conservatives maintain that committed, same-sex couples are not suited to be good parents and to create healthy home environments for children. This has not been my personal experience. So why do the social conservatives make this claim? For the FRC, who seem to be a pretty good representative of this viewpoint, it's founded on the prior claim that homosexuals are promiscuous and do not sustain long-term committed relationships. Again I turn to material from the FRC:

> Homosexuals and lesbians are unsuitable role models for children because of their lifestyle. Dr. Brad Hayton observes that homosexual households "model a poor view of marriage to children. They are taught by example and belief that marital relationships are transitory and mostly sexual in nature....And they are taught that monogamy in a marriage is not the norm [and] should be discouraged if one wants a good 'marital' relationship." (Dailey 2004)

According to the FRC, the reason same-sex couples are not suitable parents is that they sleep around. We already found that gay and straight men on the whole are just as likely to "sleep around." Additionally, the data on same-sex parenting is not reliable. In reviewing what I could find, much of it was posted by antigay groups. What some of the data do indicate is that gay men who participated in the research have trouble with commitment. (Frankly, straight men seem to have trouble with commitment too, but that is a different conversation.) One study did indicate that unfaithfulness was declining among gay men. Relational faithfulness between lesbians is much higher (Leichliter 2013).

If commitment to monogamy is the key, then our entire population needs to do some work. There are complex causes of any particular social behavior. The fact that a primary message of our culture has been that LGBT persons have to change does not encourage the pursuit of healthy relationships. There is, of course, the ghetto effect as well. Compact a particular population in a small space and unusual things can happen. Our college campuses are marvelous examples. LGBT enclaves in large urban areas are examples as well.

237

But same-sex couples with children are not likely to raise their children in such environments (see the map at end of chapter 5) (Gates 2013).

A study by the American Academy of Pediatrics released in 2013 found the well-being of children raised with same-sex parents was fine. After thirty years of research, they found no indication that children raised in a same-sex environment were any less resilient "with regard to social, psychological, and sexual health despite economic and legal disparities and social stigma" (Perrin and Siegel 2013).

I will concede some ground to FRC. I do believe that the best environment for the healthy nurturing of children is one in which parents are perceived as happy and committed. That so many must grow up without this (and I am talking of heterosexual households now) is deeply regrettable. We all can do better to support families and encourage relational fidelity for the sake of our children. This being the case, gay couples with children, like straight couples with children, have some work to do.

The Same-Sex Relationships Don't Last Problem

Social and religious conservatives assert that same-sex relationships don't last and, for that reason, should not be considered on par with traditional marriage. Unfortunately there is some truth to the claim that same-sex relationships do not last very long. This is especially true among gay men. It is less true of lesbians.

There are several social dynamics at work here, however, that conservatives do not take into consideration before jumping to conclusions. First and perhaps the most important dynamic is the rapidly evolving social acceptance of the idea that same-sex partnerships and marriage are intended to be for the long haul. Second, we have already looked at the data that suggests there is a certain percentage of gay men who are promiscuous, but that is not the subgroup within the LGBT population we should be looking at here, anymore than we would look at the subpopulation of single straight males when looking at patterns of straight marriage. So to address the question, are same-sex relationships less likely to last than straight relationships, we must focus on that portion of the LGBT community that is seeking to form loving committed relationships on the model of traditional marriage. The data on this is not extensive, in part because it has not been the focus of social research. The Williams Institute of the University of California–Los Angeles conducted a study dated November 2011 entitled "Patterns of Relationship Recognition by Same-Sex Couples in the United States" (Badgett and Herman 2011, 1-2). As a law center, their focus overall was the different legal rights of same-sex couples in the various states of the United States. Part of their research included an analysis of the percentage of gay and lesbian persons who actually formed long-term commitments and how long those commitments lasted. The following list captures some of their key findings:

- Over 140,000 same-sex couples, or 22 percent of all same-sex couples in the United States, have formalized their relationship under state law within the United States.

- In the states with available data, dissolution rates for same-sex couples are slightly lower on average than divorce rates of different-sex couples. The percentage of those same-sex couples who end their legal relationship ranges from 0 percent to 1.8 percent annually, or 1.1 percent on average, whereas 2 percent of married different-sex couples divorce annually.

- After taking into account dissolutions and divorces, about 134,000 same-sex couples, or 21 percent of all US same-sex couples, are currently in a legally recognized relationship. In just those states that offer some form of legal recognition, 43 percent of couples are currently in a legally recognized relationship.

- Same-sex couples prefer marriage over civil unions or registered domestic partnerships, even when these statuses extend almost all of the rights and obligations of marriage under state law. An average of 30 percent of same-sex couples married in the first year that their state allowed them to marry, while only 18 percent entered into civil unions or broad domestic partnerships in the first year states offered these statuses. Furthermore, only 8 percent entered into limited domestic partnerships, reciprocal beneficiary relationships, or other limited statuses in the first year that states offered those statuses, which extend a smaller subset of the rights and obligations of marriage.

- Women are more likely to marry or formalize their relationships by entering an alternative legal status than are men. In eight states that provided data by gender, 62 percent of same-sex couples who sought legal recognition were female couples.

- Same-sex couples who marry or enter other legal recognition statuses tend to be younger than the general population of married different-sex couples in those states. However, when one compares same-sex and different-sex couples who are newly married, newly married same-sex couples tend to be older than newly married different-sex couples.

These findings make the point that the whole social landscape is changing as our culture adjusts to the social structure of same-sex partnerships and marriage. It also makes the point that it is not correct to make the claim that same-sex relationships don't last. Of those seeking long-term loving relationships that result in some kind of legal formalization (based upon what one's state allows), they are just as likely to remain together on the whole as straight couples. So when Brad Hayton of the FRC says, "Homosexuals . . . are taught by example and belief that marital relationships are transitory and mostly sexual in nature," he is simply wrong[9] (Hayton 1993). He has not focused on the subpopulation of those LGBT persons seeking to enter what would be consistent with a traditional loving, long-lasting partnership.

If you want to make the point that same-sex partnerships in general do not last by looking at the total population of the LGBT community, there is evidence to suggest that among some, relationships tend to be temporary. But frankly, if you look at the straight population this way, one will draw the same conclusion. If we have a problem in our culture, it is in our trend away from seeing lifelong relationships as the goal. Conversations I have personally had with many young people reveal that they don't believe relationships can last a lifetime.

The Domestic Violence Problem

Social and religious conservatives make the claim that domestic violence is more common among same-sex couples than among straight couples, demonstrating that same-sex marriage is not a viable social structure. Again from the pamphlet *The Slippery Slope of Same-Sex Marriage*, the FRC writes: "Intimate partner violence: homosexual and lesbian couples experience by far the highest levels of intimate partner violence compared with married couples as well as cohabiting heterosexual couples. Lesbians, for example, suffer a much higher level of violence than do married women" (Dailey 2004).

The research does not support this assertion. In fact one of the primary sources referenced by the FRC says exactly the opposite. The reference to the above statement comes from a report by the Department of Justice, titled *Extent, Nature, and Consequences of Intimate Partner Violence Findings from the*

National Violence against Women Survey (Tjaden and Thoennes 2000). In the executive summary, some of the findings report the following:

- Intimate-partner violence is pervasive in US society.

- Abusive and controlling behavior regularly attends the domestic violence.

- Women are more likely to be the victims of violence than men and experience greater injuries as a result.

- Women living in same-sex partnerships "experience less intimate partner violence than women living with male intimate partners" (roughly 11 percent for same-sex women versus 30 percent for women of opposite-sex relationships).

- Men living with a male partner do experience more violence than those who live with women. This finding confirms that men are more likely to be the perpetrators of domestic violence than women. The logic here is not to be lost. In a same-sex male relationship, there are two men, doubling the possibility of violence. So the issue is not so much that homosexuals perpetrate more domestic violence. The issue is that males perpetrate more domestic violence.

- Most partner violence (other-sex or same-sex) is not reported to police mostly because they do not believe the police would do anything.[10]

For the FRC to draw from this research their assertion is a failure to properly reflect the research findings and is in fact misleading and disingenuous.

So what does the research reveal? First of all, one does not read very far in the research before realizing that domestic violence is a problem. Second, the predominance of research points to the following findings:

- The percentage of incidents of domestic violence between same-sex partners is similar to the percentage between opposite-sex partners.

- The perpetrators of domestic violence tend to be men regardless of the sex of the partner.

- Victims of same-sex domestic violence are not as likely to receive supporting and protective services as victims in an opposite-sex partnership.

241

Instead of making unfounded claims about the incidence of same-sex intimate-partner violence as the FRC does, we as a society ought to be looking for ways to mitigate the domestic violence that does occur. The church again has a role to play in this, and it is not the role of a condemning judge. Our role ought to be showing people the way of Jesus and looking for real and practical ways to help both victims and potential perpetrators get the help they need in support of human flourishing.

The Slippery Slope Problem

One of the objections against same-sex marriage and families is that it will open the door to a whole host of other "lifestyles," including polygamy, pedophilia, and even bestiality—what I am calling the "slippery slope problem."[11] I must first of all state that I think this highly unlikely. Yet in the pamphlet put out by the FRC, they open with this statement—along with a picture of a horse: "A Man and His Horse: In what some call a denial of a basic civil right, a Missouri man has been told he may not marry his long-term companion. Although his situation is unique, the logic of his argument is remarkably similar to that employed by advocates of homosexual marriage" (Dailey 2004). The kinds of relationships I am talking about in this study bear no comparison. One can only assume that the motivation for making such odd claims is to create fear among conservative people. But for clarification, I offer three brief comments.

Pedophilia

Pedophilia is morally wrong. It is behavior in which one person manipulates and abuses another. It is a predatory behavior. Although it was practiced freely in the Greco-Roman world, thankfully the influence of Judeo-Christian morality has called this practice for what it is: evil. There is no healthy, flourishing love. There is only predator and victim. The harm inflicted is beyond our imaginations. Yet it is a persistent assertion by many in the conservative religious community that there is a linkage between pedophilia and homosexuality. The Family Research Council again takes the lead. In a 2002 report titled "Homosexuality and Child Sexual Abuse," it says the following: "While many homosexuals may not seek young sexual partners, the evidence indicates that disproportionate numbers of gay men seek adolescent males or boys as sexual partners" (FRC 2002).

What follows is a list of six points that the FRC intends to argue. The logic goes like this: (1) pedophilia is mostly committed by men; (2) a large number of victims are boys; (3) homosexuals as a percentage of the total population make up a disproportionate percentage of pedophiles; (4) some homosexuals advocate for the old Greek pederasty relationship; (5) gay fiction includes "intergenerational intimacy"; and (6) therefore, gays are more likely to be pedophiles.

But again, is this true? The research does not support this. In fact, it goes in the opposite direction. A report by Harvard Medical School's Health Publications in 2010 focused on pedophilia. Along with providing definitions and such statements as, "Consensus now exists that pedophilia is a distinct sexual orientation, not something that develops in someone who is homosexual or heterosexual," it also states that "roughly 9% to 40% of pedophiles are homosexual in their orientation toward children," *but that is not the same as saying they are homosexual. Homosexual adults are no more likely than heterosexuals to abuse children* (Harvard Medical School 2010).

Bestiality

What about bestiality? Frankly, it seems silly to even bring it up. If love is the defining element in a relationship and committed love is between two sentient beings, then there is no definition under which bestiality is acceptable. Caring deeply for animals is our vocation. This is what Genesis 1 teaches us: "Then God said, 'Let us make humankind in our image, according to our likeness; and let them have dominion over the fish of the sea, and over the birds of the air, and over the cattle, and over all the wild animals of the earth, and over every creeping thing that creeps upon the earth.'" (v. 26 NRSV). Using God's creatures to fulfill one's own lustful desires instead of caring for them properly is again evil and contrary to the promotion of flourishing in God's creation.

Polygamy

What about polygamy? This is, of course, a more difficult question, and a full exploration of the topic is certainly beyond the scope of this study. But since it is part of the slippery slope objection, I must deal with it briefly. In many ways polygamy is a more difficult question than homosexuality because Bible stories include multiple examples of men with multiple wives, many of whom are fathers of the faith. Consider, for example, Abraham, Jacob, David, and Solomon, to name the most obvious ones. Yet at the same time, the Bible promotes as normative a relationship between only two people. See Genesis 1 and 2. I think that the "two people" is the key. A committed relationship is one entered mutually between two people, person A with person B.

In polygamy, one or more additional people are introduced. Most examples are of a man making commitments to multiple women.

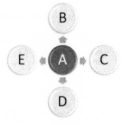

The fair question to ask of those advocating for polygamy is: Does each member of the relationship make commitments equally to all the other members? Or is the primary commitment to person A? Of course, there can be all sorts of answers to the question, but in the end, the human flourishing observation is determinative.

I realize that my argument here may come close to closing the door on same-sex marriage. If marriage is an intimate commitment between two people, does the Bible not say that these two people are male and female? Yes, it clearly does. So have I dismantled my entire argument by challenging polygamy? I don't think so and here is why. I have already made the argument that the primary focus is partnership that ends loneliness. It is clear that in more than 90 percent of the cases this will be an intimate relationship between a man and a woman. But we have also seen that nature spins out on a relatively regular basis over time a certain percentage of the population that is LGBT. That being the case, I argue that the moral calling is for two people, of the opposite sex or same sex, to make deep, loving commitments to each other that promote life. I do not believe polygamy does this.

Red Herrings All

In reality, these are all "red herring" arguments.[12] They are intended to detract from the primary question. The question of love and life remains the central criteria for viewing all of these. For example, our society knows that pedophilia is evil just as we know human trafficking and slavery are evil. That is not going to change—I hope! Bestiality fears are a reach. The percentage of the population that seeks to practice polygamy is extremely small. Where it is practiced, there exist great concerns that young women are not really given choices and too often are married barely into puberty. Most of us would consider this practice blatant child abuse. The claim that same-sex relationships do not last is far more nuanced than is often stated. The promiscuity and poor parent models claims are simply not founded on real data. Finally the charge that same-sex couples experience higher levels of intimate-partner violence is simply not true.

So why all of these claims? Each claim by the social and religious conservative community is portrayed as rooted in social or medical science research. The conclusions drawn are all intended to show that it is bad public policy to support same-sex committed relationships and same-sex families with children. As we have seen, the assertions are not supported by the research. It is my suspicion that behind it all are theological assumptions based upon their readings of the Bible and, in some cases, natural law. This is an example of domain jumping. By dressing their assertions in the language of the social sciences, these groups give the appearance of academic credibility. But it is a particular religious worldview based upon their interpretation of scripture that is the driving force forming their assertions in this manner. I am not opposed to building moral arguments out of one's theology. I have done just that. But I have not tried to use the findings of other domains of inquiry to surreptitiously legitimize my theological position.

Notes

1. I have borrowed the phrase *the good* from Miroslav Volf. In his book *A Public Faith: How Followers of Christ Should Serve the Common Good*, he talks about human flourishing. It is his way of talking about the life God wants for humans but which we so often reject in the choices we make. Whenever I use this term throughout the book, this is what I am referring to because, from my standpoint, Volf has it correct.

2. Gagnon follows this line of interpretation: "He [Paul] also apparently regarded some knowledge of moral absolutes among gentiles as possible through the 'natural' faculties of reason and conscience (Rom 2:14-16)" (Gagnon 2001, 257).

3. It is likely that Paul, as a good Jew, had in mind that one could simply look around and see creation and in the seeing conclude that there had to be a god who was responsible

for it all. To argue that Paul was in some way an incipient rationalist does not seem to be reasonable given what we know about Paul and about the worldview of Second Temple Judaism.

4. When you sort through all of the pieces of Gagnon's argument, in the end he bases much of it on this one principle of procreative possibility, which he couples with biological complementarity of male and female.

5. The classic Protestant ideal of "sola scriptura" meant that scripture alone was our basis for knowing what was necessary for salvation and for a holy life. The Westminster Confession of Faith, chapter I, section VII says, "All things in Scripture are not alike plain in themselves, nor alike clear unto all; yet those things which are necessary to be known, believed, and observed, for salvation, are so clearly propounded and opened in some place of Scripture or other, that not only the learned, but the unlearned, in a due use of the ordinary means, may attain unto a sufficient understanding of them" (Williamson 2004, 17).

6. Though Jesus is Lord of all, not all recognize that Lordship, and so laws are required. I believe those laws ought to reflect the values of the kingdom of God.

7. A review of Dailey's sources brings the credibility of his statement into question. The first study by Maria Xiridou et al., "The Contribution of Steady and Casual Partnerships to the Incidence of HIV Infection among Homosexual Men in Amsterdam" (2003, 1031), is the most recent. It was a Dutch study of HIV-infected men. To draw a percentage from this population skews the results dramatically. HIV-infected gay men is a subset of the total gay and lesbian population. The second study, which is by A. P. Bell and M. S. Weinberg, *Homosexualities: A Study of Diversity among Men and Women* (308, 309] is dated 1978. See also A. P. Bell, M. S. Weinberg, and S. K. Hammersmith, *Sexual Preference* (1981). The third study is by Paul Van de Ven et al., "A Comparative Demographic and Sexual Profile of Older Homosexually Active Men" (354) focuses on older active homosexual men and is dated 1997. A search of the quote in a magazine called *Genere* (October 1996) could not be found after multiple attempts.

8. Although certainly not an exhaustive list, other groups and an individual who repeat the negative claims about LGBT people include the following below. It should be noted that some of this is self-referencing information. That is, they quote one another and the same "statistics" regularly. They are TrueNews.org (http://www.truenews.org/Homosexuality/homosexual_myths_and_facts.html), Exodus Global Alliance (http://www.exodusglobalalliance.org/ishomosexualityhealthyp60.php), Christian Apologetics & Research Ministry (http://carm.org/statistics-homosexual-promiscuity), and Joseph Nicolosi (http://josephnicolosi.com/an-open-secret-the-truth-about/).

9. Hayton's natural law bias is also present in his statement when he says sexual relationships among homosexuals are primarily about pleasure not procreation.

10. Other data suggest this is even more the case between same-sex partners because of the stigma associated with homosexuality.

11. See Achtemeier 2014.

12. A red herring argument raises an irrelevant topic in order to divert attention from the original issue.

LGBT People, the Church, and the Future

I am ready to address the questions about homosexuality and the church that I laid out in the beginning based upon the findings of the research. I realize that what I will say will not be acceptable in some Christian circles. However, I hope that I have helped you, the reader, think through the issues. I do hope that the book has given some comfort to LGBT persons and their families who struggle to reconcile their faith and their reality. I also hope that I have changed some minds or at least opened some a bit.

Synopsis

I began this study with a set of questions. The structure of the study was designed to provide a logical process for thinking through the issues from the various domains of inquiry that are germane to this issue, including how biblical texts are interpreted. The study culminated in the presentation of a moral framework for considering the entire LGBT issue (or any issue for that matter). Here is a summary of the main points:

- God is the creator of all that is, and God's view of creation is that it is good.

- God gave creation the freedom to unfold within a framework of natural laws with contingency that has fruitfully resulted in a great deal of natural diversity in the cosmos, within the natural formation of the earth and within the flora and fauna that have evolved on the earth.

- Current biological science demonstrates that sex and gender are initially formed in utero in the interplay between a person's genes and the hormonal environment in which a fetus develops.

- Sexual orientation and gender therefore are innate traits determined before birth. They are not a choice a person makes.

- It is obvious that environmental factors do contribute to the formation of adult LGBT persons.

- This science is a game changer. If sexual orientation and desires are innate, then the homosexual person is who he or she is. The question will be what one does with that.

- The biblical texts used to condemn homosexuality have little if anything to do with the modern same-sex committed relationship that is at the center of this discussion. Almost everyone today would agree that the cultural norms of power and status in previous societies that resulted in sexual activity that was oppressive, exploitive, and abusive, are wrong and unacceptable in the modern world, even if they appear to be sanctioned by the Bible in some places.

- God's love for all of creation calls upon us to be as God and also love all of creation.

- There is a moral line, but it is not the axis between straight and gay; it is how one acts vis-à-vis the "other" that determines its morality. One kind of behavior seeks to fulfill love, while the other seeks to exploit for one's self-satisfaction.

- The Bible labels self-indulgent lifestyles idolatry, for it is making something a god and giving one's self to it. But false gods cannot deliver life. The end result of self-indulgent idolatry is the opposite of human flourishing. Human flourishing is God's intent for humans.

With these conclusions before us, we can provide short answers to the initial research questions up to the point at which we turn our attention to how the church should respond to the LGBT person.

Research Questions	Summary Answers
Is one born a homosexual or transsexual person or is homosexuality something someone chooses? In other words, is sexual orientation a choice an individual makes?	Current science supports the idea that a person's sexual orientation is an innate trait with which one is born. One does not choose to be heterosexual, bisexual, or homosexual. One is born as one of these or, in some cases, intersexual.
Is same-sex attraction sinful in itself?	No. Attraction is attraction. At the biological and psychological level, it is a natural process that is established through processes that also determine a person's orientation. Attraction serves the human community by bringing people together.
Within the scope of the healing and restoration of creation, is homosexuality a disease to be corrected?	If there is nothing that is broken, there is nothing to fix. All of us have need of healing and restoration of our sexuality, for all of us are broken in some way. What sexuality will be like when the heavens and earth become one and we are all healed, I do not know. But whatever it is, it will be good, and I very much look forward to that.
Is it true that LGBT people are more promiscuous than heterosexual people?	No, research does not support this. On the whole, gay people are no more promiscuous that straight people, though there is an extreme edge of gay males who demonstrate unusual promiscuity. This is a sad circumstance.

Is it true that same-sex relationships do not last as long as hetero-sex relationships?	It is not true if one is careful to focus only on that percentage of the LGBT community that is actually seeking to establish a lasting partnership/marriage. Sadly it can be the case for the general population of LGBT people.

Remaining Questions

"Where is the application?" we often ask. This study was designed to address some specific questions vis-à-vis homosexuality and the church. I certainly do not presume to have done an exhaustive study on the subject. Given the amount of material written on this issue, the only exhausting thing would be to read it all and try to respond to it all. I have tried to focus my analysis on what I believe to be the most germane issues, with the intent of developing the conceptual framework within which to address the church questions. In this regard, there are three areas remaining to address: (1) sexual behavior, (2) same-sex marriage, and (3) LGBT leadership in the church.

Abstinence

Is abstinence for life the only choice for a Christian LGBT person? Or can one enter into an intimate and sexual relationship and still be an active participant in a Christian community? The conventional answers to these two questions form the foundation upon which the other questions are based. The traditional view of human sexual expression is between a man and a woman who have been formally joined in marriage. That view precludes a world of sexual behaviors regardless of one's orientation. Social and religious conservatives press this one hard and have worked to have school districts teach abstinence only as the lone true birth control. Having been a school board member for eleven years, I ran into this more than once. Frankly I always thought it was naive to insist on an abstinence-only curriculum while hoping all along that the students would not be sexually active.

I believe the best approach to this question is to begin with sexual behavior in general and the basis for choices in this regard before addressing the issue of gay/lesbian sexual behaviors. I do not totally disagree with the religious conservatives who want to see people restrain from sexual behavior outside of marriage. But we get to this position from two different paths. For many conservatives, improper sexual behavior leads to the judgment of God and the prospect of spending eternity in hell. Within this conceptual world, young people are taught sex is bad unless you are married and you are bad if you practice it before marriage. In our sex-crazed world, it is a tall order to insist that young people remain chaste until that first night after they say, "I do." Consequently we have young people everywhere dropping out of our churches because their choice is between feeling guilty and condemned or turning away from God entirely.

I believe this is a wrongheaded approach to sexual morality. I also don't believe it reflects the biblical story. If love is the center out of which flows everything else, then we ought to teach our young people (and the rest of us too) that our choices ought to flow out of love for the other just as Jesus's choices for us did. Life flourishes when love is the source of an action. I realize that to some this sounds naive. What sixteen-year-old boy is going to refrain from sexual experimentation because it is "not loving"? I don't know. But what sixteen-year-old boy refrains from sex because the fear of hell or the fear of an angry God hangs over him? Not many it would appear. There are significant challenges for us humans to overcome if we are to be truly human. But where we start from is important. We too often fail to keep the big picture in mind and trust the Spirit to accomplish what has been promised. So I believe one chooses abstinence because it is the loving thing to do for the other and even for one's self. Sound familiar?

> "Teacher, what is the greatest commandment in the Law?" He replied, "*You must love the Lord your God with all your heart, with all your being*, and with all your mind. This is the first and greatest commandment. And the second is like it: *You must love your neighbor as you love yourself*. All the Law and the Prophets depend on these two commands." (Matt 22:36-40)

Now with this as our approach to sexual moral questions, what do we say to the LGBT person? I have already concluded that being gay with same-sex attraction is an innate reality. There is nothing biologically wrong with being gay. If there is nothing biologically wrong, then there is nothing wrong period any more than there is something wrong with all of us.[1] What is wrong with all of us is that we are inclined toward idolatry, toward pursuing behaviors and lifestyles that are inimical to human flourishing. The call to all of us is to make moral choices that promote life and not death. So to the LGBT person, I would say promiscuous sex is a sure path to destruction. You were intended for better than this. I do believe sex promotes human flourishing when it happens within the security and intimacy of a committed relationship on the order of marriage. I am not being a prude here. I am being a realist. What God wants for all of us is human experiences that build us up and not tear us down.

Christian Same-Sex Marriage

The next question follows from the discussion about abstinence. Is same-sex marriage acceptable from a Christian standpoint? If it is possible to have a sexual relationship that promotes life, then it is reasonable to assume there is a structure that is supportive of that. In our culture, this is marriage. Marriage is a social construct designed to protect and encourage *durative* relationships. It is not easy to get out of a marriage, and it shouldn't be. Our human nature is such that we are inclined to put away things that are difficult for us. Marriage helps protect us from that. It draws a hedge around a relationship and says, "Inside this circle of two is to be only two." It is sacred space in which intimacy, honesty, and individual safety from the outside world occur. Sacred space. Yes, marriage is a social construct, but it is also a holy construct. In that space of two is to be one other, that is, God who gives life.

Same-sex marriage would seem to me to be the place where two people who happen to be gay or lesbian make a commitment that is intended to be durative and is intended to reflect a solemn vow to God to honor that commitment and honor the vocation of loving the other. It may not feel real comfortable to those of us who are straight, especially those of us who are older. I still find that I wrestle with myself when I see a same-sex couple. But that feeling of discomfort, I believe, is the result of my socialization, not God's condemnation of LGBT people who are seeking to find what I have enjoyed since 1976—marriage. Therefore I do believe that the church ought to embrace same-sex marriage and regain the high moral ground by calling us all to love the other and therefore to promote life.

LGBT Leaders in the Church

Should LGBT persons be allowed to become ordained leaders in the church?

Let me begin with some questions. If we are going to be "biblical," why do we allow women to be in ordained leadership? First Timothy 2:12 says, "I don't allow a wife to teach or to control her husband. Instead, she should be a quiet listener." If we are going to be "biblical," why do we allow divorced persons to be in ordained leadership? First Timothy 3:2-3 says, "So the church's supervisor must be without fault. They should be faithful to their spouse, sober, modest, and honest. They should show hospitality and be skilled at teaching. They shouldn't be addicted to alcohol or a bully. Instead, they should be gentle, peaceable, and not greedy." Or in the case of deacons, 1 Timothy 3:12 says, "Servants must be faithful to their spouse and manage their children and their own households well."

Most certainly I affirm both of these groups of people, regardless of their gender or marital experience, to qualify for leadership in the church because, as I have already stated, sometimes biblical authors' writing reflects their cultural environment. This is the case in 1 Timothy. But it is not an unqualified affirmation. Not just every divorced person or not every woman or certainly not every man is, in fact, qualified for church leadership. Within my own tradition, we ordain teaching elders (pastors), ruling elders, and deacons. Each denomination has its own ordination process, but each expects to find evidence of faithful Christian life, character, and service. This is at least what we take away from 1 Timothy.

Coming to the question of LGBT persons and church leadership, I believe they ought to be granted opportunities to serve alongside their straight colleagues. But again, it is not an unqualified affirmation. I believe we need to ask the same kinds of questions of our LGBT friends in terms of prerequisites for service as we ask of straight people. Evidence of faithful Christian life, character, and service ought to be present.

So a fair question is, given what I've already said, why are LGBT persons, who fully accept Jesus as Lord and seek to live the life of love he showed us, not qualified for ordained church leadership? Obviously I believe they should be. I really do not believe it is any more complicated than this. There are clear ties that bind people of the opposite sex and the same sex together, which produce lives that flourish. There are beliefs that break our fellowship. These beliefs have been breaking us apart now for over forty years. It is surely time for that to change.

One final question needs to be considered, because it is this specific question that prodded me to embark upon this study in response to the potential requirement that I sign a document supporting marriage between a man and woman only. Does support of same-sex marriage disqualify one from leadership and teaching ministries in the church? I do not believe it should for all of the reasons and research that have brought us to this place in our study.

Now we can complete our table of question and answers.

Research Questions	Summary Answers
Is abstinence for life the only choice for a Christian LGBT person? Or can one enter into an intimate and sexual relationship and still be an active participant in a Christian community?	I do not believe abstinence for life is the only choice for a Christian LGBT person given that orientation and attraction are innate traits. But we also must insist on some moral expectations of LGBT persons like we (or at least should) expect of any Christian person. Actions should be expressions of love as God loves. Outcomes pursued should promote human flourishing.
Is same-sex marriage acceptable from a Christian standpoint?	If the above statement is true, then same-sex marriage only makes sense. It is in the context of a durative loving commitment that life is to be found.[2]
Should LGBT persons be allowed to become ordained leaders in the church? Does support of same-sex marriage disqualify one from leadership and teaching ministries in the church?	If we can affirm the validity of a same-sex committed partnership/marriage (depending upon what legal structure is available to them) and they are living faithfully within that relationship, then there is no reason to restrict LGBT persons from active leadership in the church at any level nor those who are supportive of LGBT people.

What Must Change?

To see our doors opened to the LGBT community and to see the church have a voice in calling them, like straight folk, to faithful discipleship, we must make some changes.

We must realize that our discomfort is *our* discomfort. It is no different than the discomfort many Southerners felt when suddenly blacks were granted equal status. It is no different than the discomfort many of us felt as we recognized the need and necessity of granting women equal status in society and in the church; although, I am not saying we have arrived. As Paul teaches us in Galatians 3:28: "There is neither Jew nor Greek; there is neither slave nor free; nor is there male and female, for you are all one in Christ Jesus."

Do you think Paul meant to include only three classes of people? No, Paul was speaking to the universal inclusion of all humans in the kingdom of

Jesus the Messiah. He certainly called us to a life of holiness, but is that not a life that places the love of God first and the love of the other second? Is this not the summation of Torah? Yes, that is what Jesus said! So our first change is to confront our discomfort.

The second change is willingly to redefine what Christian marriage means. I realize, even as I write this, how ominous this sounds. It is all well and good to argue back and forth and raise our righteous voices asserting this or that view. But now we are talking about changing something that has been in place for a very long time. I personally would not be proposing this if I did not have the science to inform me. As I said earlier, the science that tells us that sexual orientation and attraction are rooted in biological processes requires me to rethink all of this. So it is not lightly that I concur with those calling for a redefinition that is inclusive of all people.[3]

The third change that is called for is how we define Christian leadership. I have already indicated that there are qualifications that must be taken seriously. Frankly, I don't think we take leadership qualification seriously enough. I have watched this for over thirty years of working with churches and church agencies. Far too often the only qualification for leadership (other than being a heterosexual) was being a warm body. We have far too many people sitting in leadership positions who are not leaders or whose Christian character is not what it ought to be in order to faithfully lead the people of God. But there are LGBT people who love God and want to serve God whom we exclude from leadership unless they take a vow of celibacy. I think this must change. I do think we ought to expect of all our leaders sexual faithfulness within the context of a committed lifelong relationship. But I do not believe we should continue to exclude gay or lesbian people who are in active, committed partnerships if they live in a state in which marriage is not yet legal from serving the body of Christ as leaders.

Personal Reflections on the Work of the Spirit

Before I close this chapter, I want to take a brief excursion. In my research I have come across the notion that the issue of same-sex marriage and LGBT ordination is parallel to the social-political-religious movements that resulted in the end of slavery and the acceptance of women in church leadership. These changes came as a result of movements that sought to be true to the radical nature of the kingdom of God and to the call to be a new humanity. I have wondered, "Why did it take so long?" I don't really have an answer, but I feel this is the same process that is occurring with this issue.

Perhaps this really is the work of the Spirit. We have all of our human machinations, but in the end, the Spirit works. Today, tolerance for diversity has never been greater, at least in most Western countries shaped by Christianity in one form or another over the past two thousand years. Additionally I thought, well in God's timing, this might be on schedule, not because God is slow to work or is uncaring, but because we humans learn some things slowly and because of God's commitment to heal and restore without violating our freedom as humans.

It makes me wonder what new changes will be on the horizon as our world faces serious problems. Climate change is real, more real that many of us comprehend. Human population growth threatens our world with the inability even to feed everyone. The earth really does have finite resources that we are burning through now at an incredibly rapid rate. How will the Spirit lead us on these issues? And will the conservative nature of the church lag or lead? I don't know, but we must think about it and listen for the Holy Spirit's urgings.

Into the Future

I am certainly not the first to insist that we have all been haggling over this issue for quite long enough. I have spent much of my career working with denominations and churches. This single issue has diverted more energy and action than anything else in that time. Yet for all of these years most churches are at an impasse. However, it does appear that within the historic mainline traditions the tide has turned toward support of LGBT people, same-sex marriage, and ordination. For some of us this is now causing a new reaction. In my own denomination, a group emerged under the leadership of our "tall-steeple churches" that created an environment in which evangelicals still committed to "biblical authority on homosexuality" can find common cause. Additionally, this group spawned a new denomination for those churches and regional agencies that wanted to leave the previous denomination. Other denominations are wrestling with the same polarities and structural shifts. It all makes me deeply sad.

Finding a Way Forward

Is there a way forward? Or are we stuck in an infinite regress—an endless Groundhog Day[4]*—*condemned to continuing to haggle, to look for new political devices to move things in one direction or another? Can we do better?

Would not the love of Christ expect us to find a way to move out of this polarization without further divisions within the body of Christ?

Unacceptable in my mind is any path that seeks to exclude. Both sides in this debate have demonized and excluded the others. But there is so much we share in common beginning with our common affirmation that Jesus is Lord. I can think of many issues we could jointly engage that would play a role in "God's project of new creation."[5] Building a house for someone does not require that we agree on same-sex marriage. Fighting the plague of human trafficking does not necessitate an orthodoxy check. Fighting for housing for the many mentally impaired homeless in our communities does not require agreement on a particular reading of our Bible. Working in a school classroom as a volunteer with others does not require agreement on all moral and social issues as a people. And on and on this could go. We should join arms together for the benefit of God's creation. I cannot support actions by those whom I agree with on the homosexuality issue when they engage in exclusion of those whose conscience cannot let them embrace my position on the LGBT issue. Nor can I support actions by those who oppose my position when they seek to sideline or exclude those who advocate for full inclusion.

If Jesus is the center toward which we are all moving, we are moving together even if from different places. Therefore, the only acceptable path that I can find that is biblically sanctioned is the path of inclusion practiced by communities of people who have all found in Jesus the answers to humanity's deepest needs. This is certainly the more difficult path, but it is the path Jesus walked. The Gospel of Mark tells the story of James and John coming to Jesus to request that they sit on his right and left when he comes in his glory:

> James and John, Zebedee's sons, came to Jesus and said, "Teacher, we want you to do for us whatever we ask." "What do you want me to do for you?" he asked. They said, "Allow one of us to sit on your right and the other on your left when you enter your glory." Jesus replied, "You don't know what you're asking! Can you drink the cup I drink or receive the baptism I receive?" "We can," they answered. Jesus said, "You will drink the cup I drink and receive the baptism I receive, but to sit at my right or left hand isn't mine to give. It belongs to those for whom it has been prepared." (10:35-40)

This has always been one of many truly enigmatic texts to me. It seems so brazenly unlike how we understand the ethics of the kingdom of God as taught by Jesus. What happened to taking the lowest seat at the table and letting the host raise you? Here they are *asking* to be raised. In my mind, I picture the throne room of heaven with one seat on each side and Jesus

257

sitting in the middle. In that scenario, their request is the ultimate expression of presumption. Most of us just read over this text and think, *how silly of them*. Jesus, however, does not rebuke them for their question, as he rebuked the Pharisees for their practices. Rather, he redirects the question and tells them they really don't know what they are asking. He asks them if they are willing to be baptized as he is about to be baptized. They confidently respond, "We can." Jesus confirms that they indeed will be baptized with the same baptism; they will follow the path that he will tread. We know now that Jesus meant they would die for following him as he was about to die. But what did he mean by the last statement about who will be on his right and on his left? I again find an answer in N. T. Wright. He explains that Jesus was talking about who will be on his left and right when he comes into his kingdom, but that moment was not as James and John imagined. That moment was on the cross. There were in fact two with him, one on his left and one on his right, but it turns out they were two criminals who were guilty: "They also led two other criminals to be executed with Jesus. When they arrived at the place called The Skull, they crucified him, along with the criminals, one on his right and the other on his left" (Luke 23:32-33).

Why am I now focusing on the cross? Because I believe the way forward for all of us, regardless of the side of the issue we fall on LGBT issues, if Jesus is truly the center, is the way of the cross. But what does this mean in practical terms? Well let me explain in practical terms what Jesus did. Again, N. T. Wright has opened my eyes to a much greater insight into the significance of Jesus's death on the cross and specifically why it went the way it did (2013). Jesus did not ever draw upon evil to combat evil. He gave himself fully without recourse. And he did not call down angels for help. And imagine how it was for the Father. There is the Son with no one coming to his aid. He was innocent, though hanging helplessly between two criminals. Evil threw at him everything it could through the power of the Roman Empire and the religious authorities who saw in him a threat to their established order. Never once did he return evil for evil. When evil had nothing else it could throw at him, he died. In that moment, evil was defeated. Jesus demonstrated that evil's power has limits. The resurrection vindicated Jesus's righteousness and rightful authority. Death could not hold him.

Evil can only persist where evil is used, even against evil. Where love persists, that is, love as Jesus loved, evil is defeated. The true mark of who is the center of one's life is how we respond individually and collectively to difficult situations. And this is certainly the case when we are discussing the issue of homosexuality. When either side resorts to name calling, derision, or disrespect, that side is not following the way of Jesus, and the result is the breakup of the fellowship of God's people and the failure to live in the world as ambassadors for Jesus, the Messiah. Instead of promoting the way of flourishing, we promote the way of exclusion and death.

This calls for a choice. That choice must begin with me.

Notes

1. The only exception to this might be the transgender person if the person experiences a disconnect between their physical sex and their gender. But in these cases, this is an issue for the transgender person to determine, hopefully with assistance from qualified mental health persons.

2. I do not intend by this statement to say that life cannot be found for a single person. My point is to emphasize the need for structures that support durative relationships if relationships are to be formed.

3. I do believe we must be extremely wise and careful in this. When either side in the debate unduly forces their position on the other, only brokenness and alienation occur.

4. This is a fun reference to the 1993 Harold Ramis movie starring Bill Murray and Andie MacDowell.

5. See again, the tagline for Canvas OC: "Inviting everyone to join in God's project of new creation"

Appendix

These data extend the analysis of the religious community on the social issue questions of the Quadrennium Survey. They portray how the different Christian religious traditions responded to the four statements. The statements are provided here again for quick reference.

Of the following statements of personal belief, please indicate your level of agreement or disagreement.	Strongly disagree	Somewhat disagree	No opinion	Somewhat agree	Strongly agree
I believe religious communities should fully embrace LGBT persons (lesbian, gay, bisexual, transgender).	1	2	3	4	5
I believe same-sex marriage should be legalized.	1	2	3	4	5
I believe marriage is only a relationship between one man and one woman.	1	2	3	4	5
I believe children ought to be raised in a two-parent, mother and father family if possible.	1	2	3	4	5

"I believe religious communities should fully embrace LGBT persons."

When the traditions were aggregated, those who agreed that religious communities should fully embrace LGBT people was 39 percent compared to 34 percent who disagreed. Segment these affiliations out into the eight groups and the story changes significantly. The MissionInsite report provided this analysis:

> Broken down into their separate denominations it shows some groups ready to embrace the LGBT community while others are not. The groups with a higher percentage of agreement were Catholics, Episcopalians, Lutherans, Methodists, and Presbyterian/Reformed. The groups who had a higher percentage of disagreement were Baptist, Nondenominational, and Pentecostal/Holiness. (Regele 2012)

Should the Religious Community Embrace LGBT People by Christian Religious Affiliation

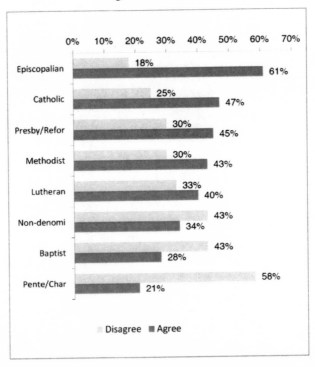

Source: The Quadrennium Project, 2012 MissionInsite LLC. The No Opinion responses have been removed. The groups represent religious traditions not specific denominations.

Not surprising, the data demonstrate a progressive to conservative orientation. Episcopalians, at 61 percent, are far more ready and willing to accept LGBT people than any other affiliation group. Baptists and Pentecostals are equally unlikely to embrace them. Presbyterians, Methodists, and Lutherans fall along the middle. There is a measurable group in these middle traditions who do not agree that LGBT persons should be embraced. It is these traditions that have had some of the most enduring internal conflict over the issue. A surprising finding is the more embracing number of Catholics given that the Catholic tradition is conservative.

"I believe same-sex marriage should be legalized."

Aggregating the eight religious affiliation groups, 49 percent believe same-sex marriage should be legalized compared to 31 percent who disagree. These percentages shift a bit to the conservative side relative to the national population with few "no opinion" responses.

Should Same-Sex Marriage Be Legalized by Christian Religious Affiliation

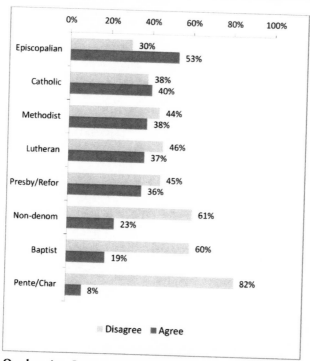

Source: The Quadrennium Project, 2012 MissionInsite, LLC. The No Opinion responses have been removed. The groups represent religious traditions not specific denominations.

The same progressive to conservative distribution plays out on this statement. While five traditions agreed they should welcome the LGBT community, there are only two that have a higher "agree" percentage that same-sex marriage should be legalized, Episcopalians and Catholics. The greater percentage of Lutherans, Presbyterian/Reformed, and Methodists do not agree that same-sex marriage should be legalized (Regele 2012).

Again Episcopalian agreement aligns on the agreement side and the Pentecostal/Holiness on the right. However the Episcopalian responses are not as far apart on this statement. Only 53 percent agree that same-sex marriage should be legalized. Three in ten do not. On the other side, over 80 percent of Pentecostal/Holiness disagrees with the legalization. The nondenominational group and the Baptists fall 20 percentage points lower than the Pentecostal/Holiness, but still six in ten disagree.

Catholics, who were second in agreeing that LGBT people ought to be embraced by religious communities, drop to 40 percent who agree with same-sex marriage with slightly less disagreeing. The other mainline traditions mostly track together, leaning on the side of nonlegalization: "This shows that these three groups are torn on this issue, they know they should be welcoming, however they are still not completely comfortable with LGBT issues" (Regele 2012). This becomes more obvious as the next two statements are considered.

"I believe marriage is only a relationship between one man and one woman."

Overall the findings indicate a more conservative shift on this issue for all eight religious traditions. In the aggregate the religious affiliation groups agree that marriage is between a man and a woman at 62 percent (Regele 2012). Only one in four disagrees. There is again a progressive to conservative distribution by tradition, but perhaps more significant is the fact that the difference between agree and disagree on the progressive Episcopalian side is minimal while the distance at the conservative end is greater than nine to one.

Marriage Is Only a Relationship between One Man and One Woman by Christian Religious Affiliation

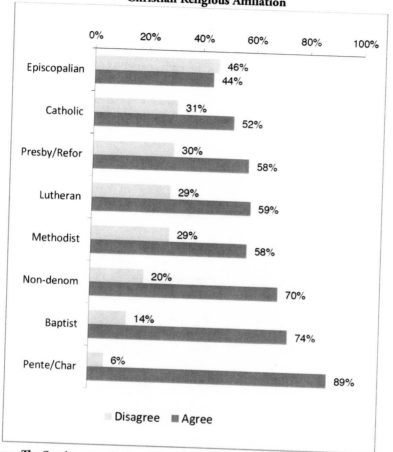

Source: The Quadrennium Project, 2012 MissionInsite, LLC. The No Opinion responses have been removed. The groups represent religious traditions not specific denominations.

Episcopalians who lead the pack in embracing and wanting to see same-sex marriage legalized fall back on how they want marriage defined. Only slightly more Episcopalian respondents disagreed that marriage is between a man and a woman than those who agreed. This is the most evenly divided yet for them. Nonetheless they were the only religious tradition with more who disagreed than agreed with a traditional marriage definition. All of the other groups agreed with the more traditional definition. For the Presbyterian/Reformed, Lutherans, and Methodists, this is the largest differentiation between agree and disagree. Almost 60 percent of the respondents from these three traditions affirm the traditional definition of marriage.

"I believe children ought to be raised in a two-parent, mother and father family if possible."

All of the traditions move to the conservative side when asked about the best environment to raise children. On average 73 percent believe the traditional two-parent mother and father family is the preferred child-rearing setting.

Children Ought to Be Raised in Two-Parent, Mother and Father Families

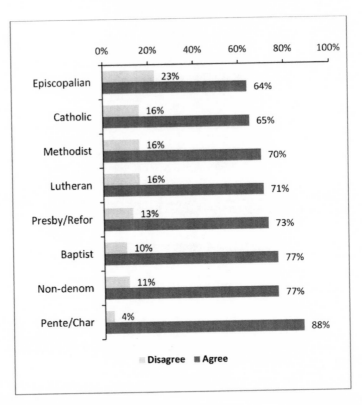

Source: The Quadrennium Project, 2012 MissionInsite, LLC. The No Opinion responses have been removed. The groups represent religious traditions not specific denominations.

This belief generates the closest opinions across the groups. The separation is only 24 percentage points, or half what is the case on the other three belief statements. The majority of every denomination still believes that children should still be raised in a two-parent mother and father home when possible (Regele 2012).

References

AAPC (American Association of Pastoral Counselors). 2012. *AAPC Code of Ethics.* American Association of Pastoral Counselors. http://www.aapc.org/about-us /code-of-ethics/.

ACA (American Counseling Association). 1998. "ACA Governing Council Meeting Minutes." American Counseling Association. March 26–27. http:// www.counseling.org/docs/governing-council-minutes/1998-march-26-27 .pdf?sfvrsn=4.

Achtemeier, M. 2014. *The Bible's Yes to Same-Sex Marriage: An Evangelical's Change of Heart* (First Edition ed.). Louisville, KY: Westminster John Knox Press.

Association for Lesbian, Gay, Bisexual, and Transgender Issues in Counseling Compentencies Taskforce. 2012. *Competencies for Counseling with Lesbian, Gay, Bisexual, Queer, Questioning, Intersex and Ally Individuals.* http://www. counseling.org/docs/competencies/algbtic-competencies-for-counseling -lgbqqia-individuals.pdf?sfvrsn=6.

Ambinder, M. 2010. "Bush Campaign Chief and Former RNC Chair Ken Mehlman: I'm Gay." *The Atlantic*, August 25. http://www.theatlantic.com/politics /archive/2010/08/bush-campaign-chief-and-former-rnc-chair-kenmehlman -im-gay/62065/.

American Psychiatric Association. 2000. "Position Statement on Therapies Focused on Attempts to Change Sexual Orientation (Reparative or Conversion Therapies)." *APA Official Actions.* http://www.google.com/url?sa=t&rct=j&q=& esrc=s&source=web&cd=1&ved=0CB8QFjAA&url=http%3A%2F%2Fw ww.psychiatry.org%2FFile%2520Library%2FAdvocacy%2520and%2520 Newsroom%2FPosition%2520Statements%2Fps2000_ReparativeTherapy .pdf&ei=LNP0U_nSLpehyASy24GICQ&usg=AFQjCNHeWyM3HOZIeE u5GXNY44_gA27Mkg&sig2=ISTbBHxf5eKlpswPkdz0Zg&bvm=bv.73231 344,d.aWw.

————. 2013. "Gender Dysphoria." In *Diagnostic and Statistical Manual of Mental Disorders.* 5th edition (DSM-V). Washington, DC: American Psychiatric Publishing.

————. 2014. "LGBT-Sexual Orientation." American Psychiatric Association. http://www.psychiatry.org/lgbt-sexual-orientation.

American Psychological Association. 2008. "Sexual Orientation and Homosexuality." American Psychological Association. http://web.archive.org /web/20130808032050/http://www.apa.org/helpcenter/sexual-orientation .aspx.

APA Task Force on Appropriate Therapeutic Responses to Sexual Orientation. 2009. *Report of the Task Force on Appropriate Therapeutic Responses to Sexual Orientation.* Washington, DC: American Psychological Association.

Aquinas, T. 1947. *Summa Theologica.* Translated by Fathers of the English Dominican Province. New York: Benziger Bros.

Augustine. 1887. *Saint Augustin: Anti-Pelagian Writings.* In *A Select Library of the Nicene and Post-Nicene Fathers of the Christian Church.* Vol. 5. Edited by Philip Schaff. New York: Christian Literature Compnay.

————. 1993. *On Free Choice of the Will.* Translated by T. Williams. Cambridge, MA: Hackett Publishing Company.

Badash, D. 2011. "70 Year-Old Stoned to Death Because the Bible Says to Stone Gays." The New Civil Rights Movement. March 18. http://thenewcivil rightsmovement.com/70-year-old-stoned-to-death-because-the-bible-says-to -stone-gays/news/2011/03/18/18138.

Badgett, M. L., and J. Herman. 2011. *Patterns of Relationship Recognition by Same-Sex Couples in the United States.* The Williams Institute of UCLA. http:// williamsinstitute.law.ucla.edu/wp-content/uploads/Badgett-Herman -Marriage-Dissolution-Nov-2011.pdf.

Bagemihl, B. 2000. *Biological Exuberance: Animal Homosexuality and Natural Diversity.* New York: St. Martin's Press/Macmillan.

Balthazart, J. 2011. *The Biology of Homosexuality.* Oxford Series in Behavioral Neuroendocrinology. New York: Oxford University Press.

Bass, D. B. 2012. *Christianity after Religion: The End of Church and the Birth of a New Spiritual Awakening.* New York: HarperCollins Publishers.

Bauckham, R. (1993) 2005. *Climax of Prophecy: Studies on the Book of Revelation.* New York: T&T Clark.

————. 1993. *The Theology of the Book of Revelation.* New Testament Theology. Edited by J. D. Dunn. Cambridge: Cambridge University Press.

Bauer, W., and F. W. Danker. 2001. *A Greek-English Lexicon of the New Testament and Other Early Christian Literature.* 3rd edition. Chicago: University of Chicago Press.

Bell, A. P., and M. S. Weinberg. 1978. *Homosexualities: A Study of Diversity among Men and Women.* New York: Simon and Schuster.

Bell, A. P., M. S. Weinberg, and S. K. Hammersmith. 1981. *Sexual Preference.* Bloomington: Indiana University Press.

Bell, R. 2011. *Love Wins: A Book about Heaven, Hell, and the Fate of Every Person Who Ever Lived.* New York: HarperOne.

Birney, J. G. 1885. *The American Churches, the Bulwarks of American Slavery.* Concord, NH: Parker Pillsbury.

"Bob Jones University Apologizes for Its Racist Past." 2009. *The Journal of Blacks in Higher Education: News and Views.* http://www.jbhe.com/news_views/62 _bobjones.html.

Bonetta, L. 2008. "Epigenomics: The New Tool in Studying Complex Diseases." *Nature Education* 1 (1). http://www.nature.com/scitable/topicpage/epigenomics -the-new-tool-in-studying-complex-694#.

Boswell, J. 1980. *Christianity, Social Tolerance, and Homosexuality: Gay People in Western Europe from the Beginning of the Christian Era to the Fourteenth Century.* Chicago: University of Chicago Press.

Bowersock, G. W., P. Brown, and O. Grabar, eds. 1999. *Late Antiquity: A Guide to the Postclassical World.* 1st ed. Cambrigde, MA: Belknap Press of Harvard University Press.

Bromiley, G. 1985. *Theological Dictionary of the New Testament: Abridged in One Volume* Edited by G. Kittel and G. Friedrich. Grand Rapids: Eerdmans.

Brown, C. 1986. *The New International Dictionary of New Testament Theology.* Vol. 2. Grand Rapids: Zondervan Publishing House.

Brueggemann, W. 1982. *Genesis; Interpretation: A Bible Commentary for Preaching and Teaching.* 1st ed. Louisville, KY: Westminster John Knox Press.

Budin, S. L. 2008. *The Myth of Sacred Prostitution in Antiquity.* Cambridge: Cambridge University Press.

Burke, S. 2012. "11-Year-Old Girl Married to 40-Year-Old Man." CNN. http:// amanpour.blogs.cnn.com/2012/08/05/11-year-old-girl-married-to-40-year -old-man/.

Burroway, J. 2008. "Today in History: The Love That Dares Not Speak Its Name Gets a Name." *Box Turtle Bulletin* (blog). May 6. http://www.boxturtle bulletin.com/2008/05/06/1942.

Catholic Answers. 2004. "Birth Control." Catholic Answers. http://www.catholic
.com/tracts/birth-control.

Chambers, A. 2013. "Exodus Int'l President to the Gay Community: 'We're Sorry.'" *Alan Chambers* (blog). June 19. http://alanchambers.org/exodus-intl -president-to-the-gay-community-were-sorry/.

Cicero, M. T. 1877. *On the Commonwealth*. Translated by C. D. Yonce. Project Gutenberg, 2005. http://www.gutenberg.org/files/14988/14988-h/14988-h .htm.

Cohick, L. H. 2009. *Women in the World of the Earliest Christians: Illuminating Ancient Ways of Life*. Grand Rapids: Baker Academic.

Cohn, D. 2011. "How Accurate Are Counts of Same-Sex Couples?" Pew Research: Social and Demographic Trends. http://www.pewsocialtrends.org/2011/08/25 /how-accurate-are-counts-of-same-sex-couples/.

Dailey, T. J. 2004. *The Slippery Slope of Same-Sex Marriage*. Family Research Council. http://downloads.frc.org/EF/EF04C51.pdf.

———. 2014. "Comparing the Lifestyles of Homosexual Couples to Married Couples." Family Research Council. Accessed August 19. http://www.frc.org/get .cfm?i=IS04C02.

D'Ambra, E. 2006. *Roman Women*. Cambridge: Cambridge University Press.

de Vaux, R. 1965. *Ancient Israel*. Vol. 1 of *Social Institutions*. New York: McGraw-Hill.

Dittenberger, W. 1905. *Orientis Graeci Inscriptiones Selectae: Supplementum Sylloges Inscriptionum Graecarum*. Vol. 2. Lipsiae: S. Hirzel.

Dobson, J. 2001. *Bringing Up Boys: Practical Advice and Encouragement for Those Shaping the Next Generation of Men*. Carol Stream, IL: Tyndale.

Dover, K. J. (1978) 1989. *Greek Homosexuality*. Cambridge, MA: Harvard University Press.

Duke, R. K. 1996. "Baker's Evangelical Dictionary of Biblical Theology: Hospitality." Edited by W. A. Elwell. StudyLight.org. http://www.studylight.org/dictionaries /bed/view.cgi?n=354&search=hospitality#hospitality.

Dylan, B. 1979. "You Gotta Serve Somebody." *Slow Train Coming*.

Evans, F. B. 1996. *Harry Stack Sullivan: Interpersonal Theory and Psychotherapy*. London: Routledge.

Evans, R. H. 2012. *A Year of Biblical Womanhood*. Nashville: Thomas Nelson.

"Exodus International Shuts Down: Christian Ministry Apologizes to LGBT Community and Halts Operations." 2013. *Huffington Post*, June 20. http://www.huff ingtonpost.com/2013/06/20/exodus-international-shuts-down_n_3470911 .html.

Falcon, A. 2012. "Aristotle on Causality." *The Stanford Encyclopedia of Philosophy.* Edited by E. N. Zalta. http://plato.stanford.edu/archives/win2012/entries /aristotle-causality/.

Fife, S. 2012. "Augustus' Political, Social, and Moral Reforms." Ancient History Encyclopedia. January 18. http://www.ancient.eu/article/116/.

FRC (Family Research Council). 2002. *Homosexuality and Child Sexual Abuse.* Family Research Council. http://www.frc.org/get.cfm?i=is02e3.

Gagnon, R. A. 2001. *The Bible and Homosexual Practice: Texts and Hermeneutics.* Nashville: Abingdon Press.

Galli, M. 2011. *God Wins: Heaven, Hell and Why the Good News Is Better Than Love Wins.* Carol Stream, IL: Tyndale.

Garcia-Falgueras, A., and D. F. Swaab. 2010. "Sexual Hormones and the Brain: An Essential Alliance for Sexual Identity and Sexual Orientation." *Endocrine Development* 17: 22–35.

Gates, G. J. 2006. "Same-Sex Couples and the Gay, Lesbian, Bisexual Population: New Estimates from the American Community Survey." The Williams Institute. October. http://williamsinstitute.law.ucla.edu/research/census-lgbt -demographics-studies/same-sex-couples-and-the-gay-lesbian-bisexual -population-new-estimates-from-the-american-community-survey/.

———. 2011. "How Many People Are Lesbian, Gay, Bisexual and Transgender?" The Williams Institute. April. http://williamsinstitute.law.ucla.edu/wp -content/uploads/Gates-How-Many-People-LGBT-Apr-2011.pdf.

———. 2013. *LGBT Parenting.* Los Angeles: The Williams Institute.

Gates, G. J. and A. M. Cooke. 2014. "United States Census Snapshot: 2010." The Williams Institute. Accessed August 19. http://williamsinstitute.law.ucla.edu/wp -content/uploads/Census2010Snapshot-US-v2.pdf.

General Social Survey. 2014. *GSS 1972–2012 Cumulative Datafile.* General Social Survey. Accessed August 20. http://www3.norc.org/GSS+Website.

George, R. P., and C. Tollefsen. 2008. *Embryo: A Defense of Human Life.* New York: Doubleday.

Ghose, T. 2012. "Identical Twins Are Genetically Different, Research Suggests." LiveScience. November 9. http://www.livescience.com/24694-identical-twins-not -identical.html.

Green, J. 2010. *The Gospel of Luke.* The New International Commentary on the New Testament. Grand Rapids: Eerdmans.

Greenberg, G. 2007. "Gay by Choice? The Science of Sexual Identity." Mother Jones. http://www.motherjones.com/politics/2007/08/gay-choice-science-sexual -identity?page=2.

Haldeman, D. C. 2002. "Gay Rights, Patient Rights: The Implications of Sexual Orientation Conversion Therapy." *Professional Psychology: Research and Practice* 33 (3): 260–64. http://www.drdoughaldeman.com/doc/GayRightsPatient Rights.pdf.

Harrell, J. A. 1999. "The Vice of Slave Dealers in Greco-Roman Society: The Use of a Topos in 1 Timothy 1:10." *Journal of Biblical Literature* 118 (1): 97–122.

Harvard Medical School. 2010. "Pessimism about Pedophilia." Harvard Health Publications. http://www.health.harvard.edu/newsletters/Harvard_Mental _Health_Letter/2010/July/pessimism-about-pedophilia.

Hayton, B. P. 1993. "To Marry or Not: The Legalization of Marriage and Adoption of Homosexual Couples." Newport Beach: The Pacific Policy Institute.

Hiebert, P. G. 1994. *Anthropological Reflections on Missiological Issues*. Grand Rapids: Baker Academic.

Horsley, R. A. 2003. *Jesus and Empire: The Kingdom of God and the New World Disorder*. Minneapolis: Augsburg Fortress Press.

Janus, S., and C. Janus. 1993. *The Janus Report on Sexual Behavior*. New York: John Wiley & Sons.

Just the Facts Coalition. 2008. "Just the Facts about Sexual Orientation and Youth: A Primer for Principals, Educators, and School Personnel." American Psychological Association. http://www.apa.org/pi/lgbt/resources/just-the-facts.pdf

Kennard, D., G. Haines-Stiles, and A. Malone (Producers). 1980. *Cosmos: A Personal Voyage* (TV series). Directed by D. Oyster, R. Wells, and T. Weidlinger. PBS.

Kirkpatrick, D. D. 2009. *The Conservative-Christian Big Thinker*. New York Times Magazine, December 16. http://www.nytimes.com/2009/12/20 /magazine/20george-t.html?pagewanted=all&_r=0.

Koritansky, P. 2007. Thomas Aquinas: Political Philosophy. Internet Encyclopedia of Philosophy, December 29. http://www.iep.utm.edu/aqui-pol/.

Kreitner, R. 2012. "The Stoics and the Epicureans on Friendship, Sex, and Love." *The Montreal Review*. http://www.themontrealreview.com/2009/The-Stoics -and-the-Epicureans-on-Friendship-Sex-and-Love.php.

Kuhn, T. S. 1996. *The Structure of Scientific Revolutions*. 3rd ed. Chicago: University of Chicago Press.

Laertius, Diogenes. 1972 (First published 1925). *Lives of Eminent Philosophers*. Translated by R. D. Hicks. Perseus Digital Library. Cambridge, MA: Harvard University.

Laumann, E. O.1994. *The Social Organization of Sexuality: Sexual Practices in the United States*. Chicago: University of Chicago Press.

Lauter, D. 2013. "Even Most Foes Say Gay Marriage Rights Are Inevitable, Poll Finds." *Los Angeles Times*, May 7. http://eeditionmobile.latimes.com/Olive /Tablet/LATimes/SharedArticle.aspx?href=LAT%2F2013%2F06%2F07&id =Ar01507.

Leichliter, J. 2013. "Temporal Trends in Sexual Behaviour among Men Who Have Sex with Men in the United States." *Journal of Acquired Immune Deficency Syndrome* 63 (2): 254–58.

LeVay, S. 1997. *Queer Science: The Use and Abuse of Research into Homosexuality.* Cambridge, MA: The MIT Press.

———. 2006. "The Biology of Sexual Orientation." Homepage of Simon LeVay. http://members.aol.com/slevay/page22.html#_Brain_studies%97function. Site discontinued.

———. 2010. *Gay, Straight, and the Reason Why: The Science of Sexual Orientation.* New York: Oxford University Press.

Lewis, C. S. (1952) 2009. *Mere Christianity.* New York: HarperCollins.

———. 1976. *The Last Battle.* Vol. 7 of The Chronicles of Narnia. New York: Collier Books.

———. 2001. *The Weight of Glory.* New York: Harper Collins.

———. 2009. *The Great Divorce.* New York: HarperOne.

Liddell, H. G., R. Scott, and H. S. Jones. 2014. *The Online Liddell-Scott-Jones Greek-English Lexicon.* Edited by M. Pantelia. Thesaurus Linguae Graecae (TLG): A Digitial Library of Greek Literature. Accessed August 20. http://www.tlg.uci .edu/lsj/#eid=1&context=lsj.

Markie, P. 2013. "Rationalism vs. Empiricism." *The Stanford Encyclopedia of Philosophy.* Edited by E. N. Zalta. http://plato.stanford.edu/archives/sum2013 /entries/rationalism-empiricism/.

McLaren, B. D. 2004. *A Generous Orthodoxy: Why I Am a Missional, Evangelical, Post/Protestant, Liberal/Conservative, Mystical/Poetic, Biblical, Charismatic/Contemplative, Fundamentalist/Calvinist, Anabaptist/Anglican, Methodist, Catholic, Green, Incarnational, Depressed-yet-Hopeful, Emergent, Unfinished Christian.* Grand Rapids: Zondervan.

Mikkelson, B. 2012. "Letter to Dr. Laura." Snopes.com. November 7. http://www .snopes.com/politics/religion/drlaura.asp.

MissionInsite. 2012. *The Quadrennium Project 2012: A Survey of US Religious Preferences, Practices and Beliefs.* MissionInsite, LLC. http://www.missioninsite .com/wp-content/uploads/2013/01/QuadrenniumWhitePaper.pdf.

Morales, L. 2011. "U.S. Adults Estimate That 25% of Americans Are Gay or Lesbian." Gallup Politics. http://www.gallup.com/poll/147824/adults-estimate -americans-gay-lesbian.aspx%29.

Moulton, J. H., and G. Milligan. 1995. *Vocabulary of the Greek Testament*. Grand Rapids: Baker Academic.

Mounce, W. D. 2000. *Pastoral Epistles*. Vol. 46 of Word Biblical Commentary. Nashville: Thomas Nelson Publishers.

Mustanski, B. 2012. "Author of Controversial Study on Therapy to Change Sexual Orientation Apologizes." *Psychology Today*. The Sexual Continuum. May 11. http://www.psychologytoday.com/blog/the-sexual-continuum/201205/author -controversial-study-therapy-change-sexual-orientation-apolog.

National Committee on Lesbian, Gay, and Bisexual Issues. 2000."'Reparative' and 'Conversion Therapies' for Lesbians and Gay Men: Position Statement." National Association of Social Workers. http://www.naswdc.org/diversity/lgb /reparative.asp.

Newport, F. 2012a. "Half of Americans Support Legal Gay Marriage: Democrats and Independents in Favor; Republicans Opposed." Gallup Politics. http://www .gallup.com/poll/154529/half-americans-support-legal-gay-marriage.aspx.

————. 2012b. "Religion Big Factor for Americans Against Same-Sex Marriage." *Gallup Politics* (blog), December 5. http://www.gallup.com/poll/159089 /religion-major-factor-americans-opposed-sex-marriage.aspx.

Nicolosi, J. 2013. Thomas Aquinas Psychological Clinic. http://josephnicolosi.com/.

Nicolosi, J., and L. A. Nicolosi 2002. *A Parent's Guide to Preventing Homosexuality*. Downers Grove, IL: InterVarsity Press.

Nissinen, M. (1998) 2004. *Homoeroticism in the Biblical World: A Historical Perspective*. Translated by K. I. Stjerna. Minneapolis: Augsburg Fortress Press.

Nittle, N. K. 2014. "How Four Christian Denominations in the U.S. Atoned for Racism." About.com Race Relations. Accessed August 20. http://race relations.about.com/od/historyofracerelations/a/How-Four-Christian -Denominations-In-The-U-S-Atoned-For-Racism.htm.

O'Connell, M., and S. Feliz. 2011. "Same-sex Couple Household Statistics from the 2010 Census." SEHSD Working Paper 2011-26, Fertility and Family Statistics Branch Social, Economic and Housing Statistics Division, U.S. Bureau of the Census. http://www.census.gov/hhes/samesex/files/ss-report.doc.

Oden, T. C. 1989. *First and Second Timothy and Titus: Interpretation: A Bible Commentary for Teaching and Preaching*. Louisville, KY: Westminster John Knox Press.

Paglia, C. 2013 "Gender Roles: Nature or Nurture?" October 8. http://motif .janetoakes.com/gender-roles-nature-or-nurture.html.

Perrin, E. C., and B. S. Siegel. 2013. "Promoting the Well-Being of Children Whose Parents Are Gay or Lesbian." *Pediatrics* 131 (4): e1374–e1383. doi:10.1542 /peds.2013-0377.

Philo. 1993. *The Works of Philo Judaeus.* Translated by C. D. Yonge. Peabody, MA: Hendrickson Publishers.

Pickett, B. 2011. "Homosexuality." *The Stanford Encyclopedia of Philosophy.* Edited by E. N. Zalta. http://plato.stanford.edu/cgi-bin/encyclopedia/archinfo .cgi?entry=homosexuality.

Polkinghorn, J. 2000. *Faith, Science and Understanding.* New Haven, CT: Yale University Press.

Queen Mary University of London. 2013. *The Biology of Sexual Attraction.* Queen Mary University of London. Accessed June 6. http://www.qmul.ac.uk /research/mind_society/mind_society_stories/65407.html. Site discontinued.

Quinn, K. 1982. "The Poet and His Audience in the Augustan Age." *Aufstieg und Niedergang Der Römischen Welt* II.30.1: 75–180.

RBC Ministries. 2013. *RBC Ministries.* http://rbc.org/.

Regele, K. 2012. *The Quadrennium Reports: National Findings.* MissionInsite, LLC.

Rice, W. R., U. Friberg, and S. Gavrilets. 2012. "Homosexuality as a Consequence of Epigenetically Canalized Sexual Development." *The Quarterly Review of Biology* 87 (4): 343–68.

Ritter, K. 2014. "Therapeutic Issues for Same-Sex Couples." American Association for Marriage and Family Therapy. Accessed August 19. http://www.aamft .org/iMIS15/AAMFT/Content/Consumer_Updates/Therapeutic_Issues _for_Same-sex_Couples.aspx.

Ritter, M. 2001. "Study: Some Gays Can Go Straight." *WashingtonPost.com.* http:// www.washingtonpost.com/wp-srv/aponline/20010509/aponline013921 _000.htm.

Rogers, J. 2010. *Jesus, the Bible, and Homosexuality.* Louisville, KY: Westminster John Knox Press.

Rosik, C. H. 2012. "Spitzer's "Retraction" of His Sexual Orientation Change Study: What Does It Really Mean?" Lifesite News. May 31. http://www.lifesitenews .com/news/spitzers-retraction-of-his-sexual-orientation-change-study-what- does-it-rea.

Satcher, D. 2001. *The Surgeon General's Call to Action to Promote Sexual Health and Responsible Sexual Behavior.* Rockville, MD: Office of the Surgeon General (US). www.ncbi.nlm.nih.gov/books/NBK44216/.

Schmitt, B. E. 1960. "The Peace Treaties of 1919–1920." *Proceedings of the American Philosophical Society* 104 (1): 101–10.

Scroggs, R. 1983. *The New Testament and Homosexuality.* Minneapolis: Fortress Press.

Seligman, M. E. 2007. *What You Can Change...and What You Can't: The Complete*

Guide to Successful Self-Improvement. New York: Knopf Doubleday Publishing Group.

Spitzer, R. L. 2003. "Can Some Gay Men and Lesbians Change Their Sexual Orientation?: 200 Participants Reporting a Change from Homosexual to Heterosexual Orientation." *Archives of Sexual Behavior* 32 (5): 403–17. http://www.stolaf.edu/people/huff/classes/Psych130S2012/LabDocuments/Spitzer.pdf.

Sprigg, P. and T. Dailey. 2004. *Getting It Straight: What the Research Shows about Homosexuality*. Washington, DC: Family Research Council.

[Sprigg, P. and T. Dailey]. 2014. "What Causes Homosexuality?" Family Research Council. Accessed August 19. http://downloads.frc.org/EF/EF08L41.pdf.

Stedman, R. C. 1995. *Body Life: The Book That Inspired a Return to the Church's Real Meaning and Mission*. Revised edition. Grand Rapids: Discovery House.

Steffan, M. 2013. "Alan Chambers Apologizes to Gay Community, Exodus International to Shut Down." *Christianity Today*/Gleanings, June 21. http://www.christianitytoday.com/gleanings/2013/june/alan-chambers-apologizes-to-gay-community-exodus.html?paging=off.

Stolberg, S. G. 2013 *Strategist out of Closet and into Fray, This Time for Gay Marriage. New York Times*, June 19. http://www.nytimes.com/2013/06/20/us/strategist-out-of-closet-and-into-fray-this-time-for-gay-marriage.html?pagewanted=all&_r=0.

Tickle, P. 2008. *The Great Emergence: How Christianity Is Changing and Why*. Grand Rapids: Baker Books.

Tjaden, P., and N. Thoennes. 2000. *Extent, Nature, and Consequences of Intimate Partner Violence: Findings from the National Violence against Women Survey*. U.S. Department of Justice. https://www.ncjrs.gov/pdffiles1/nij/181867.pdf.

US Census Bureau. 2011. *Census Bureau Releases Estimates of Same-Sex Married Couples*. US Census Bureau. http://www.census.gov/newsroom/releases/archives/2010_census/cb11-cn181.html.

Vandenbergh, J. G. 2003. "Prenatal Hormone Exposure and Sexual Variation." *American Scientist* 91 (3): 218–25. http://www.jstor.org/stable/27858211.

Van de Ven, P., et al. 1997. "A Comparative Demographic and Sexual Profile of Older Homosexually Active Men." *Journal of Sex Research* 34.

Venter, C., and D. Cohen. 2004. "The Century of Biology." *New Perspectives Quarterly* 21:73–77.

Volf, M. 2013. *A Public Faith: How Followers of Christ Should Serve the Common Good*. Grand Rapids: Brazos Press.

von Rad, G. 1995. *Genesis*. Revised edition. Louisville, KY: Westminster John Knox Press.

Webb, W. J. 2001. *Slaves, Women and Homosexuals: Exploring the Hermeneutics of Cultural Analysis*. Downers Grove, IL: InterVarsity Press.

Wesley, J. 1835. *The Works of the Reverend John Wesley, A. M.* Vol. 7. Edited by John Emory. New York: B. Waugh and T. Mason.

Wildermuth, J. "Prop. 8 Battle Draws in $46 Million." 2008. *San Francisco Chronicle*, October 8. http://www.sfgate.com/bayarea/article/Prop-8-battle-draws -in-46-million-3266288.php.

Williams, C. A. (1999) 2010. *Roman Homosexuality: Ideologies of Masculinity in Classical Antiquity*. New York: Oxford University Press.

Williamson, G. I. 2004. *The Westminster Confession of Faith for Study Classes*. Phillipsburg, NJ: P&R Publishing.

Wilson, G., and Q. Rahman. 2008. *Born Gay: The Psychobiology of Sex Orientation*. 2nd ed. London: Peter Owen Publishers.

Wright, N. T. 1992. *The New Testament and the People of God*. Vol. 1 of *Christian Origins and the Question of God*. Minneapolis: Fortress Press.

———. 1993. *The Climax of the Covenant: Christ and the Law in Pauline Theology*. London: T&T Clark.

———. 1997. *Jesus and the Victory of God*. Vol. 2 of *Christian Origins and the Question of God*. Minneapolis: Fortress Press.

———. 2002. "Romans." In *New Interpreter's Bible*. Vol. 10. Edited by L. E. Keck. Nashville: Abingdon Press.

———. 2003. *The Resurrection of the Son of God*. Vol. 3 of *Christian Origins and the Question of God*. Minneapolis: Fortress Press.

———. 2009. *Justification: God's Plan & Paul's Vision*. Downers Grove, IL: InterVarsity Press Academic.

———. 2011. *The Monarchs and the Message: Reflections on Bible Translation from the Sixteenth to the Twenty-First Century*. International SBL Meeting. http://ntwrightpage.com/Wright_SBL_Monarchs_Message.htm.

———. 2012. *How God Became King: The Forgotton Story of the Gospels*. New York: HarperOne.

———. 2013a. *Evil and the Justice of God*. Downers Grove, IL: InterVarsity Press.

———. 2013b. *Paul and the Faithfulness of God*. Vol. 4 of *Christian Origins and the Question of God*. Minneapolis: Fortress Press.

———. 2014. "Your Questions to N. T. Wright." Beliefnet: Inspiration, Spirituality,

Faith. Accessed August 21. http://www.beliefnet.com/Faiths/Christianity/2000/07/Your-Questions-To-N-T-Wright.aspx.

Xiridou et al. 2003. "The Contribution of Steady and Casual Partnerships to the Incidence of HIV Infection among Homosexual Men in Amsterdam." *AIDS* 17 (7): 1029–38.

CPSIA information can be obtained at www.ICGtesting.com
Printed in the USA
LVOW08s0716161014

408885LV00001B/1/P